Huawei Wisdom

"There is no end on the way to success for an enterprise, but accomplishments and growth. Every change and transformation present critical challenges for the growth of the enterprise. In this book, Lan Tao reviews the three major transformations in Huawei's growth, from which we can see Huawei's business wisdom at the critical moment. This book can serve as an excellent reference for other Chinese enterprises."

—Peng Jianfeng, *Professor of Renmin University of China, leader of the drafting group of Huawei Basic Law, Chairman of Huaxia China Stone Management Consulting Ltd.*

"The strategic choices made in the face of major changes determine the life or death of the enterprise. With the records the causes of Huawei's three major changes and various issues to be solved in the process of transformation, this book highlights the two keys of enterprise operation and development: ensuring the unity of the formulation and the implementation of strategy, and ensuring the matching of strategy and organization construction."

—Zhang Zhixue, *Professor, Guanghua School of Management, Peking University*

"Changes and transformations in the product development model, the market strategy, and the core business model are all related to the life or death of an enterprise. Upon reviews over the background and tortuous course of Huawei's three major transformations, this book presents a set of effective methods for strategic transformations through the combination of the systematic theory with the practical operations for the careful study by enterprise managers."

—Li Donghong, *Deputy Director of Department of Innovation, Entrepreneurship and Strategy, School of Economics and Management, Tsinghua University, Institution for Global Industry (IGI), Vice President*

"Enterprises, either large or small, will face the fatal challenges of life or death, rise and fall. Upon his experience of the three changes in Huawei, Dr. Lan Tao summed up a refined series of modes and methods for the changes of enterprises at different stages of the development of the enterprise, which is worth reading."

—Wu Jihong, *Founder of AIBusinessLab, Former Chair Professor of Haas School of Business, University of California, Berkeley, USA, and now Visiting Professor of Peking University*

"The most advanced management theories and the best practical experience assimilated, internalized as the corporate governance structure for the future development through effective change management, and implemented in each unit and to each person through strategies, processes and rules, this is just "Huawei Wisdom" presented by Dr. Lan Tao."

—Zhu Xingming, *Chairman and General Manager of the Inovance Group*

"We began to learn Huawei's enterprise management methods in 2013. Six years passed, and we have seen an average annual growth of more than 50%. Huawei's management starts with the formulation of strategies. Based on the BLM model of IBM, Huawei has explored and summed up its own strategic methodology, consisted of a set of methods from strategic insight and vision description to the setting of process and organization, to measures centering talent, atmosphere and incentive, and from headquarters platform to the front-line combat unit.

Personally going through three major changes together with Huawei, Mr. Lan knows not only what Huawei's strategic evolution is, but why it is. This book, as Mr. Lan's summary and sublimation of Huawei's strategic evolution in the past 20 years, will serve as a valuable guide for developing enterprises to learn from the benchmark enterprise."

—Yan Hua, *Chairman and President of Farben Information Technology*

"Based on his experience as the first director of Huawei's strategy department, 17 years of work across departments of Huawei, as well as his rich experience in strategic management consulting and counseling of dozens of enterprises, Dr. Lan Tao has summarized the practical experience of enterprise transformation and strategic choice at critical moments in this book within 3 years. Our enterprise has seen the effect upon the practical application of the contents of this book during the strategic management reform under the guidance of Dr. Lan Tao for one year."

—He Weixiao, *General Manager of Hangzhou Boiler Group Co., Ltd.*

"With Huawei's three fatal transformations as the main line, the author deeply analyzes the evolution process and the underlying reasons of strategy, business model and innovation path of Huawei, a world-renowned enterprise in the past 20 years. This book, depicting the huge contrast between the increasingly fierce competition among the global ICT industry and Huawei's persistent pursuit of power within itself for revolutions, provides an important reference for the sustainable development of today's enterprises!"

—Li Yuan, *Secretary-General of Digital Industry Innovation Research Center and Founder of JN Expert*

"The critical moment of transformation may be the darkest moment of an enterprise's development, but the highlight of the enterprise's wisdom as well. In this book, Dr. Lan Tao shows us Huawei's great wisdom in strategic decision-making and implementation."

—Ke Zhou, *CEO of Bijixia*

"Having personally experienced three fatal transformational changes of Huawei during his 17 years in Huawei, the author presents us a lot of details in the process of key strategic decision-making and implementation of Huawei in this book, which may serve as a valuable reference for domestic enterprises facing similar challenges."

—Ni Qikong, *Founder and CEO of MBAlib*

Lan Tao

Huawei Wisdom

Develop Strategy to Execution at Critical Moments

人民邮电出版社
POSTS & TELECOM PRESS

Springer

Lan Tao
ShenZhen, Guangdong, China

ISBN 978-981-19-1168-2 ISBN 978-981-19-1169-9 (eBook)
https://doi.org/10.1007/978-981-19-1169-9

Jointly published with Posts & Telecom Press
The print edition is not for sale in China (Mainland). Customers from China (Mainland) please order the print book from: Posts & Telecom Press.

This Springer imprint is published by the registered company Springer Nature Singapore Pte Ltd.
The registered company address is: 152 Beach Road, #21-01/04 Gateway East, Singapore 189721, Singapore

Foreword

Since 1978, with the further reform and opening-up of the country, stimulated by the incentives and dividends like national policies, natural resources, and human resources and driven by the huge demands for products from scratch, and pushed by the huge wealth effect of GDP growth from $700 per capita to nearly $10000 per capita, countless excellent enterprises and entrepreneurs have mushroomed in various industries of our country, from which went out numerous talents and heroes. However, only a few of these enterprises see the chances of growing into global enterprises, because in this century of competition of enterprise globalization, participants must build core competitiveness around technological progress and management improvement. Some of our enterprises, being "big but not strong", found it is difficult to cope with the global political and economic uncertainty, and even more difficult to face the attack of international competitors alone in market competition.

The present days saw the world experiencing great changes once in a century, for which Chinese enterprises are bound to shoulder the important responsibility and historical mission entrusted by the times. Our enterprises must grow bigger and stronger with the courage to go abroad and serve the world customers with our advanced technology and products, so that people all over the world can enjoy the high-tech products and high-quality services from Chinese enterprises. To pursue global expansion, enterprises should continue to adapt themselves to the changes of the internal and external environment, for the steady enhancement of their core competence. Change is an important management method for enterprises to redeem themselves through improved scientific management and further evolution, which will not shift the enterprises from being "ruled by man" to being ruled by law, but also help entrepreneurs grow from individual heroes to wise leaders, and finally from successful businessmen to respected entrepreneurs, and even to industrial leaders or business thinkers. Huawei is such a representative of Chinese enterprises, who seizes the premise of changes, that is, to put the customer at the center and to create values for customers, which harvested as the core competence for Huawei to ground in an invincible position.

Founded in 1987 as a private enterprise, after 32 years of development, Huawei realized revenue of US 100 billion dollars from scratch. Today, we value Huawei not only for its tremendous growth in business revenue, but also for its important successful practices in the span, difficulty, and depth of management from merely a company of switching technology to an enterprise of multi-technology research, from single product to multi-product line development, and from B2B to B2C and B2b[1] full-service operation. The crises, problems, and uncertainties faced by Huawei in its four critical periods and stages, from entrepreneurship, domestic growth, and internationalization to global leadership, are the management challenges that many Chinese enterprises are likely to encounter again. Especially at the critical moment of the current global industrial chain reconstruction, Huawei's top-down strong will, collective organizational strength, and resilience against attacks in its forward-looking performance are even more admirable.

So what makes Huawei's core competence? From a strategic perspective, this book presents an in-depth analysis of Huawei's motivation for change, strategic choices, and construction of core competence at three critical moments after its entrepreneurial period through theories as well as an abundance of case studies. Through the analysis of Huawei's reform and growth process in this book, it is found that from 1998 to 2018, Huawei's management investment (scientific knowledge, formulation of rules, talent empowerment, management system optimization, etc.) accounted for an average of 1.38% of its revenue annually for 20 consecutive years, which makes the settled the uncertainty of management improvement through the determination upon the rules of management investment. Through reform, Huawei has injected the expertise and wisdom of the world's top talents into itself and promoted the growth and ability of the company's internal managers and talents, making reform a testing ground for managers and talents. Huawei makes its judgments of managers and talents with excellent values upon whether they take the lead, embrace the really, or practice the strategy of reform. At the same time, Huawei also takes that change to the cradle of managers and talents. Managers and talents with potential can be sorted out by examining employees' understanding, experiences, and progress during the changes. It is the respect for talents, knowledge, and wisdom, as well as the control of the application of wisdom, scheme co-creation, and integration of training and practice if the enterprises can lower themselves down to the position to study, grow, and overcome.

Facts have also backed the truth that more than half of the enterprises in most of the economic powers strive to improve their management vision, level, and ability through definite and continuous management investment and the introduction and utilization of consulting firms. Among them, 80% of British enterprises seek help from consulting firms, 75% of American enterprises, and only 8% of Chinese enterprises.

As an author with 28 years of practical work experience, Dr. Lan Tao has worked in state-owned enterprises for five years, especially from 1997 to 2013, during which time he worked in Huawei for 17 years, being responsible for Huawei's innovation management, strategy formulation, and marketing reform. Since 2014, he has been devoting himself to management research and enterprise reform practice, providing

[1] The "b" in a B2b here refers to small and medium-sized enterprises.

quality reform and consulting services for dozens of companies with his rich management wisdom and enterprise practical work achievements. With the common concept of "putting the customers at the center, as well as spreading management wisdom to Chinese enterprises to help them grow bigger and stronger", we are here with each other.

As the Chinese sayings go, "A journey of a thousand *li* begins with the single-step under your feet" and we should "handle it before it happens and govern it before it falls into chaos". Based on the integration of Huawei's practical cases, combined with the training he offered to more than 100 enterprises and the consultation for dozens of enterprises, Dr. Lan Tao completed this book in three years. Seemingly a talk about Huawei, but actually the book explains how Chinese enterprises cope with the ups and downs, crises, and problems in their growth. Whether for exploring the domestic market or implementing globalization, whether for B2B or B2C, you will find the management practice and practical methods of reform from this book valuable for you in keeping pace with the times.

At a time when Huawei is facing the fourth critical moment, through this book, the author hopes to bring immersive experience and management reference to Chinese enterprises, entrepreneurs, and managers upon his summarization of management experience in more than 30 years through the three most important critical moments, with an expectation that our Chinese enterprises will work together to create a better society! The grand pass is as iron as iron is, and now it's all over from the beginning again!

ShenZhen, China

Fan Houhua
Former Vice President of Huawei
Overseas Market

Preface

Upon his 17 years of working experience in the strategic department of Huawei and following the three major transformations of Huawei along with its history, the author of this book introduces how Huawei changes its product strategy from "R&D as the center" to "customers as the center", how Huawei alters its market strategy from developing domestic market to global market, and how Huawei shifts its business model from B2B to terminal consumers and small and medium enterprises oriented. Based on the author's own personal practice in Huawei and nearly 100 cases of consulting services, the author summarizes a set of systematic methods for enterprises to formulate transformation strategies and implement them in key periods, which provides effective guidance for enterprises in different development stages but facing similar challenges in their growth.

This book serves as a suitable reference for domestic managers of various enterprises facing product transformation, market transformation, and business model transformation.

ShenZhen, China　　　　　　　　　　　　　　　　　　　　　　　　　　　Lan Tao

Contents

About the Author

Lan Tao, Ph.D. He has 28 years of work experience, including 17 years in Huawei. He held the positions as the Directors of the Corporation Strategy Department and the Regional Marketing Department. Now as a senior consultant, he is focusing on strategy and marketing consulting project. He obtained the copyrights of the Enterprise Marketing Capability Assessment Model and the Enterprise International Maturity Assessment Model and published several articles, which were well received by readers.

Chapter 1
Huawei's Successful Transformations and Revolutions

Under the severe impact of the global political and economic situation and the development of Internet technology, the Chinese economy, which has been reformed and opened for more than 40 years, found itself step into the key period of transformation. Many enterprises, such as real stores, have to transform due to the huge impact of the Internet economy; many state-owned enterprises have encountered the bottleneck of growth in China, and started market transformation and went overseas; some enterprises feel powerless when they want to sprint towards higher goals after completing the initial "small goal"; there are also some Unicorn companies, are eagerly taking the initiative to transformation after problems arising when the internal and external environment changes and the performance growth slows down due to the less-developed management covered by high-speed growth. To sum up, transformation remains the eternal theme of enterprise development.

All enterprises want to develop through transformation, but "non-transformation equals to die passively while ill-transformation means to die actively", which presents a paradox for enterprise management. Here is a typical case of enterprise transformation.

Initially, Nokia made a successful transformation for the first time from wood to feature phone and occupied first place in the global mobile phone market for 17 years and left a record unbroken by any other mobile phone manufacturer even till today. Apple launched its first-generation smartphones in 2004, when Nokia reached its peak in global market share in history at 40%. Nokia met its waterloo in the process of transforming its feature phone to smart phone, simply because its feature phone is over successful. Nokia's former CEO wrote a book in which he said that although Nokia had already realized that smartphones might be the trend for the future, no one in the enterprise thought the era of smart phones would come so soon, even less believe that Nokia's dominance would be shaken so early. Consequently, with no one being really willing to face it, the enterprise failed to formulate a response strategy. Therefore, if the senior management of the company does not pay attention to and formulate the corresponding transformation strategy from the ideological point of view, the transformation is sure to fail.

L. Tao, *Huawei Wisdom*,
https://doi.org/10.1007/978-981-19-1169-9_1

The transformation from Suning Appliance Co., Ltd. to Suning.com also serves as a typical case. To meet the challenge from the Internet, Suning actively constructs the O2O business model. Nine of the top ten retail enterprises in the United States have successfully developed from the traditional retail mode through O2O transformation. Therefore, Suning made a very determined strategy for transformation with crystal clear orientation and warm applause from the senior management. To that end, Suning introduced a set of very advanced systems to establish Suning e-commerce platform. However, Suning still encountered many problems in the process of transformation, but why?

First of all, the imported online system is very advanced, but also very complex, which calls for "outside experts", who know not much about the offline business of Suning to manage online business, making it difficult to integrate online and offline processes before a long time. At the beginning of the transformation, customers often compare prices on the Internet first before they go to Suning's real stores to experience them, and then go back to order on the Internet after experiencing them. Because such deals have nothing to do with the performance of the salespersons in the real stores, where the salespersons reject such customers. Secondly, the sales settlement system is relatively independent in the initial stage, with one set online, but the original POS system for the real, and there is no integration between the two either in terms of price update or settlement. Many reasons like lack of support for business process, organization, or assessment resulted in a lot of problems in the early transformation of Suning. In the 3–4 years of the transition period, Suning has been suffering a loss. However, due to the firm transformation strategy as a guide, with the deepening of the transformation, Suning online and offline business integrated with each other better. In 2017, Suning's online business saw a profit, when its offline business surpassed its biggest domestic competitor Gome for the first time.

Therefore, in order to succeed in the transformation, the transformation strategy must be correct. The mindsets, process, organization, as well as the cultivation and assessment of abilities, must be in tune with the strategy for transformation, otherwise, the transformation strategy will fail in vain.

Huawei announced its annual report in 2019, unveiling its revenue in 2018 at RMB 721.2 billion! Started from RMB 20,000 yuan, after the start-up period, Huawei has experienced three critical transitions in its development. At present, can Huawei make another successful transformation under the changing global trade environment? What are Huawei's preparations for the rainy day? The growth experience is worth other Chinese enterprises to learn from systematically.

Now many enterprises visit Huawei to study, where they come into contact with a large number of advanced management concepts. In fact, Huawei's management methods today may not apply to some enterprises. Enterprises must learn from them with the consideration of the reality of their own development. The author has had the honor to work in Huawei for 17 years and has personally experienced the three major transformations in Huawei's development, as shown in Fig. 1.1.

After the survival of the enterprise, in 1998, Huawei carried out an active reform in the context of the good momentum of development, which is marked by the change of the customer-centered integrated product development process. In 2002, Huawei

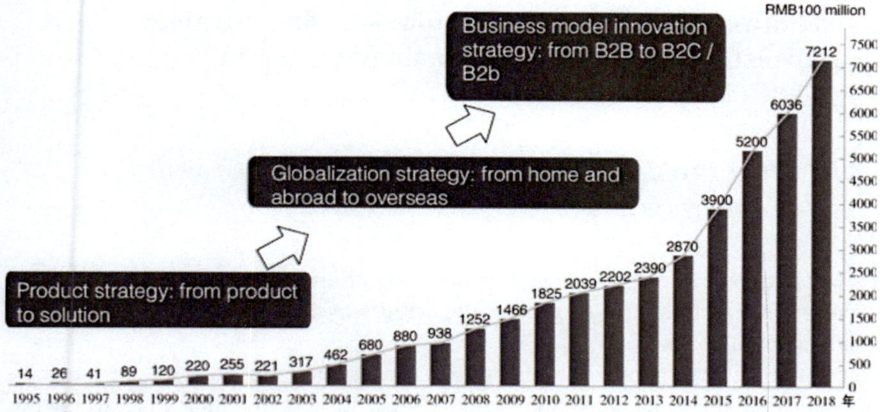

Fig. 1.1 Huawei's three major transformations and sales over the years from 1995 to 2018

experienced the first and only negative growth in history. At that time, faced with domestic difficulties and foreign troubles, Huawei carried out the second reform, moving from the domestic market to the global market, through the construction of the governance structure adaptable to the development of globalization. The third change of Huawei lasts for a relatively longer time, for the expansion from the operator market to the consumer market and enterprise market, which is actually marked with Huawei's official announcement on the establishment of consumer BG and enterprise network BG in 2011, thus realizing the transformation of business model from B2B to B2b and B2C.

By comparing the time points and revenue curves of the three transformations, periods of slow growth, zero growth, or even negative growth can be found at the critical moment of the transformations of Huawei. Therefore, enterprises should have the psychological expectation of the cost for transformation or changes. In the process of change, there is a need to replace the old process with the new one, when organizations need to adapt themselves to the changes and people need to improve their competence and change their mindsets, for which they need to experience a period of maladjustment when performance will be temporarily affected by these factors. However, once survived the painful period of transformation, the growth of enterprises will be exponential, and the potential for future development gigantic!

In the first chapter of this book, a summarization will be made upon the transformations of Huawei at three critical moments (product strategy transformation, globalization transformation and business model transformation), as well as the major problems and the essence of the management philosophy in the transformations. Chap. 2 to Chap. 7 of this book will detail product innovation strategy and decision management, global strategy formulation and path selection, business model innovation strategy, enterprise strategy formulation and strategy implementation system, in addition to case analysis. The author hopes that these practical management theories and methodologies can be helpful to the development of Chinese enterprises.

1.1 Huawei's First Transformation—Product Strategy Transformation from "Technology-Centered" to "Customer-Centered"

1.1.1 What Problems Are Covered by the Rapid Growth of Enterprises

Huawei had been seeing an annual growth rate at around 100% during the years before 1998, so quite a lot of people wondered why Huawei took to transform in such a favorable backdrop.

Just like the large number of unicorn enterprises emerging now, seizing a certain entrance along the value chain, they achieve great success in a short time, following their own philosophies of development, and become famous through explosive growth. According to the report of the analysis by some relevant consulting company, in 2018, 36 new unicorn enterprises emerged in China, accounting for about 1/3 of the global total, second only to the United States, as exemplified by Xiaomi, Ant Financial and Didi. However, the temporary advantage overshadowed the weakness in the enterprises' overall organizational ability, and enterprises fail to foresee the risks and take the initiative to transform will suffer heavy blows when encountering the turning points. Take Xiaomi, whose products feature high-cost performance, as an example. At the early stage, through online channels and Internet marketing, Xiaomi, with its brand of public praise, created a miracle of booming growth. However, with the rapid growth of shipments, management problems exposed along the supply chain of Xiaomi, who was caught at the turning point due to the challenges in launching its new products for the insufficient supply of key components in the period of 2015–2016. Realizing the significance in improving the organizational ability of the enterprise, Xiaomi started to increase investment in fields like product development, patent application, supply chain management, and the construction of offline channels. In 2017, after a brief rebound in sales, Xiaomi quickened its steps to get listed in Hong Kong. However, internal management could not be perfected overnight. In the context of international politics and economy, with the forced return of Huawei, the domestic market will see even more intense competition, where Xiaomi will face great pressure for its future development.

In 1998, Huawei carried out transformation at the critical moment of its development after problems found through active self-exams at the time of rapid development, which reflected the foresight and strategic vision of the enterprise. At that time, after comparing the two business systems of R&D and the market, Huawei found that R&D was not suitable for the future development of the enterprise. In the early days of its development, Huawei made the switch as its only product, before it developed more categories of products later by following the footsteps of the model enterprises in the industry. The reason why these iconic enterprises are regarded as the benchmark of the industry is that, when it comes to the requirements of customers and the trend of development, they know exactly which way the wind blows, for which they win the market recognition. However, if we only "know the effects but not the cause", and we fail to perceive the requirements of the customers, then following the benchmarking enterprises will result in not only the low efficiency in R&D and the unsurmountable difficulties in surpassing the competitors, but a giant waste in development.

To draw the attention of leaders and developers of R&D department to the issues concerning R&D, at an annual meeting of 10,000 people, Huawei presented a "Golden Raspberry Award" to the R&D department and product line, together with products, designed and launched but remained dead stock after coldly welcomed by the market, to the leaders of R&D departments and product line directors as "awards". Back then, many "innovative products" were blind innovation even at the beginning, and the product development process was no more than repetitions of the same thing at a low level for they cannot do it well at one time, for which the products developed then failed to meet the requirements of the customers either concerning the function, performance, quality or marketing cycle. In addition to the great investment waste for the company, the lame-duck products greatly injured the staff's morale in R&D. Behind the apparent prosperity, crisis lurked every corner within Huawei.

Although the "award" has impacted greatly on the mindset of the R&D department, the whole company still felt quite in the cloud about the right direction. Seeing this, Huawei introduced the integrated product development (IPD) of IBM, for the revolutionized reform of Huawei's mode of product R&D. This IPD revolution, with customers as the center and driven by the market, marked the first reform of Huawei and realized the transformation of R&D from "technology-centered" to "customer-centered", and even the transformation from product to solution.

As shown in Fig. 1.2, the process of IPD[1] contains two key concepts. First, product development should be based on requirements of customers to form the product concept satisfying the requirements of the market, that is, to do the right things; second, through the structured product development, the product should be made perfect at one time, that is, to do the things right.

By grasping the market and customer requirement, spells can be woven into products to solve customers' troubles, and create an emotional resonance that can not be separated from customers. By further discovering the exciting points and tapping the potential needs of customers, the requirement can become the fundamental force driving the development of the company. Huawei has established a offering requirements management (OR) system for the whole staff to collect requirements, to standardize input of requirements, to support process its platform and to manage the special requirements management team.

First, it is to solve the problem of sources of demands, which are divided into external sources and internal sources, with the former includes customer communication, project bidding, standards, expert consultants, friends and merchants, industry analysis, technical support center and hotline, user conference, various marketing activities, etc. and the latter mainly includes product line, general office, service,

[1] IPD: Integrated Product Development, refers to a set of mode, concept and method for product development.

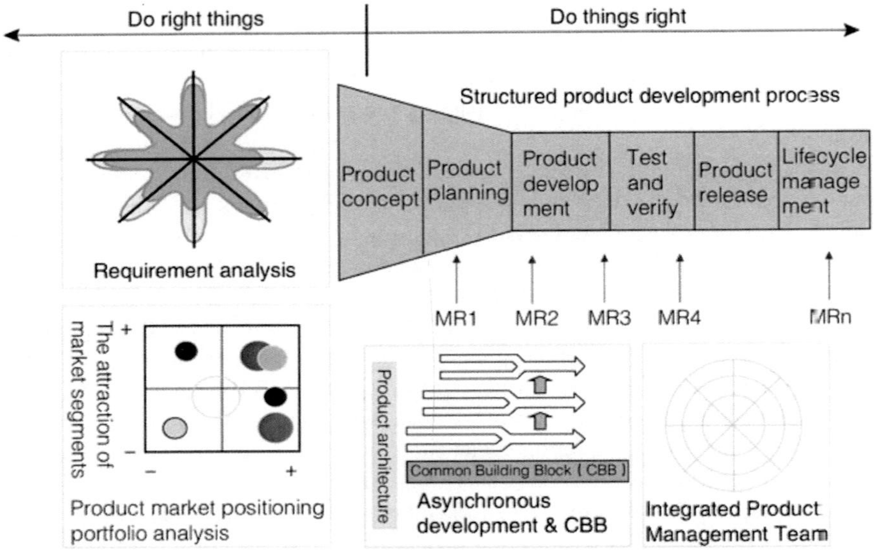

Fig. 1.2 Diagram of the Integrated Product Development (IPD)

pre-research, market, R&D, and even production supply chain. Enterprises should formulate unified standards to ensure the quality of submitted requirements and centralized management through a unified demand library.

Secondly, the problem of demand management should be solved, namely, to eliminate the false and save the truth and to remove the essence from the rough. We cannot take the demands put forward by customers as real demands. We also need to make a comprehensive analysis and priority on the value of this requirement to customers, the value of the company, the importance of customers, the difficulty of development, the return on investment and the role of forming competitive advantage through a set of methods such as portfolio analysis, and then by the market, R&D, supply chain key departments such as finance set up the integrated management team to make decisions and judgments. From the original "technology-centered" product decision-making mode, to "customer-centered, achieve win–win enterprise and customer" product decision-making mode.

After the product concept meets the market needs has been formed, the enterprise can start product development. Of course, the IPD process itself is also in continuous optimization, in which the implementation and verification of requirements are constantly strengthened in practice. When Huawei began to enter the developed countries' market, BT, the first bridgehead in Europe, conducted a very strict and complete strategic supplier certification for Huawei. BT requires its technical experts to join the decision-making process of key review points for BT product development. Huawei did not understand at the time and thought that the R&D process should be confidential. In fact, in order to ensure the consistency of both parties' understanding of requirements and to respond to necessary requirement changes, it is necessary for strategic customer opinion leaders, technical experts or market representatives who can represent customers' voice to join the decision-making process of key review points of product development. The Information and Communication Technology (ICT) industry is changing rapidly. It is necessary to make necessary adjustments according to the changes in market requirement. Therefore, Huawei added MR, the market review point, in the subsequent IPD process. For the consumer market, users are both consumers and content/product producers, and the necessity of users participating in the product creativity and design process should be emphasized. Enterprises generally seek opinion leaders and professional users in the user and potential user group through social media and user community. By making them express creative opinions, they can participate in the product design process and try the early products as friendly users. This makes the user participate in the whole management process of requirement collection, analysis, realization and verification.

So the core of the IPD integrated product R&D process is "customer-centered". From the collection and analysis of initial customer's needs, to the realization and change management of mid-term customer needs, and then to the later product launch, in the whole life cycle of the product, R&D work closely surrounds the closed-loop management process of market and customer.

After establishing the "customer-centered" product strategy and IPD integrated product development process, according to the business-driven process organization design principle, the enterprise will inevitably adjust the old organizational structure, which will bring great impact on the original interest groups, management thinking and the requirements of staff ability.

There will be a technical authority department in many enterprises to review and make decisions on technology or product projects, such as an office for the chief engineer or the department for the comprehensive management of technology, quality, safety and civilization. Huawei also had such an organization before the product change, called the general office. When Huawei's products are only switches and their derivatives, the technical authority of the general office has a deep technical background, makes timely and accurate decisions, and can grasp the key points of the problem. With more and more Huawei products, technical authorities need to constantly learn new knowledge and technology. Although with their own learning ability, experience and long-term accumulation, decision-making can still be relatively correct, the efficiency of decision-making begins to decline. When Huawei's product field has developed from wired technology to wireless technology, due to the large technology span, the decision-making difficulty is also increasing, the knowledge update of technical authorities is relatively lagging behind, the accuracy of decision-making is significantly reduced, and even there are major decision-making errors. From the delayed decision to the wrong decision, the general office has encountered a technical bottleneck. The most important thing is that the IPD development process runs horizontally. The product line integrates the market, R&D, supply chain and finance, and the company gives decision-making power to the cross-department product integration management team. The result of the process change is the adjustment of the organization and the cancellation of the general office. At that time, Huawei's sales volume was about RMB 10 billion, 10% of which was

RMB 1 billion for product R&D expenses, while 10% of which was RMB 100 million for product pre-research/innovation. Even today, this is not a small amount of innovation R&D expenses. Although it is also collective decision-making, the general office and the pre-research department play a key leading role in it. The abolition of departments means the loss of power. The impact of change on organizations and individuals is enormous, and many of them do not understand or even oppose the change. At that time, the author was the general manager of pre-research technology, and he was negative about the reform "The sound development is strong evidence that our model has original advantages and is suitable for the development of our industry. Why can IBM, who does not understand our industry, teach us how to do it?" Similar words, when the author engaged in consulting, are quite familiar in many enterprises.

In a sense, change means the redistribution of interests. In order to ensure the success of the reform, we must be firm in strategy. Especially for the first change, there will be more resistance, because at this time, the culture for changes has not been formed, the change management system is not perfect, especially the change management ability is not enough. To this end, Ren Zhengfei proposed to "cut one's feet to fit one's shoes", first with an open mind and an open mind to learn from the experience of IBM summed up in the past hundred years, first rigid, then optimized, and then solidified. For cadres who hinder reform, they should either "change their heads" or change themselves. At the same time, we should adhere to the guiding ideology of improvement, oppose drastic and rash progress. It is the so-called "pull one hair and move the whole body", the price of random improvement is high cost. Huawei's approach is to let everyone realize the importance of change, to achieve "still water undercurrent" in operation, to find and promote cadres who adapt to change in the process of change, and to make the vast majority of people, especially middle and high-level cadres, embrace change.

1.1.2 Transformation and Upgrading from "Crying up Wine and Selling Vinegar" to Customer-Value-Oriented Solutions

After this transformation, Huawei's product R&D is increasingly in line with customer needs, which greatly promotes the development of the company's business. The advancement of business and changes in management join each other into a virtuous circle of mutual promotion. Customers have higher and higher expectations with the increasing variety of products offered by Huawei, which pushed product development mode further forward to the deep-water area of change, that is, from product development to solution development. This transformation spans longer and yields a far-reaching impact on Huawei.

The full implementation of IPD saw Huawei's product R&D capability substantially improved, with its product differentiation advantage more outstanding. The customer's request to Huawei goes beyond a specific product feature to build a network most suitable for customer development to solve an operation problem or pain point, which was not fully understand by Huawei's sales team at the time when the sales staff focus mostly on the multiple functions, strong performance, high quality and low price of their products.

In Hong Kong, there is a Dr. Kong, a brand of shoes professionally designed for flat foot correction. When a customer visits its store for the first time to buy shoes, the salesperson will not directly go out of his way to sell shoes like the salesperson in other shoe stores will do, instead, he will first test the feet of the customer before recommending the most suitable shoes to the customer according to the measurement. For female customers who are not quite satisfied with the appearance of shoes, the sales staff will recommend customers to buy shoes from other stores to match the shoe-pads from Dr. Kong. If customers visit the store again to buy shoes, the sales staff will track the improvement of their flatfeet on the computer, which not only solves the customer's problems, but also greatly increases the user's loyalty. The shoe-seller provides solutions for his customers with the start from the pain point of them, while Huawei, an enterprise of high-tech products, has long been arguing about "solutions". Clearly, Huawei's early solutions are but a means of marketing.

"Incident of TM", which is a typical solution project across multiple product lines, serves as one of the major events to promote Huawei's solution transformation. Upon an email sent directly from the top management of TM to the chairman of Huawei complaining that Huawei failed to deliver IPTV services as required for a long time, Huawei asked the relevant departments to reflect from the top to the bottom, for which the conclusion was basically as "weak sense of responsibility". The root of the problem lies in the lack of process and organization systems in the way of solution delivery, and the lack of core capabilities such as business consulting, network planning and traffic management, and scenario-based design and delivery. At that time, the then leaders laid a rigid rule that the solution development department was "not authorized to develop one line code", which inevitably led to the solution development department into the dilemma of "crying up wine and selling vinegar" in a long-term. In 2008, when bidding for the project of Deutsche Telekom AG, the last barrier in Europe, Huawei found the tender of Deutsche Telekom involved the integration and interconnection of the whole network equipment and multiple equipment manufacturers. The premise of winning the bid is that the supplier should promise to do integration, otherwise it will be out automatically. Thong not being strong in integration at that time, in order to win the bid, Huawei had to compromise. So at the initial stage transformation of Huawei was completely "led by the nose" by customers concerning its transformation upon solutions.

Driven by customers and businesses, and with the deepened understanding of customers' concerns, IBM told Huawei that it should meet 100% of customers' needs with 30% of its products, and it must be equipped with the ability to integrate solutions. In order to facilitate the management, Huawei decomposes the solutions, and distributes the products and solutions based on the product line to the product line of the product. Therefore, Huawei officially renamed its "XX product line" as "XX product and solution department"; in addition to the company level solution system set up for cross-product line solutions, especially for system-level whole network solutions. With the establishment of organizations like the customer service consulting department and network design and research institute, Huawei's solution system goes closer to the requirements of customers and the market due to the delivery mode of site solutions and the setting of scene engineer's responsibilities.

At the Huawei Ping'an Park solution report meeting in 2017, Ren Zhengfei made a summary, in which he believes that in order to accelerate the accumulation of solutions, it is necessary to develop products and solutions that are easy to be integrated and can be replicated on a large scale. Starting from the end, from the perspective of future marketing, the company should plan the system architecture, think about the pricing model, find the strategic control points, and explore the operation and management model after the construction. He also proposed that starting with the change of R&D budget mechanism, the company should take Ping'an Park Project as a typical case to optimize the management mechanism of solutions, in which IRB should play a role to truly realize IPD from an opportunity to realization, and enhance the competitiveness of the company's products and solutions. Driven by the "customer-centered" philosophy, Huawei has gradually gone through the transformation from centering on technology to focusing on customers' requirement, and then to solving customers' problems and creating value for customers, so that the enterprise "customer-centered" strategy has been continuously enhanced and carried forward.

The innovation of IPD R&D not only resulted in a huge impact upon Huawei's R&D system, but also a great enhancement of Huawei's marketing capability, which developed from originally marketing upon relations, to the technology marketing highlighting features of its products and the satisfactions of customers, then to the solution marketing highlighting solutions to solve the problems and pain points of customers, and ultimately to value marketing to find and prevent risks in advance and create cost value for customers. Huawei had every once asked the General Manager of China Mobile why Huawei couldn't beat Ericsson in the Chinese market for 30 years? The answer is that whenever China Mobile issues a bid, Huawei will always invest a sea of people trying to persuade and convince China Mobile in an all-round way, while Ericsson will discuss the development strategy, do business planning and formulate standards with China Mobile together in advance. If this is the case, how can Huawei win Ericsson? For what Ericsson was doing presents the highest level of customer value orientation, which is the consultant marketing and value marketing with the customer's strategy, business development and operation improvement in the heart.

1.1.3 The Basic Elements of Successful Transformation: Strategy, Process, Organization and People

In the process of transformation, in addition to clearly formulated strategies for transformation, the corresponding process and organization should also change with the change of strategies, while people often serve as the decisive factor. First to be concerned should be cadres. An entrepreneur in Zhejiang once complained that it seems that the boss is the only one that is eager about the reform of the enterprise, but none of the business of the senior executives. The culture for transformation should come first before the consensus upon the strategies of the transformation and driving force among the senior management, who, together with the boss should take the lead to call up all employees into thinking and actions. Second comes the powerful organization and management of changes. Reforms, as "top leader" projects can't be thrown to the carelessly organized makeshift team or entirely to consultants. The core leadership team, such as the company-level Steering Committee for Changes, should stand out as the first level of the management; followed by the second level of the permanent management of changes and IT department for the accumulation and inheritance of the methods and experience of the changes; the third level is the teams of projects for different changes led by the business department. The guarantee of cadres and organizations serves as the key to the success of the transformation.

Equal as the problem of cadres, the introduction and training of professional talents carry a lot of weight as well. Huawei's first IPD transformation pilot failed, for at that time, there was no concept of the Solution Responsibilities in the company, but only hardware managers and software managers, leaving no one responsible for the whole life cycle of the product, while in many successful enterprises, the CEO acts just as the CPO. Steve Jobs and Pony Ma (Ma Huateng), both of whom are responsible for the innovation and design of products and the release of ideas on the market, exemplify Solution Responsibilities very well. Without a suitable Solution Responsibilities to organize the cross-department team for efficient and orderly operation, the project of changes is doomed to fail. The same as that the transformation of products to solutions is but merely empty talk without solution experts and the understanding of customers' pain points, or knowing how to turn customers' pain points into solutions and deliver them to customers.

In short, in order to succeed in the transformation, a consensus upon the clearly-stated strategic intention and driving force of the transformation should be going hand in hand with the well-matched organization for the management of changes as well as the firm implementation; a complete change process should be established and gradually optimized in practice, in addition to process organization driven by business and major talents for transformation prepared and cultivated in advance. Only in this way can the strategy of the transformation practically be implemented.

1.2 Huawei's Second Transformation: Global Strategic Transformation from the Domestic Market to Overseas Market

Huawei's second transformation, a passive transformation, is to go to the global market from the domestic market, which is just like what many companies have to do upon problems. At that time, Huawei was in a dangerous situation of internal difficulties and external troubles, resulting in only one way left to follow, that is, to dive into the overseas market from the domestic market. But despite the impassioned article entitled *Brave across the Pacific with High Spirit* by Ren Zhengfei, yet within Huawei, the middle and senior managers collectively saw a cut in their salaries, so it was a tragic and passive transformation with all means of retreat cut off. However, it is just this transformation that has laid the solid foundation for the future development and management transformation of Huawei.

1.2.1 Efforts to Break Through Under Internal Difficulties and External Troubles

Back in 2002, the global telecom market saw gloom development shortly after the burst of the dot-com bubble. The domestic market share of Huawei's mainstream products has exceeded 40%. When deciding upon their suppliers, the customers are always avoiding making one company dominate, which is very disadvantageous to the risk prevention of the supply chain and business negotiation, and will leave the customers kidnapped by the supplier. For this reason, Huawei experienced weak growth in the domestic traditional market, besides, the 2G wireless communication market that Huawei is eager to break through has been firmly controlled by powerful international giants such as Ericsson and Nokia, so Huawei hit the "ceiling" of its growth. Although Huawei took the lead in developing 3G products among domestic manufacturers, due to shrinking investment, immature industrial chain and unclear 3G standards, domestic 3G licenses have yet wait to be issued. The three years' of waiting but ended with the emergence of the listing of PHS, the backward wireless technology, with an average annual equipment market scale of about 20 billion yuan, has been built for four years. Together with the supporting mobile terminal market (about RMB 20 billion per year), Huawei's biggest domestic competitors UT Starcom and ZTE have expanded, who have invested their profits to tackle 3G problems and promote overseas markets, making their gap with Huawei gradually narrowed. At the same time, some important executives of Huawei left together with more than 600 R&D backbones, the Harbor Network Co., Ltd. formed by whom also entered the ranks as Huawei's competitor.

In 2002, Huawei's IPD management reform entered the deep-water period, when all product lines were required to operate in full accordance with the PTD 2.0 process by the end of the year. Despite the intensified pains of reform, no obvious financial effect meets people's eyes. To make matters worse, as soon as Huawei occupied the beachhead of Asia, Africa and Latin America in the overseas market, Cisco, an international rival, began to accuse Huawei of infringing its intellectual property rights in an attempt to stop Huawei's overseas progress. As Ren Zhengfei said, Huawei was on the verge of collapse facing internal difficulties and external troubles from 2001 to 2002. As seen from the financial data, 2002 saw the first negative growth in the history of Huawei. Under the internal difficulties and external troubles, Ren Zhengfei felt into his deepest reflection about how to get out of the predicament.

From the perspective of market structure, to vigorously expand overseas markets left as the only way to follow. Ren Zhengfei once said frankly that failing to cover the world as soon as possible will be a waste of investment and a loss of opportunities for Huawei, believing that Huawei shouldn't act reactively upon problems, but to get familiar with the market, win the market, train the cadre team in the exploration of the overseas market, for if Huawei failed to build an international team within three to five years, it is to see its bankruptcy once the Chinese market is saturated.

1.2.2 Success as the Necessity from the Possibility

1.2.2.1 High Vision of Huawei People

As early as 1994, Ren Zhengfei made his "crazy assertion" that "Ten years later, Huawei will play a role in the world's communication manufacturing industry dominated by three giants", with an implication that Huawei will, with no means of retreat, inevitably embark on the road of globalization. But where comes the strength of Huawei to go abroad?

China is the largest emerging market in the world, for which the world's giants gathered in China. In the beginning, Huawei encountered the most fierce competition in the world at its own door. In the domestic competition, Huawei, with an open and enterprising attitude, like a sponge, humbly absorbs the world's advanced R&D mechanism, marketing methods, management means, and competition rules. Huawei put on "American hat" in human resource management, and "American shoes (IPD, ISC[2])" in product development management and supply chain management, while "German heart" in production and quality management. Through continuous management reform, the company has gradually built an "end-to-end" process-oriented organization with customers as the center and the market as the drive. These globally consistent business logic and management essence laid a solid foundation for Huawei to compete in the world. Huawei has never been influenced by policy support, nor did it follow the Internet upstarts in focusing on "down-to-the-earth" in China. Because it is crystal clear in the heart of Ren Zhengfei that competing the world-class rivals in the global market is the only way for Chinese enterprises to reach the world-class level.

[2] IPD stands for integrated product development, and ISC stands for integrated supply chain.

1.2.2.2 Low Hands of Huawei People

Although Huawei has learned a lot from its international rivals through the domestic competition, and the continuous management reform has also strengthened its body, Huawei's still suffered difficulties and risks in "sailing out to overseas markets".

1997 marks the initial stage of Huawei's internationalization. Hearing that lots of international businesspersons from China had hit oil in Russia, Huawei also entered the Russian market following its nose. However, without market analysis or strategies for the market, plus the barrier of the language difference, even the basic life of its employees became a challenge when Huawei arrived in Russia. After one year's efforts and through agents, Huawei finally succeeded in its international trade in Russia, whose worth is but tens of US dollars. In order to establish a relationship with the local government, Huawei also built factories there. However, the Russian market, which remained "hot in politics but cold in the economy", did not improve much. Failing its move in Russia, Huawei shifted its main force to South Africa to look for other opportunities, but only resulted in "looking across the fertile land of South Africa, it has long been occupied by western companies", consequently, until 2012, Huawei was still working hard to enter the core cities of South Africa to cooperate with mainstream operators.

So far, many Chinese companies are still repeating Huawei's story of trials and errors like "crossing the river by feeling the stones" in those years. They prefer BRICS countries and take it for granted that the development status and business environment of these countries must be similar to those of China, so they can play it well there. However, due to the high tariffs in Brazil, Huawei did not make any profit until 2014; Indian seems to be a very large market, but the requirements for ultra-low-cost, the low efficiency of the government and political factors have made most companies sacrifice their profits to boost their existence. Therefore, how to choose the most suitable path for internationalization and regional markets is the first hurdle for Chinese companies to overcome. After repeated defeats, Huawei reconsidered its strategic direction and returned to the strategy of "encircling the city from the countryside".

Africa, the Middle East, Southeast Asia and other regions have become Huawei's major "granaries". After more than four years of exploration, Huawei's overseas market analysis ability, marketing methods and front-line "iron triangle" organization have gradually taken shape, marking the completion of the task of "seizing the beachhead" in the first stage with its marketing system basically internationalized.

If "brave across the Pacific Ocean with high spirit" in 2001–2002 seemed somewhat tragic, Huawei has entered the second stage of internationalization since 2005, that is, to actively start its global layout, especially for developed markets and strategic customers, when the market-driven integrated product development and management reform has entered the harvest period, and product internationalization has become a false proposition. The products that meet the domestic market only add the necessary domestic characteristics on the basis of the global baseline version, for China is but a large global regional market. On the other hand, the acquisition of Harbor

Network Co., Ltd[3] and the exit of UT Starcom have given Huawei a solid base in China. In 2005, Huawei began to advance toward global operation when its overseas sales exceeded domestic sales for the first time.

Success doesn't come easily, sometimes even at the cost of life. If employees in developing countries and regions are struggling in the material sense, then employees in developed regions are fighting spiritually, when the "soldiers" needed to constantly search for the glimmer of hope in the dark. Here, I would like to share the "three battles" I have been personally involved in.

1. Quick Response: Battle for British Telecom (BT), the Bridgehead of Strategic Customers in Developed Markets

At the beginning, Huawei couldn't even get the tender. But with persistent efforts, BT gave Huawei two tentative projects in 2003, one of which is the BluePhone project, a project of high innovation and high uncertainty as well. BT left this project, a dual-mode integrated solution involving cable and wireless telecommunication, for which only the world's giant like Alcatel dares to have a try, as a hard nut to Huawei. Huawei organized research and development teams across four product lines and demonstrated the outcome to BT's senior management in less than half a year, when BT's CTO visited Huawei headquarters in Shenzhen for the first time, making BT understand how Huawei's innovative ability in the solutions quickly created through market-driven process organization to meet customers' needs through the "awkward" collaboration between the front line and the headquarters. Although this project failed as a "martyr", it marks the beginning of Huawei's full participation in BT's network construction in the twenty-first century. Years later, the CTO joined Huawei.

2. A "unwise" Company with Overpromise Conquered the Last Bastion of Europe, Deutsche Telekom (DT)

In 2008, Deutsche Telekom launched the NGF project for the next generation network, for which the cooperation consultants who know Deutsche Telekom well have repeatedly warned Huawei that there is no need to meet all the features of the project, especially some old ones. However, as a latecomer, how can Huawei win the project if it "acts choosily" on the condition that it is not clear about the internal contradictions of Deutsche Telekom? Later, the fact proved that the strategy of fully meeting the requirement of features brought down the competitors, in addition to the full verification of the feasibility of NGF, and achieved a win–win situation between Huawei and Deutsche Telekom. Just upon this "unwise" approach through taking the trouble in doing what is considered "dirty" or "tiresome" upon the comparative advantage of human resources, Huawei wins the trust of customers and wins the battle. According to the statistics of a famous consulting company, the average requirement satisfaction rate of the world's giants stays around 80%, while that of Huawei stands at more than 95%. Since then, one of the key problems that call for lasting optimization and treatment in the transformation process when "the front-line cries for weapons" is to retain the truth while eliminating the false and priority of the

[3] Harbor Network Co., Ltd was acquired by Huawei in 2006.

requirements. Huawei is constantly optimizing the operation mode of the "iron triangle" in the front line, gradually implementing the financial settlement and incentive system based on the project, so that the front line will realize that "they need pay for the weapons", so as to enable long-term balanced development of the enterprise.

3. Braving in the Direction of the Earthquake Radiation Cloud—The Hard-Won Breakthrough in the Japanese Market

Japan is a market featuring high standards and excellence in European and American markets, and the humanistic feelings of the Oriental people. In 2006, NTT requested Huawei to provide a new product without a primary contract, with very detailed requirements for technology and unprecedentedly high requirements for quality. In order to finish the task on time, the R&D department worked for 60 consecutive days. During the days around Fukushima nuclear accident on March 11, 2011, back in China, I would always ask my colleagues who were still in Japan with concern, "How is everything going in the representative office?", "Is the air safe in Tokyo?", for which the reply from the front line came as "Ericsson has withdrawn, so it leaves the opportunity for us, and the day after tomorrow, we will be in the disaster area. Just wait for our good news." The Japanese were truly moved, for which in 2013, Huawei's sales in Japan increased by four times, nearly $2 billion, from less than $500 million in 2011. That is just the Huawei people of iron and steel will.

1.2.2.3 The Management of "People" as One of the Main Challenges in International Management

To achieve internationalization in its real sense, localization turns out to be the only way. Especially for Chinese enterprises grow up underdeveloped business culture, when involved in developed markets, they should not only equip themselves with courage but smartness in the management of their foreign employees, so as to avoid the same mistakes made SAIC's acquisition of Korean SSANG YONG Motor Company or TCL's acquisition of French Thomson.

1. People's Heart as Core Values

To deliver and optimize the core values with an "open, enterprising and inclusive" attitude serves as an anchor for Huawei's global expansion. Ren Zhengfei has ever personally demonstrated how to explain Huawei's core values to foreign employees: to be customer-centered, first of all, is to implement solutions formulated according to customer needs, while the solution is to be customer-centered, and only after doing this can we get the contract. Why should he be better paid? It's because he works more. Foreign employees are also clear that they would be better paid for harder work, which is definitely striver-centered? Ren Zhengfei believes that Huawei culture is open and inclusive, so it is not good to require foreign employees with Chinese mindsets, instead, we should be open to absorb their cultural essence to enrich Huawei culture with an open mind. Due to the practices and examples of Huawei leaders at all levels, Huawei's core values of "customer-centered, striver-centered, persistent diligence" have become the universal codes of actions for Huawei employees all over the world. In an interview with BBC in Davos in early 2019, Ren Zhengfei depicted vividly the stories of local Huawei employees struggles in disaster relief after Chile's magnitude 9 earthquake.

So, it calls for our reflection upon what motivates foreign employees to risk their lives in their work?

2. Who to "be in Charge"

Different companies follow different ways in doing things, and Huawei's regional presidents, representatives of representative offices and other top leaders are basically Chinese, most of whom are sent abroad from home, which is often criticized by the outside world, saying that Huawei is not acting as an international company. Lenovo is a typical company that internationalized through mergers, where foreign employees are favored with more opportunities to become the top leaders. However, Liu Chuanzhi, believes that the so-called management by Chinese lies in the top leader, who determines the direction of the enterprise. So it is the best policy where integration, but not balance comes as the main idea to greet the international employees with a feeling that you are an international company before they later will gradually integrate themselves and establish the values recognized by both sides. This is what Huawei has done. As a self-growing company, in addition to the recognition of core values, the understanding of the company's strategies, the compliance to the process, and even the communication with superiors and peers are equally of great significance.

3. The Issues Concerning Incentives

As a non-listed company with employees as the shareholders, Huawei's long-term incentive to foreign employees has always remained a long-standing problem due to various reasons such as different laws of different countries. 40% of my staff were foreign employees, who have worked in Huawei for more than four years and agree with Huawei's values, but much disturbed by the lack of long-term incentives. In 2013, Huawei began to implement a new TUP (Time Unit Plan) shareholding plan for foreign key employees, which solved this long-standing key problem and played an important role in accelerating Huawei's globalization. For such a company that constantly criticizes itself and improves its management, what else can hold its steps moving forward?

1.2.3 Globalized Vision and Pattern

Ren Zhengfei does not favor the term "internationalization" for it always suggests "peeping" from China. Ren believes that in this era, it takes an enterprise needs to have a global strategic vision to develop strong; a nation needs to absorb the essence of globalization for its prosperity, and a company needs to establish a global business ecosystem to survive and develop. Only after going global, can the enterprises effectively improve the utilization rate of resources.

Well-known enterprises like Apple, IBM, Hon Hai, Google all maximized their interests and global resource utilization through the global operation. These enterprises generally adopt the "sandwich business model", as shown in Fig. 1.3, with the main purposes as follows.

- Hardware manufacturing moved to countries with low labor costs;
- Tax reasonably avoided by setting up overseas sales companies in low tax countries;
- High profitability through soft capabilities (software, design and intellectual property).

Apple put its system design and development in the United States (with the industrial design done mainly by British employees), software activation and sales are in Ireland (one of the tax havens), and production and manufacturing in China. In 2012, Apple paid only about 6% of its overseas income of about US$35 billion for taxes, which maximized the profit of the enterprise. IBM constantly strengthens its software capabilities (software products, professional services, etc.) and lowers the price of

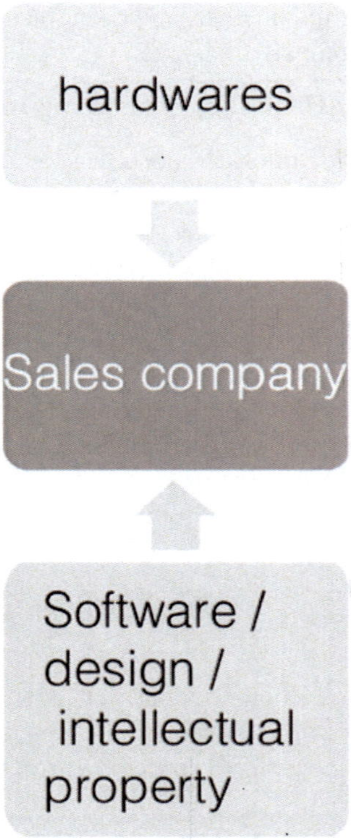

Fig. 1.3 Typical global sandwich business model

hardware to crack down on low-cost manufacturers, or sells hardware systems (such as low-end servers) to improve the overall profitability. Foxconn's hardware products only see a 2% profit, while the high-profit core business unit of design and mold technology is kept in the company's headquarters and will never be listed, so as to maintain the overall profit requirements of Hon Hai and realize the effective utilization of global resources.

1.2.3.1 Huawei's Second Qualitative Change of Management Realized by the Promotion Through Internationalization

1. Front-Line Elite Combat Supported by a Large Platform

"What is Huawei's core competence?" This is a question that puzzled many, the answer to which someone says being Huawei's corporate culture, or R&D capability by someone else, or human resource by still someone else. Ren Zhengfei gave the standard answer as the governance structure of "front-line elite combat supported by large platform", a management mode comes from Huawei's management gene, which is the core competence that is hard to be copied by other enterprises. And it is just through the process of internationalization and continuous practicing that this mode is formed, which happened to coincide with the modern combat mode of the US military.

The so-called front-line elite combat mode is the combat mode at the front-line following the pattern of an "iron triangle", which is composed of AR (Account Responsibility), SR (Solution Responsibility) and FR (Fulfill Responsibility). The "iron triangle model", firstly proposed by Huawei's North Africa Sudan representative office in a difficult environment, was promoted and improved in the whole company with its essence to seize market opportunities (to create value for customers), break functional barriers, and form a project-centered team operation mode, so that 70% of the problems can be solved in the first line, while the remaining 30% can be quickly responded and solved by the rear support platform through the "first line's calling for weapons". With global operation with increased business, in order to speed up the response of the rear end, Huawei not only continuously strengthens the highest tenet of "customer-centered" in leadership mindsets, action and assessment, but also combs and optimizes the process and organization from the front line, resolutely cuts off the non-value-added departments, so as to focus on the front line through simplified management. Besides, Huawei moved cadre training and selection, decision-making authorization, and strategic management planning and so on forward to the front line, which ensured the mechanism for the efficient operation of the "front-line elite combat supported by large platform".

2. "Adult Ceremony" in Developed Markets

In the process of involving in the markets of developed countries, strategic customers such as BT started the certification of Huawei as a strategic supplier, which promoted the second qualitative change of Huawei's management. BT's certification covers

Fig. 1.4 Multiple dimensions of BT's strategic supplier certification

12 major projects and more than 100 minor projects, ranging from production and operation to employee accommodation, as shown in Fig. 1.4.

Sun Yafang, chairman of Huawei, who is in charge of the certification program, has a deep impression about this, saying that "the BT's three-year continuous certification of Huawei has cost Huawei people a lot of efforts like losing a layer of skin." She believes that through continuous improvement, Huawei will realize the transformation towards internationalization, during which Huawei people will gain a deeper understanding of the value and role of customers in the company's business process. Not only do they need customers to input requirements at the initial stage, but they also need customers to participate in intermediate control and later delivery. Related systems also need to be connected with customers' systems. After continuous iteration, Huawei's process system has been comprehensively improved generation after generation, laying the foundation for its global operation.

1.2.3.2 The Global Layout of Huawei

To make effective use of global resources, after 18 years of planning and layout, Huawei has established a number of global operation centers and resource centers.

1. Administrative center: Board of directors and advisory committees were set up in among areas of the gatherings of business leaders such as in the United States, France and the United Kingdom to enhance interaction with high-end business. An administrative center was established in the UK and a transcontinental business center in Germany to improve the efficiency of global operations.

2. Financial centers: Financial centers were established in Singapore, Hong Kong SAR of China and Romania, in addition to the global financial risk control center established in the UK to reduce financial costs and prevent financial risks.
3. R&D centers: Antenna R&D center in Russia, wireless system R&D center Sweden and Finland, security certification center and 5G innovation center in Britain, technology innovation center and chip R&D center in the US, software R&D center in India, a terminal industrial design center in Korea, and Industrial Engineering Research Center in Japanese were established to make effective use of global intellectual resources.
4. Supply chain centers: European Logistics Center (reaching out to Europe, Central Asia, Middle East and Africa) in Hungary, manufacturing base in Brazil, network operation center in Poland were established improve the quality of global delivery and service.

Hu Houkun, Huawei's rotating CEO, believes that in today's worldwide flow of capital, talents, materials and knowledge, and highly developed information, the concepts of "global company" and "localized company", which were often separated in the past, have gradually become unified. Huawei should combine the two in its business practice to integrate the best resources in the world, build a global value chain, and help local enterprises create global value. This kind of global operation layout also reduces the company's operation risk by shaking off the dependence on a single region in technology acquisition, supply chain, finance and market. In today's difficult environment, Huawei's global layout plays a crucial role in achieving "good performance in some areas if not in the other areas".

1.3 Huawei's Third Transformation—Business Model Transformation from B2B to B2C, B2b

In 2012, Huawei announced the establishment of consumer business group (CBG) and enterprise network business group (EBG), which means that Huawei's business model has officially transformed from B2B (telecom operators, big business users) to B2C (individual consumers) and B2b (small and medium-sized enterprises). Why does Huawei's third transformation expand from the operator market to the individual consumer and small and medium-sized enterprise market? Apart from the need to maintain sustained growth, what is the profound business logic behind it?

As a matter of fact, Huawei has been involved in the mobile terminals as products for the personal consumer market for a long time, but instead of being willing, it is forced to do so at the beginning.

As mentioned earlier, due to the late issuance of 3G license, the biggest investment in the communication industry in 2001 fell in PHS system of China Telecom, with its total investment in system equipment and supporting mobile phones as high as RMB 40 billion per year, whose market is mainly divided up by UT Starcom and ZTE. At that time, ZTE's sales exceeded 3/4 that of Huawei, closest to Huawei for the first time in its history. The most important thing is that ZTE and UT Starcom started to threaten Huawei's main channel by speeding up their pace of R&D in the 3G field with the profits they have made. Huawei has been forced to join the competition of PHS mobile phones through OEM in order to "burn the granary of its competitors". Under the guidance of the strategies that "kill one thousand enemies at the loss of eight hundred", the long-term development goal of the mobile phone has been a hot debate within departments of Huawei, but through the practice in the market, Huawei has earned some certain understanding of the consumer market. At the end of 2008, the era of 3G has finally arrived, when the types of mobile phones available for users are seriously insufficient due to the less-developed industry chain, which presents one of the important reasons hindering the development of 3G technology. Operators of 3G communication require equipment providers to provide corresponding types and quantities of mobile phones, and encourage other terminal manufacturers to participate in the competition of 3G mobile phones, when the operators are very dominant, trying to control the whole industry chain, demanding that the mobile phone must be sold exclusively through the channel of the operator, with only the brand of the operator and the logo of the manufacturer in the battery or a corner only. Although Huawei occupied dominant positions in the mobile phone market in the 3G era, together with ZTE, Coolpad and Lenovo, most consumers never know Huawei as a producer of mobile phones for quite a long time. For at this time, the business model is still B2B, and Huawei provides but one more product for the operators.

Although the sales model has not changed much, the mobile phone products have pushed Huawei into the research and development of mobile phones in an all-round way. On the one hand, Huawei has started the research and development of mobile phone core technologies and chips, upon its long-term accumulation in the field of wireless systems and chips, and extended to the high end of the mobile phone value chain. On the other hand, to promote the development of mobile business, master the business needs of the final consumers and activate the whole value chain, operators have carried out various business innovation attempts. Huawei has also taken the initiative in establishing joint innovation laboratories with operators, hoping to grasp the other end of the value chain through the actual effect being not ideal. Operators just remain Huawei's major purchasing customers, but not the ultimate consumers. Operators have no clear understanding of what the final consumer's requirement is, either what business to develop. Huawei, with "customer-oriented" as its highest strategy, is full of panic at this time, just as Ren Zhengfei once thought pessimistically: "why does the information industry end up in trouble? Because the information requirement of consumers is limited in that people just have two eyes, and there are but 24 h in a day, while information resources are unlimited. The basic material of information industry is silicon, which is inexhaustible on the earth. The limitation of demand and the infinity of supply are the fatal weakness of the information industry."

From the perspective of the development of the communication industry value chain, the traditional telecom services are mainly voice communication and certain text information, such as SMS, MMS and so on, when the communication terminal remains simple for the business content is not complex. Therefore, the most high-end and largest investment area of the value chain is communication systems and equipment. However, the development of Internet technology has accelerated the integration of information technology and communication technology, especially the emergence of the Apple intelligent terminal ecosystem, which makes mobile Internet a new development direction, and the industrial value chain of ICT has been reversed. As shown in Fig. 1.5, the top two ends of the value chain are intelligent terminals and content services. With the development of intelligent terminals to broadband, intelligent and diversified, many Unicorn enterprises emerged with fast development. Business content has also been greatly enriched, evidently proved in that the income and market value of Tencent, Alibaba and other representative enterprises turn out to be much higher than those of telecom operators. The investment-related to content and intelligent terminal far exceeds the investment in system equipment, while the vigorous development of intelligent terminal and business content, in turn, calls for the growth of communication speed, which promotes the investment in communication systems and equipment. That explains why Ren Zhengfei believes that thanks should be given to Apple for it has changed the world, and Huawei would not have enjoyed today's achievements if not for the development of the mobile Internet.

Driven by the market, Huawei acts sensitively to the changes in the value chain and begins to develop to both ends of the value chain. In addition to intelligent terminals, Huawei began to provide equipment and services to content providers at the other end (such as Tencent and Alibaba), build a business ecosystem similar to that of Apple, with an attempt to provide cloud technology and content services. With the development of these two tentacles, Huawei has obtained a large amount of first-hand requirement information from end-users and content providers. The highest guideline of "customer-centered" makes Huawei a duck in water, who gradually grasps the essence of mobile Internet business, and a relatively independent consumer business group came into being as a natural outcome. At the same time, driven by the

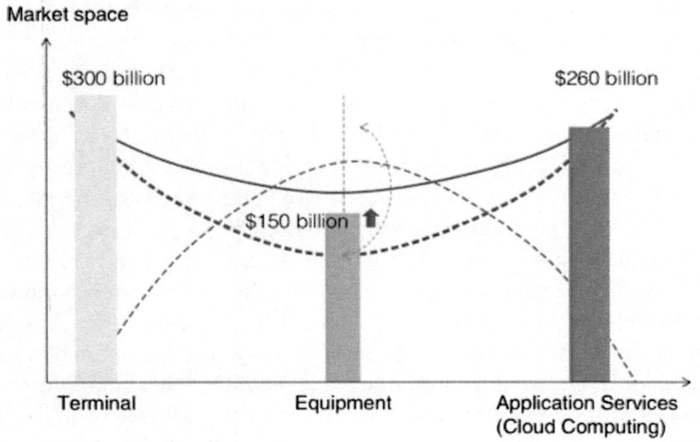

Fig. 1.5 Changes in value chain of communication industry (reversal of smiling curve of value chain)

technology of the Internet of Things, industry 4.0 and the concept of robot, society, government and traditional enterprises are quietly transforming towards the direction of digitization, informatization and intelligence, which lays the urgent demands for informalized transformation and upgrading of digital enterprises with ever-increasing investment year by year. The enterprise business group for enterprise users also arises at the historic moment upon Huawei's sensitive reaction to this trend, which was formally established in 2012 as the consumer business group (terminal) (CBG) and enterprise network business group (EBG), representing an active change based on deep insight into the changes of the industrial value chain with the business model transforming from B2B to B2C and B2b. Once the rulers of the world, why did Dinosaurs become extinct later? The reason is simply that dinosaurs didn't know how to adapt themselves to their environment. If Huawei does not transform in time, but remains unchanged with its successful experience, relying only on operators but not the active perceptions of the changes in user needs, it will not embrace the development of itself today. Not a few complacent enterprises have already tasted the bitter fruits of sleeping over their temporary achievement instead of pursuing changes.

Every industry should have a deep insight into the changes of its own industry's value chain and take the initiative to make positive adjustments, which is the important enlightenment that comes from the transformation of Huawei.

1.3.1 Huge Impact on Process and Organization System by Business Model Transformation

Huawei operator BG has no more than 1000 customers in the world. Taking the Chinese market as an example, after the operators adopt the policy of centralized equipment procurement, Huawei has only three major customers in China. For key customers, Huawei has formulated a complete and clear key customer strategy: externally, through strategic interaction with key customers, business consultation, joint innovation, and establishing organizational customer relationship, Huawei deeply understands customer needs, discovers market opportunities, and creates value for customers; while internally, Huawei has formed a mature key customer organization system and excellent operation management methods. The customers of enterprise network BG include government, transportation, electric power, energy, finance, manufacturing and other industries, among whom, except for financial industry with investing relatively larger in informatization construction upon the earlier realization of the importance of informatization, the informatization construction of most industries still remains in the aspect of office automation. Failed in taking informatization construction as an important means to ensure the development of main business, the investment in it generally will be no more than 10% of their total investment. Huawei has to deal with tens of thousands of customers of different sizes, various requirements and diversified decision-making modes. Compared with the operator customers, most of the contract amounts are small and medium-sized contracts, some of which even at the worth of only thousands. The successful experience earned from dealing with operators, such as direct selling model, customer management, contract management, etc., is obviously not applicable, besides, the management cost remains high, which seriously hinders the development of enterprise network BG. In the consumer market, Huawei has to face tens of millions or even billions of ordinary consumers. How to obtain the requirement information of consumer groups? Consumers have higher requirements on the appearance, software interface and function of consumer products than industrial products, and the upgrading speed of consumer products is obviously faster than that of industrial products. How shall Huawei transform the gene of producing items featuring the characteristics of "being hard, black and coarse" in industrial manufacturing? How to build their own brand and sales channels, so that consumers can have quick access to its products? These are all great challenges posed to Huawei.

1.3.2 Transformation and Revolution Like "Starting a New Undertaking"

The implementation of strategies for business model transformation calls for the support of corresponding business processes, organization system and talent guarantees. Due to different customers, Huawei has undergone a major organizational division and established BG for various clients, namely, enterprise network BG and consumer BG. As the BG business of operators is relatively stable, to improve their excellent operation ability from the market opportunity to contract management to payment collection stands out as the most urgent task. However, it leaves no much experience to import due to the fact that enterprise network BG and consumer BG are quite different from operator BG in the way of customer management, access to opportunity and service delivery. In order to improve its ability and adapt to the new business model, Huawei began to implement the transformation of marketing process and organization system of Marketing to Leads (MTL) and Leads to Cash (LTC) in its marketing and sales delivery system with the help of external forces again, which filled the gap of marketing process system in Huawei's process system. The introduction of these two processes is an important symbol of the third transformation of Huawei.

The process architecture of MTL and LTC is shown in Fig. 1.6. The general working process is to select market segments and customers through market insight and judgment. Match the process from cognition to purchasing decision of the customers, design reasonable marketing activities, and identify potential customers according to customer feedback in marketing activities. According to the problems and needs of potential customers, requirement analysis, lead incubation and tracking are carried out, with those meeting the judgments transformed into sales leads and enter the sales lead pipeline. Based on the leads provided by the marketing system,

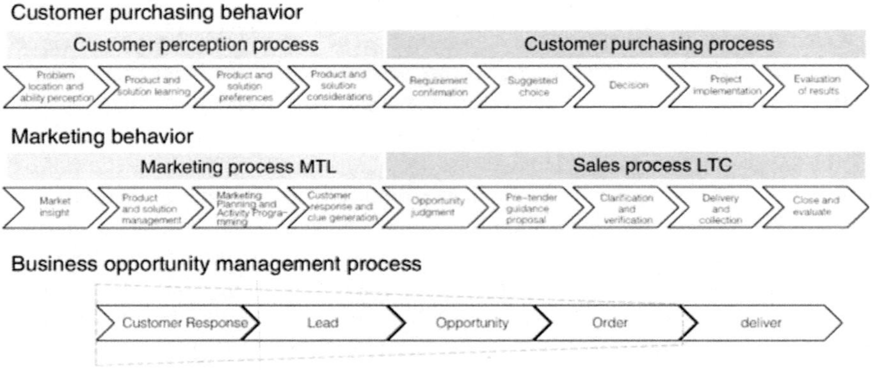

Fig. 1.6 MTL and LTC process architecture

the sales system further verifies and judges the opportunities, and enters the sales project management stage for the confirmed sales opportunities. The contract will be gained through the process of pre-sales guidance, technical advice and test verification. The payment collection will be done upon the completion of the delivery of products. Finally, the contract is closed, the overall project evaluation is carried out, and improvement methods are proposed. In this way, the whole closed-loop management process of Marketing to Leads (MTL) and Leads to Cash (LTC) is completed.

How to improve marketing efficiency and reduce marketing costs in the face of many small and medium-sized customers? Traditional marketing activities, including advertising, exhibition, forum, product release, promotion and so on, will be of high cost, so besides improving the company's brand awareness, what is its contribution to sales? How to measure the output of marketing upon the input? The successful practice of Xiaomi turns out to be stimulants to Huawei's faster pace of transformation, especially when digital marketing (online marketing) has become an efficient and low-cost marketing method with the development of Internet technology. Under the guidance of MTL/LTC process, not only the marketing system, but the whole operation mode of Huawei has quietly changed.

1.3.2.1 Marketing Mode

Huawei introduced digital marketing in an all-round way, for which internally, started from the optimization of the company's website from the original one-way push to two-way interaction, with increased analysis on user behavior over the website. The product lodging page was optimized for the users' efficient search of the desired content. The marketing materials were comprehensively updated from the perspective of solving customer problems and creating cost value for customers, with videos, online forums, micro websites and mobile applications, as well as internet marketing content such as online live broadcast added. Externally, the online advertising delivery mode was optimized through the cooperation with excellent portal websites, and increased customer clicks realized through SEO (search engine optimization) and social media. Among them, the Huafans Community of Huawei consumer BG not only as a way for enhanced customer loyalty and sales, but also as a platform for users' needs, designing and optimizing products with opinion leaders and friendly customers. For commercial users, the establishment of the user community is relatively difficult, for which based on the existing commercial customer base, Huawei has taken the initiative in establishing a user community and setting up an incentive fund. The customers who put forward important requirements for Huawei's innovative products, or who put forward suggestions for improvement upon the problems found in Huawei's equipment, will be highly rewarded. Now, Huawei is more and doing with the operation mode of digital marketing with high proficiency.

After that, Huawei further organically combined the traditional offline marketing activities with the online digital marketing mode to realize the three-dimensional interactive joint marketing. An automatic marketing IT system (please refer to the relevant content in Chap. 4 for the details of MTL/LTC) composed of marketing campaigns and lead management database, PRM & CRM (Partner Relationship Management & Customer Relationship Management) database, etc. is established.

The MTL/LTC process, first piloted in China and Europe, has qualitatively improved Huawei's marketing ability, after being optimized and carried out globally. In addition, this change has also solved Huawei's long-standing "world problem" of disconnection between "marketing" and "sales", which makes it difficult to clearly evaluate the performance of "marketing".

1.3.2.2 Products and Solutions

IPD product development process needs to be adjusted adaptively due to the changes in customer orientation and customer requirements. Customers like Operators have high expectations on the reliability of communication equipment, and generally require that the equipment can operate safely for more than 10 years. While the changes and replacements of IT products go much faster than that of communication products, with the average service life of terminal products being only about 3 years. Based on the uncertainty of business development, content service providers expected that the computing capacity and storage capacity of the system can be flexibly configured, and the quotation methods of equipment can be flexible (such as charging by consumption, charging by users, etc.). The IPD integrated product development process, being suitable for communication products, turns out to be too lengthy for IT equipment. Especially for software business development, a lot of agile development concepts are greatly needed. When learning from Huawei's IPD process reform, other enterprises must learn both from Huawei's experience and lessons, refer to the optimized version, and optimize the development process according to the characteristics of the industry and the features of their own products.

While adhering to the R&D strategy of "principle of focusing on the pressure of the main channel", Huawei began to make a comprehensive layout along the whole value chain.

Same as the transformation and upgrading of "Made in China", Huawei has been continuously investing more in R&D of core technology at the innovation end, as shown in Fig. 1.7. Huawei has gradually marched into the forefront of the industry in terms of chips for mobile phones, chips for ICT devices, terminal operating systems, server operating systems, antenna and cloud computing and other algorithms, distributed cloud computing architecture, etc. The equipment system architecture is developing and upgrading to cloud computing, and becomes more modular, component-based and shared. At the other end of the value chain, because of the complexity and changeful business requirements of consumers, Huawei terminal has built an open and shared business platform, EMUI, which continuously enriches business content and actively promotes the construction of ecological chain development through various ways such as developer conference and reasonable distribution of benefits. Faced by many industries with many customized requirements, upon the continuous improvement of understanding of various industries, after painful reflection, enterprise network BG put forward the clear strategy of "integrated" strategies of products and solutions, in order to balance the contradiction between scale and customization. With Huawei focusing on standard products and solution platforms, while partners being responsible for customized solutions, a win–win development model for multiple parties was established.

In September 2019, Huawei announced to fully launch the computing strategy based on "Kunpeng + Ascend", of which on one end of core technology and chips, Huawei has released 10 commercial chips, namely Kunpeng 916 and 920, Kirin 970, 980, 810, 990 and 9905G, Ascend 310 and 910, and Honghu 818 less than three years, before a number of chips to be released later. While on the other end, Huawei announced to open the source server operating system, GaussDB OLTP

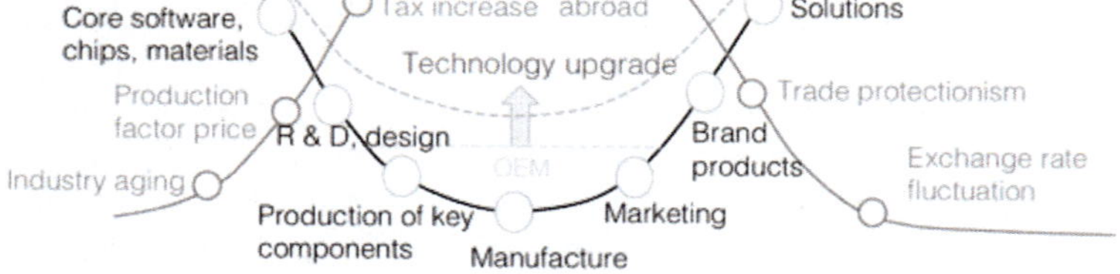

Fig. 1.7 Transformation and upgrading from "Made in China" to "Created in China"

(Huawei Gauss Database) stand-alone database, as well as Kunpeng motherboard. By opening up its hardware and software, Huawei enabled its partners and promoted the common development of the industrial chain.

As a result, Huawei's dual-engine strategy of products and solutions focusing on "high end and platform of the value chain" has been fully established and has begun to make explosive breakthroughs.

1.3.2.3 Construction of Core Professional Competence

According to the market environment and the trend of the development, Huawei's three BG build core professional competence.

- Operator BG: traditional B2B mode. With the focus on Key Account Strategy and excellent operation, Operator BG provides end-to-end solutions of end-channel-cloud management for operators with focuses on improving business consulting, network planning and delivery capability for scenarios.
- Consumer BG: B2C model is brand new for Huawei. In terms of product industrial design, Huawei introduced a large number of professionals and established research centers in Japan, South Korea and other countries. Huawei focuses on improving the ability of channel and store management, O2O marketing, supply chain and inventory management, and has made drastic changes in the organizational system and assessment incentives.
- Enterprise network BG: a new B2b mode. The "integrated" strategy was implemented up products, with the sales no longer done through direct sales, but through partners, for which Huawei focuses on improving the closed-loop management capabilities of independent software vendors (ISV), system integrators (SI), solution providers and service providers (SP), customer account representatives (CAR), value-added distributors (VAD) in the acquisition, classification, enabling and evaluation.

In terms of contract management and payment collection, considering the common credit and operational risks of small and medium-sized customers, enterprise network BG carries out hierarchical management for different customers, upon which the sales to all small and medium-sized customers are done through channels and standard contracts to avoid the complexity of management and the problem of payment collection. The smaller the company is, the stranger their requirements can be, for example, an enterprise consulted by the author even has as many as 83 contract texts, causing the management cost sky-high. For large customers, the "high-touch" cooperative sales mode is adopted, through which the needs of customers will be understood, in addition to the full play given to the advantages of partners. After the contract framework is determined according to the customer's needs, leaving only the statement of work (SOW) and bill of quotation (BOQ) to be negotiated each time, which greatly improves the efficiency of management. For even smaller customers, the purchase can be done directly through the e-commerce platform. Huawei terminal company has an independent Huawei mall, and enterprise BG has established an e-commerce platform on its website. On the e-commerce platform, Huawei integrates different solution design, configuration and quotation tools base on the consideration of different scenarios, so that small and medium-sized customers can select solutions and equipment models according to their own needs and place orders online directly, which greatly saves costs for the transactions. Therefore, the contract management and transaction methods simplified through different sales channels upon the classification of customers greatly reduced the management cost and operational risk.

Under the new business model, it turns out to be an ability and a lesson Huawei, who is used to the wolf-like direct selling model in the operator market, must-have, from being the chaser to being the leader, ensure the healthy growth of the industry value chain and lead the partners in the industry to grow bigger and stronger together.

1.3.3 System Model of Huawei's Transformations

From the three transformations of Huawei, it can be seen that, at every transformation, Huawei was challenged by difficulties and paid a price, which, however, is also an important reason why Huawei widened the gap with its competitors. These three hard-won transformations have laid a solid foundation for Huawei to grow into an industry leader. The system model of Huawei's transformation includes the following four aspects.

- Create a positive change-oriented culture under the vision and core values of the enterprise.
- Develop a clear strategy for transformation to lead the direction of changes.
- The business-driven process system guides the methods and steps for enterprises to realize the strategic transformations.
- Organize and motivate employees to execute efficiently through process organization and incentive mechanism.

From three transformations of Huawei, it can be seen that the formulation and effective implementation of a clear transformation strategy not only calls for the ability of systematic thinking, but also the grasp of the main contradictions of the enterprise in different development periods, as well as the main aspects of the main contradictions. Through health assessment, enterprises can find out the key weaknesses of enterprises from nine aspects (a total of 37 management behaviors), namely, orientation and strategy, leadership, cultural atmosphere, organization and responsibility system, coordination and control, organizational and executive ability, dynamic mechanism, open cooperation, and change and learning, to determine the direction and focus of each stage of the transformation of the enterprise.

At present, Huawei has launched a new round of reform at the fourth critical moment, which will take place in three steps.

The first step is to make clear that the representative office is the combat center. BG of the headquarters and BG of the regional departments jointly build the resource center and the capability center, of which the resource center operates and assesses through the market mechanism, and the capability center operates and assesses based on the achievement of the strategic objectives and the market mechanism.

The second step is to reform the regional division and the operational departments of BG, among which the regional division is responsible for the formulation and implementation of regional strategies, and provides regional operational resources, operational capabilities and administrative service platforms.

The third step is to reform the administrative organs, which should take the lead in opposing the repeated construction and repeated labor of the platform. The basic principle of this reform is to take the responsibilities and results as the guidance and "select people from the front-lines and promote them from the trenches", so as to nurture a large number of new leaders through inspiration and encouragement and to attract heroes and talents. Establish the "corps" combat mode, with emphasis on collective fighting, collective achievements and collective award. The employees should be both radical and conservative in the competition in the markets, with the marketing striving forward and quality of operation strengthened, in addition to increased strategic investment in the R&D, so as to "piercing the sky upward and taking root deep into the ground downward".

As it can be seen from the steps of this reform, Huawei continues to deepen the reform of its corporate governance structure of unique competitive advantages, that is, the "front-line elite combat mode supported by the large platform and high efficiency". The original "major general squad leader" formulation is self-denied because the management through the "iron triangle's calling for weapons" turns out to be rather weak, after being revised to "major general team leader" with the representative office and system department as the combat center, it is more in line with the actual operation of the front line, and can better balance the short, medium and long-term interests within the jurisdiction. In the construction of regional division, Huawei makes a further step in following the US military operation mode in strengthening the construction of the platform capability of the regional division and the unified management of the three BG in the regional division, and further moving the platform capability of the headquarters down to the regional division, thus speeding up the response of the platform to the front-line operations and the collaborative efficiency of the front and rear end. As for the headquarters, Huawei will greatly "streamline its troops and simplify its administration", with the reduced cadres either transferred to professional posts or eliminated as redundant personnel. The reform follows Huawei's consistent practice in principle on the whole. And "piercing the sky upward" indicates that Huawei's global investment in core technology and basic technology will be greatly increased, and the cultivation mode of the whole ecological chain will be more active and open, while "taking root deep into the ground downward" means "returning the grains to the granaries". Huawei will operate more finely in its advantageous market. In the domestic market, Huawei will take root in the third and fourth-tier markets that it did not pay much attention to, or even in the deeper grassroots.

"A rising force will emerge every time after we survive the critical moments in history, with a mission to occupy the global market." Huawei's experience born of its growth, a best interpretation of "the heaven will trust great responsibility to it", is worthy of systematic learning and reference for Chinese enterprises.

Chapter 2
Management of System and Strategies for Product Innovation

Under the guidance of national innovation strategy, many enterprises expect to promote the transformation through innovation. Huawei's top performance in standards, patents and other aspects, especially Huawei's Kirin chip and graphene technology, which are highly respected in the industry at present makes many enterprises eager to know the way how Huawei innovates with an expectation that they can, following Huawei's example, formulate enterprise transformation and reform strategies in combination with innovation. Many enterprises show great interest in the research of various modes for innovations, the innovation upon the absorption of the imported technologies, independent innovation in a gradual manner, independent innovations upon breakthroughs, just to name a few. While in Huawei, "independent innovation" is taken as a kind of "reactionary" formulation, in that Mr. Ren Zhengfei has always been emphasizing on "open innovation", especially those with the "customers at the center". This is a controversial formulation, because many industrial revolutions in human history are done through breakthrough innovations, so isn't it inhumane for Huawei to attribute such emphasis on "customer-centered" innovation" and why does this company with the emphasis on "customer-centered" innovation perform so well in technological innovation and product innovation in China and even in the world? Huawei ranked 397 when it was first listed in the Global 500 by *Fortune* in 2010 before in 2016, it soared to be the 129th of the Global 500, and topped the list of domestic technology companies for many years. Meanwhile, HUAWEI has entered as the only candidate from the Chinese mainland in the *2016 Global Innovation Institutions* and the *World's Most Innovative Company 2016*. But the question is, why did many enterprises speaking highly about independent innovation end up with few convincing successful innovations?

As a big manufacturing country, China boasts many indicators ranking the first in the world. The output of pen ranks the first in the world, but disabled in producing ball point pen core; the output of computer tops the globe, but with the main chips imported, numerous industries and enterprises fall into this category. After the outputs in the original fields topped in China and even in the world, these enterprises are burning to find a new direction for their growth, that's they favored "independent

L. Tao, *Huawei Wisdom*,
https://doi.org/10.1007/978-981-19-1169-9_2

innovation" much. For many enterprises that found themselves weak in R & D, it is understandable and justifiable for them to drive the transformation of enterprises, especially the change of mindsets of the leadership in this manner, though a little bit over-corrected. However, the direction and mode of innovation of many enterprises are questionable, for instance, when the photovoltaic industry saw prosperity, every enterprise jumped into the hot speculation; when rechargeable technologies such as lithium batteries prove to have a bright future, every enterprise run in eagerly for a share, the same is with the Internet plus, Internet of Things, cloud computing and big data. It seems that if people are shy to open their mouth if not about the hot topics. However, what actually meets the people's eyes is the fact that such industries mostly feel unable to grow into their maturity for the core technology left unconquered for lack of investment in R & D, after experiencing overcapacity, vicious competition and dumping. In the end, we have held our horses long for relevant policies or the "chances" but only to meet the state's regulation and restriction of the production and the cancellation of subsidy policies, with the new business falling into deep darkness... So, what are the features of Huawei's three major transformations, especially the innovation management, which are worth learning from for Chinese enterprises?

2.1 Huawei's "Customer-Centered" Product Innovation Strategy

Generally speaking, the evolution of Huawei's mode for innovation can be divided into two stages, with the comparison of the performance between Huawei and Ericsson, the last super competitor of Huawei in the world as the great division.[1] In the first stage before 2012, Huawei adopted the innovation mode as an industry catcher; in the second stage after 2012, Huawei adopted the innovation mode as an industry leader after entering the "untouched world".

In the first stage, Huawei used to compare its competitor Ericsson to a learning benchmark with a metaphor vividly going like "Ericsson is the beacon light in the vast sea, when which is off, Huawei will find no direction." During this period, Huawei's product development and innovation mode can be further divided into the following two phases.

- **The phase of learning and imitating:** To catch up with the best performers in the industry, Huawei set its own learning benchmark and main competitors in each segment, and has worked hard to surpass its competitors in different stages, with its goal to enter the top three in the world in the segment for being "big" as well as being "strong". From the early simple "cost performance" competition to the gradual replacement of key components and technologies, efforts were made

[1] In 2012, the overall revenue of Huawei's three major businesses exceeded that of Ericsson; In 2014, Huawei's operator business surpassed that of Ericsson (Ericsson run operator business only).

to enhance the core competitiveness, like to realize over 60% gross profit rate in optical transmission products through making the key components chip-based.

This mode of product development offers a realistic path for the growth of Chinese enterprises. The reason why some enterprises can serve as the industry benchmark is that they can grasp customer requirement and development trends accurately. It is nothing wrong for the following enterprises to carry out incremental development on the shoulders of giants, while if they are just satisfied with imitation like "knowing what but not knowing why", they are sure to waste a lot of development, not to mention to surpass their competitors. At that time, Huawei set seven or eight benchmarks, whose current product and whose product roadmap in the next three or even ten years was presented for the comprehensive study by the pre-research department and the product strategy department of Huawei. Considering the fact that the product roadmap of each benchmarking enterprise is based on its own market positioning, understanding of technology development trend and customer requirement, as well as its own ability, it is quite conceivable that what a big cake it will be to set the teeth on for a Chinese enterprise, Huawei at the same time, not to mention the possible "Star Wars" kind of traps, like the all-optical switch that has never come into being so far, for which Huawei had been pre-researching in 1999.

- **The stage of differentiative innovations during imitations:** Huawei is not alone, but with many successful enterprises doing the same. QQ, the money printer of Tencent, growing up out of the imitation of ICQ, won the market after adding such differentiated innovations as address book synchronization, cross terminal login, personalized avatar and quick file transfer. Even the business model of Apple was created upon the integration of its intelligent terminal and the open application platform based on the imitation of the iMode from Japan. In this stage, the innovation of enterprises must be built on the basis of reference, before transforming the customers' requirements into the features of products after a deep understanding of the customer requirements (often starting from the understanding of local customer requirements at the beginning), so as to build the differentiation advantage of products. The management reform of integrated product development (IPD) determines that Huawei's product innovation mode shifts from "technology-centered" to "customer-centered".

The key of the IPD process framework is to "do the right thing", that is, to correctly understand customer requirements upon which to define a sound product concept according. From the view of practice, the investment ratio among front-end product concept research, product development and product launch is 1:10:100, that is, if the enterprise did wrongly in product concept without timely correction, it will suffer a waste at 100 times of the investment after the launch of the product.

How to obtain information of requirements? What categories do the requirements fall into? How to prioritize requirements and meet them in order, and how to manage the changes in requirements and ensure the consistency of the requirements? In order to solve these problems, Huawei established a marketing system with the focus on the management of the requirements of customers and the planning of its products.

The management of requirements reached the market nerve endings of the front-line "iron triangle". It established a three-level requirement management process and integrated product decision-making system, in addition to the optimization of the IPD process, with a market review (MR), even with the involvement of the participations of the strategic customers added, upon the key review points of the process product development, which not only quickened the respond to the requirements of the customers with the consistency of the requirements maintained, but also helped the transformation of the requirements into products with differentiated competitive advantages. With Huawei's continuous growth in the global market, its process and IT system for management of global requirements, as well as its methods for product planning to meet customers in different regions on the basis of fundamental version, have injected new connotation into Huawei's product innovation strategy.

After 2012, Huawei saw the second stage of its innovation, when it came to be "on an equal footing" with the world's leading competitors, especially after entering the "untouched fields", where Huawei found little to imitate or learn from, when Huawei emphasized more on the "customer-centered" inclusive innovation, for which many scholars and entrepreneurs hold different views.

In fact, Mr. Ren Zhengfei is a man with a strong technical complex. In 1978, he showed his great respect to many Nobel Prize-winning inventions of Marconi and Lucent Bell Laboratories when he attended the National Science and Technology Conference as a representative "science and technology pacesetter" from the army. However, when he saw these former benchmarks and competitors fall at his feet one by one, he fully realized that the innovation of a business organization must serve to "ensure the business success of the company", while after entering the "untouched fields", customer-oriented policies would serve well as the foundation of business success. Ren Zhengfei stressed that Huawei must focus on the main channel in the case of limited financial resources (even if when the financial resources are in abundance). It is necessary to clearly define the boundary of innovation and master the trend and the rhythm of the development of business, for "one step ahead, you may sacrifice a lot".

Talents are never in full supply, for which enterprises can't afford to wait for talent to appear, for even if there come the talents, they don't necessarily favor your enterprise. Therefore, in the process of the second global transformation, Huawei realizing inclusive innovations through global R & D layout carried out on considerations of the varied requirements and regional advantages, in addition to the full use of global intellectual resources. Inclusive innovation means drawing the essence of the "universe", including even learning from its competitors. Some people satirize Huawei for its copying the Internet model of Xiaomi, which Huawei never denies, besides, Huawei is also learning about the offline store layout and the ways to maintain high-profit margins by OPPO /vivo, the R & D of key devices and supply chain monopoly of Samsung, and the business model and ecological chain construction of apple... Don't you feel scared by such a competitor? And isn't such a competitor inspiring your respect?

2.1.1 The Innovation Strategy and System Architecture of Huawei—"Inclusive Innovation with Customer-Centered and Focus on the Main Channel"

Huawei had ever invested in many new products and new fields, with failures following like a shadow, including some major wastes in investment, in addition to detours in innovation strategy and organizational structure.

For greater development in the future, an enterprise needs to upgrade the product development mode for a greater advance of technology and market visibility after it has basically survived. To this end, Huawei established the pre-research department in 1998. In the initial stage, the pre-research department determines the roadmap for product development upon the understanding of the trend of technologies with their focus on tracking, learning and digesting the product roadmap of benchmarking enterprises. In terms of mechanism, Huawei established a two-level system of company-level pre-research management and product line pre-research management, and correspondingly broadband fixed network development pre-research project and future wireless network development pre-research project at the company level, as well as the pre-research project of each product line. In terms of investment, it was made sure that the pre-research investment accounts for 10% of the overall R & D investment, especially when considering the total number of personnel, Huawei ensured that 10% of the manpower from the product development system would be allocated to the pre-research department. Due to effective management and proper measures, the pre-research department has greatly enriched and promoted the planning and development of products. The 5G today is also a natural result of the development through 4G on the basis of the 3G blueprinted in 2003. The essence of the "server pool" proposed at that time was actually the "cloud" in today's cloud computing, though there had never been such a term at that time, besides, it was predicted that CT and IT would be integrated into ICT, a shred of great evidence that the pre-research has greatly improved Huawei's market visibility, and major reserves for relevant technologies and talents.

However, with the improvement of Huawei's R & D, they found fewer and fewer products of benchmarking enterprises to be referred to, and the product roadmap of benchmarking enterprises that can be pursued is even designed for the next decade. At this time, innovation gradually deviated from the market requirements. Huawei turned to copy the all-optical switch that led to the bankruptcy of Nortel, resulting in the declining conversion rate of innovative products. At the same time, IPD product R & D management reform is right on the way in Huawei, with emphasis on the requirements of the customers, which is taken as the main driver of product R & D. In 2001, the first Internet bubble burst, when Huawei experienced its first financial downfall. Under the circumstances of the company's overall investment reduction and streamlining of its department, the pre-research department, the key innovation organization of the enterprise was abolished, with most of its original leaders at the same level sent to the marketing department.

In the process of Huawei's full-scale global expansion, a major event happened, that was, Cisco's lawsuit against Huawei on intellectual property rights (IPR), which impressed Huawei and Ren Zhengfei deeply that how intellectual property rights and necessary technical reserves weighed, and how IPR was critical as a global passport. Therefore, in 2004, Huawei reconstituted the Pre-research and Standards Department with the core task to ensure Huawei's technologies be incorporated into the industry standards and apply for basic intellectual property rights through measures like pre-research with the focus on quality rather than quantity, for the purpose to exchange intellectual property rights with friendly enterprises to prevent similar lawsuits like that of Cisco, and to realize self-protection in terms of intellectual property rights. Since then, Huawei has gradually adapted to the rules of the global game. By exchanging intellectual property rights with its cooperators upon paying reasonable license fees, Huawei advanced a lot in the global market. At the same time, the layout of Huawei's global intellectual resources has basically done, and the continuous investment in technology accumulation and intellectual property rights not only realized greater financial returns, but also constituted Huawei's technological strength. The inclusive innovation strategy is back on the right track. Especially in 2012, after its total sales revenue exceeded Ericsson, Huawei set higher requirements and goals for innovation investment and strategic layout when the application of 5G and graphene technologies has won Huawei the global leading position in certain fields. In the same year, inspired by the movie *2012*, the Pre-research and Standards Department officially inaugurated as Huawei's Innovation Technology Center for the exploration of the future and management of risks with its new name as "2012 Laboratory".

From the ups and downs of Huawei's innovation, it can be concluded that different innovation strategies needed to be formulated at different stages of development for different enterprises, and consequently, it is particularly important to establish an innovation system suitable for the development of enterprises if they want to lessen their lost during the innovations. Huawei's three-level innovation system has been constantly improved through practices.

As shown in Fig. 2.1, Huawei's three-level innovation management system allocates the most uncertain technologies that may be applied in production in 5–10 years to the first level innovation system, which mainly includes domestic and foreign key universities, cooperative research institutions, innovation companies with cooperative investment and "Huawei 2012 Laboratory". The second level innovation system sees to the preliminary commercial verification formulated by Huawei's strategic marketing system based on the development roadmap of products and technology for 3–5 years upon the analysis and judgment of technology maturity for business and market opportunity window. The third level innovation system belongs to the product realization system, which is about the confirmation of the customer requirements and the development of products and marketing management. The three-level system forms a trumpet-shaped opportunity convergence process to make the

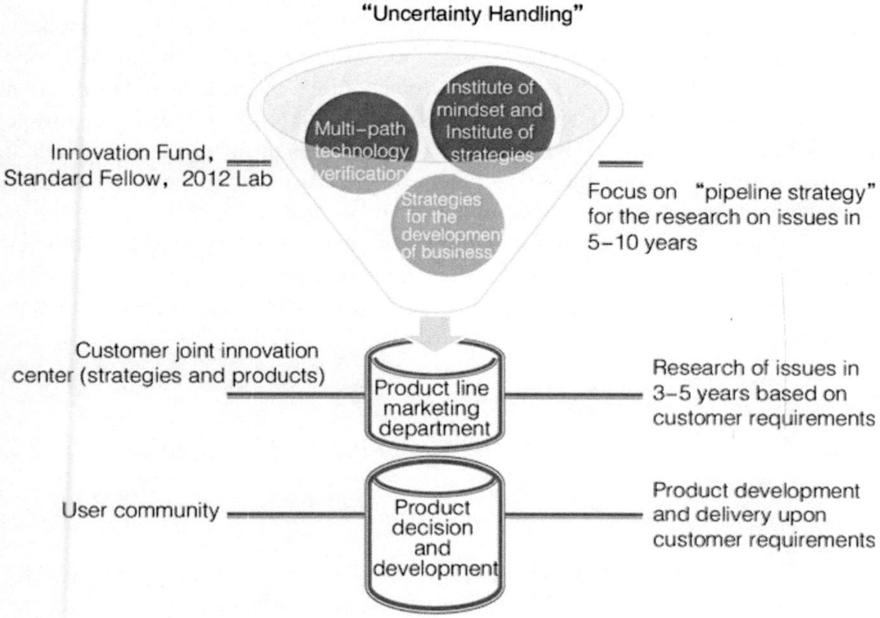

Fig. 2.1 Three-level innovation management system of Huawei

uncertainty of the future under control through strengthened the internal requirement management process, extended strategic customer joint innovation center and the requirement management with users' in-depth participation, as well as accurate evaluation of business opportunities and the pace of development of innovation mechanism. In the field of business with operators, Huawei actively encourages its customers/users to find problems with Huawei products and with feedbacks of their requirements, which once adopted, the proposer will be rewarded handsomely. In the field of terminals, Huawei has dug out many effective requirements, which were gradually implemented in different versions of its products, through Huawei Fans Community and super users.

In terms of innovation investment management, Huawei's R & D expenses account for 10% of the revenue, while innovation (pre-research) investment expenses account for 10% of the total R & D expenses. With the gradual increase of innovation risk, the investment intensity of a product from pre-research to prototype to mass production is 10 times and 100 times respectively. Therefore, the proportion of Huawei's innovation (pre-research) investment sees a steady increase, and may reach 20% of the total R & D expenses in the future. Increasing the investment in exploration can help accurately grasp the direction of product development.

On the choices of innovation, Huawei sticks to the main channel. Huawei has photovoltaic products and solutions as well, but this product line, as the escort of main channel products, is mainly to solve the problem of power consumption of wireless base stations in the regions like Africa. Even the innovation of graphene is primarily meant to solve the problem of poor user experience of mobile phone battery, which also means to serve the requirement of the main channel. However, in the choice of new business, many enterprises often fail to form a mutually supportive relationship with the original business, with their modes of management and talent structure failing to support the development of new business; In terms of mindset, these enterprises are keener on "speculation" in new concepts and follow the trend of new industries, instead of devoting themselves to the research of core technologies and products, not to say the spirit of "sitting on the cold bench for ten years to realize their great will", but are only interested in financing or raising stock prices or creating a "novel" theme.

2.1.2 Leader and Management Mechanism of Innovative Business

Many enterprises have encountered the problems that, being aged, the senior executives are insensitive to new business and feel unwilling to walk out of the comfort zone of the business. Therefore, the organizational configuration of innovation leaders presents as the priority. When choosing investment projects and start-ups, the people and the team also come as the first concern of the investment community. Huawei adopts basically the same method in the process of new business development of mobile terminal and enterprise network. Leaders with high prestige and strong interpersonal skills will be assigned to complete the organizational construction and basic business sorting of new business, before the aggressive and entrepreneurial leaders are selected for the breakthrough of new business. Under the leadership of Yu Chengdong, Huawei consumer BG has established its position in the industry; Yan Lida (literally means powerful in Chinese), the current leader of enterprise network BG, is as powerful as his name. Mr. Yan had once increased Huawei's business in Japan from US $200 million to US $2 billion, and it is believed that given time, the enterprise network business will develop even better under his leadership.

In terms of innovation management, especially in the evaluation mechanism, Huawei adopted a relatively tolerant attitude towards failures, with no requirements on immediate effects on investment in new fields, but generally 2–3 years of exploration. Ren Zhengfei said that there would never be failures for innovation, and even a "failure" can be a success in knowing which road will not work.

Innovation and changes are two powerful engines for Huawei's sustainable growth. Ren Zhengfei believes that Huawei's core competitiveness is management, because management, compared with technologies, is relatively hard to copy. Therefore, it has become a routine for Huawei to carry out "one minor change in three years and one major change in five years". In fact, in the process of Huawei's growth from a catcher to a leader, it has always complemented management with changes, with its innovation model constantly changing, whether for technological innovation, management innovation or business model innovation. Although there are great differences in mode of innovation, motivation and mode of management among large enterprises, small and medium-sized enterprises and start-up enterprises, innovation concept and management connotation should be consistent. Opportunism is the enemy of innovation. Of course, the development of new business calls for entrepreneurial leadership, new organizational style and new talents. However, without appropriate product strategy, sufficient strategic strength and supporting organizational changes, it is difficult to build core competence, and it will get little outcome for much effort.

2.2 Options on the Mode and Strategies of Innovation

The basis of "customer-centered" strategies for product innovation is the understanding of the requirements of the customers, on which, however, there are many misunderstandings, such as:

- Requirement means what the customers want;
- Overemphasizing the function and performance index of the products;
- Eyes on the cost or price of the product itself.

Correspondingly, some enterprises only care about "Me too" and competition through low prices when they make product strategies, but not finding the suitable market entry point upon the core competence and control points of products based on their own capabilities and market positioning instead.

2.2.1 Modes of Innovations for Enterprises

Innovation and change serve as two powerful engines for Huawei's sustainable growth. Geoffrey A. Moore classified innovation well in his book entitled *Dealing with Darwin – How Great Companies Innovate at Every Phase of Their Evolution*, as shown in Fig. 2.2. Huawei's successful practice is strong evidence that the modes of innovations mentioned in the book are also applicable to Chinese enterprises. However, many Chinese enterprises failed to formulate innovative strategies and themes of changes at different stages gradually on consideration of their own strategic positioning and product/business life cycle.

The life cycle of a business is generally divided into the growth period, mature period and recession period.

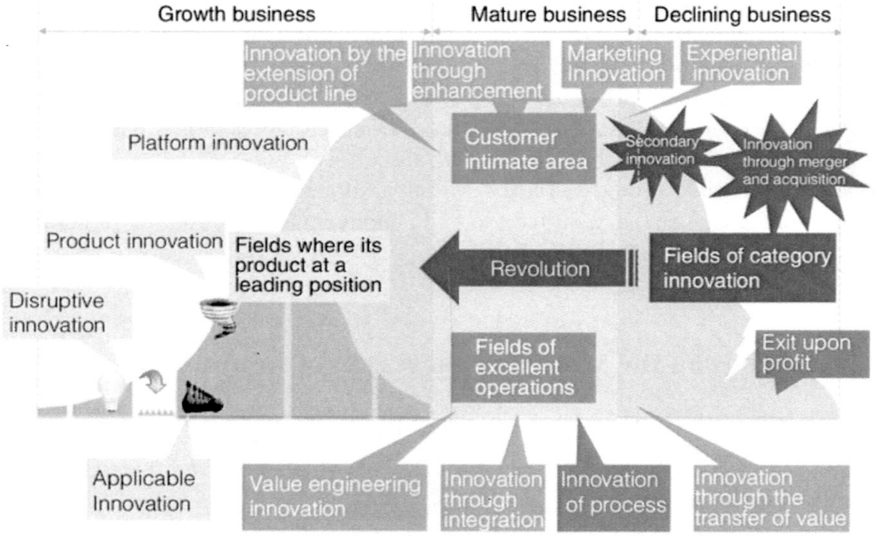

Fig. 2.2 Modes of innovation in a broad sense

2.2.1.1 Mode of innovation for business in the growth period

Business in a growth period usually comes with a new product that has never appeared in the industry, with great risks in investment and innovation, including the following modes of innovations.

1. **Disruptive Innovation:** Disruptive innovation refers to the creation of new products or services through disruptive technologies or business models. The planning of his kind of product calls for a strong grasp of customers' implicit needs and disruptive technologies. The biggest risk of this kind of innovation is to overcome the gaps, in addition to the technical difficulty, it also needs to meet the market requirements in terms of industrialization, utilization and operation. Typical successful cases include Sony tape recorder, DJI UAV (technology) and smartphones, etc.
2. **Applicable Innovation:** Applicable Innovation refers to developing new functions or combinations of new products, with the focus on customers to meet their extensive, urgent and potential needs. It is a solution innovation, and usually a kind of complex and customized application. For example, the application of X-ray technology for medical treatment, robots and UAVs as firefighting solutions for high-rise buildings.
3. **Product Innovation:** Product Innovation means to provide features or "killer" businesses that are not provided by current products. With the obvious differentiation advantages, it can meet the important needs of the customers well, and the key of whose success lies in its swift entrance into the market. The essence

of product innovation is actually a complete change of the original products in the market, which will impact much on product development, marketing selling propositions, brand and financial contributions. New energy vehicles, Taobao (innovations in the modes of credit guarantee and business), etc. can serve as examples of product innovation.

4. **Platform Innovation:** Platform Innovation means to reuse and create new value for the next generation of products through a simplified or relatively normalized product platform. For example, Tencent steadily creates new value through the new WeChat payment platform and financial platform by adding credit cards of the customers through WeChat red envelope over WeChat platform. BMW, a typical representative of the manufacturing industry, has accelerated the speed of product innovation with the reduced overall cost through the normalized automobile platform.

To occupy a share of the market during the growth of a business, enterprises must maintain a long-term firm strategy in the aspects of innovative mindset, innovation mechanism (gene or foundation), innovation investment, innovative talents, etc. The investment will go hand in hand with risks, while once succeeded, the enterprise will gain the leading position in the area of similar products, with a great leading edge and high profits as natural results. For example, as the forerunner of UAV, DJI UAV, holds a stable control in the medium and high-end machine market with more than 70% of its sales revenue comes from overseas because of its absolute leading technology, for whom the channel dealers must pay the deposit before queuing for delivery, while the main responsibility of sales is to follow the bill, and the core of the business lies in product innovation and marketing.

The transformation process from "Made in China' to "Created in China" for Chinese enterprises started from the declining business relying upon the business of "processing of imported materials or according to supplied samples, assembling of supplied parts, and compensation trade". After the construction of basic industrial capacity, Chinese enterprises develop to relatively high-end mature business, and the "trade-production-R&D" manufacturing enterprises represented by Lenovo and the manufacturing enterprises represented by Huawei, who develops their products and markets simultaneously. At present, under the pressure of industrial upgrading and the guidance of national innovation strategy, an increasing number of enterprises started to invest in growth businesses with greater risks and higher requirements for innovation ability.

2.2.1.2 Mode of innovation for a mature business

More Chinese enterprises started from the mature business on consideration of their actual strength. The business in this area has been verified in the market, and the investment risk is relatively small. But the supply market is rich in products, and the enterprise's innovation strategy and ability are the keys to occupy a place in the Red

Sea market. At this time, innovation can be divided into product and marketing innovation mode for customers, namely "customer close area" innovation, and innovation mode to improve the internal operation efficiency of enterprises, namely "excellent operation area" innovation.

1. **Mode of innovation by extension of product line**

Leading enterprises in the market improve the market penetration through developing from one product to multiple related products, or from domestic version to overseas version through the mode of innovation by the extension of the product line. But in doing so, they need to balance the customization and efficiency caused by customer segmentation. Huawei successfully did so through the establishment of limited product platforms, such as European standard product platform for emerging markets based on the Chinese version, low-cost product platform based on Indian version, high-end European standard product based on European developed operators, product platform based on American Standard, and product platform conforming to Japanese standard in later stage, on the basis of each of whose standard, to carry out the necessary customized development according to the needs of different countries and key customers.

2. **Mode of innovation through the enhancement of product**

The upgrading, enhancement of the function, improvement of the quality, beautification of the appearance, optimization of the interface, increase of the application the basis of the original product can further stimulate the desire of customers to decide on the purchase, during the process of which, there is generally no major product platform switching, such as iPhone 6/7/8… There are no essential changes in the actual experience, but partial optimization and enhancement. When the iPhone first came out, it meets the maximum at almost any point on the $APPEALS, with its simple and environmentally friendly packaging, its appearance more exquisite than any mobile phone at that time, its interface friendly and easy to use, its powerful function and abundant applications, its compact structure, its excellent quality, as well as its store open to experience, but at the same time, the price stands at the highest, which completely subverting the industry standard and customer experience perception. For the enterprises entering the market for competition, they usually choose a small number of products, deeply understand the market requirement and customer pain points, and form distinctive enhanced functions in the market segments, so as to build a differentiated competitive advantage, rather than just compete through low prices. When Huawei opened up the domestic market in the early days, it conducted a lot of customized product design by approaching customers to meet their needs to the greatest extent upon full play given to the advantages of local manufacturers, before it has to strike a balance between standardization and customization as the customer base becomes larger and larger in the later stage. Interestingly, when Huawei plans to continue to launch "customized" services in the European market, developed European operators tell Huawei instead that they want to be provided with standardized products, which is convenient for them to choose suppliers, which is an exact interpretation that different development stages and different customers call for different innovation strategies.

3. Product marketing and experience innovation

Both product marketing and experience innovation belong to the category of product marketing strategy innovation. Due to the impact of the Internet, the offline and online integrated innovative marketing mode is used by more and more enterprises, of which the digital marketing and marketing automation technology constitutes the key to ensure the success of such marketing innovation. Marketing innovation and experience innovation draw great attention from B2C consumer goods market, so more and more B2B markets are taking the initiative to adopt them, the core idea of which is to transform the original one-way bombing marketing mode into a two-way, active and targeted marketing mode. The new product on-site release broadcasted through the global network personally presided over by the top leader of the enterprise, various characteristic experience stores and communities, and Virtual Shopping Festival by various opinion leaders activated, became an innovative mode to go to the customers. Even the traditional product displays can contribute to the steady improvement of customer experience. For example, the "novel scenario" strategy of Gome offers intelligent life solutions based on kitchen scenario and family entertainment solutions based on living room scenario through the marriage of electric appliances and housekeeping appliances, with its offline physical stores transforming from electrical stores to innovative retail experience areas that customers can make biscuits, learn photography, play video games and watch VR movies, which prolongs the customer's lingering with the enhanced shopping experience. In addition, VR technology can be further developed as the main tool of online experience to realize a seamless connection with offline shopping. BG, the manufacturers mainly producing industrial equipment, tries to offer customers the benefits of Huawei equipment to customers' business through different scenarios and solutions in product marketing events such as the design of exhibition halls and world-class exhibitions. With cloud computing technology, Huawei enables experience "in-person" of its most advanced technology and latest products to customers in remote areas or overseas through shared resources of the global exhibition halls by linking them together.

In the innovation area of "excellent operation", the so-called value engineering innovation just means to reconstruct the function and cost of products to improve the value of products to customers. As improved functions have already taken as the focus of the innovation in the areas "led by products" and "close to the customer", the value engineering innovation is more about changing the cost structure of products and reducing the overall cost.

4. Value engineering innovation

Value engineering innovation mainly refers to structural cost reduction, commonly used means are as follows.

(1) **Replacement of key parts**. For example, Huawei's optical network products saw a gross profit at a rate of over 60% thanks to its early self-made optical devices and components. The later Kirin mobile phone chip kit lowered the unit purchase price from $200 to $20, which not only cut the cost, but also reduced the risk from the supply chain and set Huawei free from the dependence on key upstream suppliers.

(2) **Reduction of labor costs**. With the increase of labor cost year by year, more and more enterprises gradually transfer their factories to the mainland of China and even the underdeveloped overseas areas. Here, enterprises need to consider the qualifications of the local labor force, environments, social and government services. While on the other hand, through the introduction of "intelligent manufacturing", enterprises saw declined dependence on the labor force through the automation of production line and management automation by the applications of a large number of industrial robots for heavy repetitive work. For example, Foxconn has completed the deployment of 1 million robots for its Foxbot Project in addition to its rational layout of factories around the world. In this way, it not only forms the future competence by opening up the channel of growth in career from ordinary blue-collar workers to workers in the science and technology industry, in addition to the reduction of the number of ordinary workers.

(3) **Platform cost reduction and normalization of procurement**. Platform cost reduction and normalization of procurement mean cutting the number of product platforms and normalize the main parts. For example, many models of BMW 5 series adopt the same chassis and engine, with the engine set to different swept volumes through software. From the perspective of a single engine with high configuration and low utilization, it is not cost-effective, but from the perspectives of the overall purchase quantity discount, quality assurance, delivery accuracy, assembly and other comprehensive costs, the cost advantage can be thoroughly obvious.

The best way to reduce the cost is to open the self-owned platform and convert the cost into income. The biggest cost difference between traditional retailers such as Gome and Suning and Internet retailers such as JD.com and Tmall is that they have their own logistics system and stores. In order to realize the O2O transformation, Suning takes the lead in opening the offline resource platform, realizing the marketization and socialization of resources, forming a third-party logistics system, transforming the original huge cost into a new source of income.

(4) **Reduction of the cost for the product life cycle**. Product cost consists of Capital Expenditure (CAPEX) and operating expenditure (OPEX), which come together as Total Cost of Ownership (TCO). Enterprises need to identify the cost structure of products, find out the key points, and reduce costs from the perspective of the whole rather than the part.

For example, Haidilao found that the fastest growing and most suitable part of the cost for tapping potential was the store rent and storage, transportation and distribution, although the total cost increased year by year. Therefore, on the one hand, to reduce the cost of storage, transportation and distribution and the loss during the process, Haidilao jointly built distribution centers in Beijing, Shanghai, Xi'an and Zhengzhou with HAVI Group of the United States, and adopted innovative semi-finished product preservation technology. Each logistics center was equipped with a set of advanced cleaning, inspection, refrigeration and freezing equipment, in addition to a strictly standardized production chain, whose advantages in health and safety, quality and freshness have been certified by Beijing Paralympic Games and designated as the special distribution center for the Olympic Games; On the other hand, the planned consumption management of the backstage distribution center and the front restaurants is highly standardized, and constantly moving towards the ultimate goal of reducing the rent by "cutting kitchens for the branches". The standard "unmanned" process in backstage ensures the safety, high efficiency, low inventory and low store area of the logistics system, which not only greatly reduces the operation cost, but also forms the core competence of the enterprise.

For the pan-manufacturing industry, the whole process cost involves links like marketing, R & D, production, procurement, logistics, technical services, and management, all of which should work together to reduce the cost, instead of "fighting on their own". The platform operation and flat management of Huawei's marketing system featuring "supports for the frontline" can effectively reduce the marketing cost. Accurate requirement management makes the products more marketable, while clear market planning and accurate sales forecast also play an important role in back-end supply chain business negotiation and reduction on production cost. Through centralized procurement and optimization of the supplier management process, Chinese operators greatly reduce costs on equipment procurement and supplier management. For example, Cisco has greatly reduced the cost of global technical support, maintenance and equipment upgrade by adding remote intelligent maintenance function in the equipment, which increases the profitability of the enterprise on the one hand, and improves customer satisfaction on the other.

(5) **Reduction of other comprehensive costs**. In addition to the optimization of product cost composition, enterprises can reduce comprehensive operating costs by ways like establishing overseas financing channels. For example, through the rational global distribution, especially taking advantage of the loopholes in Irish and American company laws, Apple has imported nearly 30 billion US dollars of profits into its Irish subsidiaries in four years to achieve the purpose of tax avoidance. Because according to the local policy of Ireland, those who actually control the company need to pay tax, and the subsidiaries of cross-border enterprises do not need to pay tax to Ireland. However, according to the policy of the United States, only enterprises with their address in the United States need to pay taxes. Huawei established financial companies in many regions and countries around the world to obtain financing channels at a much lower cost than domestic financing. In addition, Huawei also built factories in Brazil to avoid Brazil's high tariff of 25% for machine imports.

Therefore, enterprises should systematically formulate a "value engineering" innovation strategy according to the characteristics of the industry and their own situation.

5. **Innovation through Integration**

Through the solution and centralized management system, enterprises can help reduce the maintenance cost of complex products for customers. Functional intelligence and operation by a "fool" can be realized by a gradual shift from the original need for professional operation and maintenance to a lot of items as small as smart phones or portable computers, or as big as complex industrial machinery. For example, Komtrax system, an intelligent management system of Komatsu machinery, can extract real-time information such as the location of machinery, start-up situation, operation and wear of various parts, for which Komatsu can not only flexibly adjust production, logistics and sales of spare parts internally according to Komtrax data, but also inform customers in advance of the existing problems and maintenance methods of machinery, which not only reduces the operating costs of the enterprise, but also improves service revenue, customer satisfaction and product brand image.

6. **Innovation through the transfer of value**

Innovation through the transfer of value means shifting to the high-profit area of the value chain, including the repositioning of the mode of business. After decades of rapid economic development, all walks of life have gone out of the traditional mode of extensive development to "stake out their turf". For example, the TMT industry, industrial machinery industry, engineering construction industry, animal husbandry and so on, which the writer has consulted deeply, are undergoing profound industry value transfer, on one end of which is innovation through transfer to the core equipment, core components, core technology, core materials and other key technology, while on the other end of which is the innovation through transfer to integrated solutions, operation management and other comprehensive ability. In the process of the transformation of the value chain, enterprise strategy, organizational process and talent structure should be changed accordingly.

7. **Innovation of process**

Changes and innovations of the process can be a very big topic in that they will fundamentally change the operation mode and organizational system of the enterprises upon breaking the original business model of the enterprises. For example, Fuyao Glass achieved a gross profit margin of 40% by optimizing the production process and manufacturing process, while the average gross profit margin of the industry remained only 5%. Three years after the implementation of IPD in IBM, the product development process has been greatly improved, with a number of indicators refreshed: (1) the time of the launching of products has been reduced from 70 to 20 months for high-end products, 50 months to 10 months for middle-end products, and less than 6 months for low-end products; (2) The proportion of R & D expenditure in total revenue decreased from 12 to 6%: (3) R & D losses fell from 25 to 6%. With the shortening of the R & D cycle and the reduction of R & D expenditure, came the improvement of quality, the substantial increase of per-capita output rate and the reduction of cost.

2.2.1.3 Mode of innovation for business in the declining period

For businesses in the declining period, enterprises must hunt for new "cheese" through three main innovation modes, namely, starting a new undertaking, conducting acquisition and merger, and admitting exit, in carrying out each of which, enterprises need to face huge challenges, naturally.

1. Starting a new undertaking: Enterprises need to reorient themselves by using their internal resources for a growth product, or developing new growth business through innovation. The new business should be relatively independent of the original business and conform to the law of the development of the new business in organizational structure, talent introduction and incentive mechanism. In addition, the difficulty of initial market development of the new business can be better reduced by using the original excellent internal and external resources. For example, Huawei's terminal product department has continued to use the original internal sales platform for quite a long time after its establishment, and the original operator customers have also continued to be used in the sales channels; In terms of brand, there had ever been a debate about whether to continue to use Huawei brand or to use a totally independent brand. Finally, it was determined that Huawei's brand advantage will continue to be used, but in terms of products, different sub-brands will be adopted to suit the different customer groups. In terms of internal resources, Huawei gave full play to its human resources reserves, as well as the technology accumulation of wireless product line, Hisilicon and 2012 Laboratory, in addition to the introduction of a large number of external intellectual resources.

But in the perspective of the product development process, marketing management process, supply chain management, the process for a new business can differ from the original business process very much. In terms of organizational setup and mode of management, it should conform to the "entrepreneurial" culture. For example, GE it can be taken as "starting a new undertaking" when GE experienced its digital transformation from giving up finance and other businesses to returning to intelligent manufacturing. Instead of learning from the old IT giants such as IBM and Oracle, GE completely imitates the model of Silicon Valley start-ups in terms of culture and methodology, such as lean entrepreneurship and agile development process, which completely overturned Welch's practice.

2. Innovation through M & A: It is a quick way to obtain innovation resources and solve the issue of business innovation through merger and acquisition, the advantage of which is that it can achieve rapid results, but with the risk that whether the trend of technology can be accurately understood, and whether the two sides can really integrate into the perspective of the corporate culture, process of business and mode of management after M & A. The case of the greatest failure can be TCL's M & A of Thomson, in which the technology of imaging tube, a technology that is on the verge of elimination, can not bring innovation, but become a burden after the merger. Lenovo has experienced difficulties from contradiction to integration in the acquisition of IBM PC business, low-end server business and Motorola mobile phone business. Whether the merger of server business and mobile phone business can be successful remains to be tested. The relatively successful case is Geely's acquisition of VOLVO. Although the restrictions on technology sharing at the time of acquisition signed between both sides, yet over time, Geely has seen significant improvement in its production technology, design and management, while during the development of the new model of SUVlink, Geely has been sharing the platform with VOLVO, which serves as a proof of the obvious improvement of Geely's innovation capability.

3. Exit upon Profit: It means to close, shut down, merge or transform the old business, leaving only a small number of personnel for product life cycle maintenance for the system running in the market. For the old business, we need to consider extending its life cycle under the premise of limiting resource investment, such as selling products to new underdeveloped areas. PHS from Japan is a very successful case in doing so, taking advantage of China Telecom's eagerness to develop mobile services when China's delayed in issuing 3G licenses Japanese enterprises successfully extended the service life of this obsolete product in China for more than 10 years through China's agent UT Starcom by taking advantage of the loopholes in communication control.

2.2.2 Finding the right position and establishing the right strategies for innovation

The choice of an innovation strategy should be aligned with the strategic positioning of enterprises.

- **Enterprises with strengths in core technologies:** Enterprises in this category can lead the development of industry and technology with their own innovation ability and R & D advantages, typical representatives of which include new energy vehicle Tesla, mobile communication chip manufacturer Qualcomm, UAV enterprise DJI, etc.
- **Enterprises with strengths in recourses:** This category sees enterprises of particular relations with governments, customer relations or strong financial supports, such as the enterprises under the Japanese Consortium; or those who control the key links of the ecological chain after years of development, such as Samsung, as well as enterprises like Alibaba and Tencent, whose huge customer resources have become the core advantageous resources of enterprises.
- **Enterprises as quick followers:** Until Huawei entered the "untouched fields" with attempts to act as a leading company, it has been a quick follower. OPPO and vivo are typical fast following enterprises. Duan Yongping, the founder of OPPO and vivo, put forward the slogan of "dare to follow", which is actually the innovation strategy established upon the characteristics of the enterprise itself.

- **Enterprises with strengths in manufacturing:** The enterprises of this type boast core mold design technology, precise manufacturing technology, efficient engineering and quality control. For example, boasting a number of invention patents in mold design technology and precision manufacturing technology. Foxconn claims that no one dares to say it can when Foxconn says can't.
- **Enterprises as unique suppliers in the market:** Many small and medium-sized specialized enterprises fall into this type, which have great strength and unique advantages in quality, cost and supply for being long engaged in the design and manufacture of single products. For example, Wanxiang Group focuses on the design and manufacture of "universal joint", and develops its own famous brand gradually from the "OEM or ODM" business in the world.

2.3 Formulation of Strategies on Product Innovation and Decision Management

From the practical point of view of the development of Chinese enterprises, a "customer-centered" product innovation strategy presents the most realistic choice for enterprises.

2.3.1 Steps of Product Innovation Strategy Formulation

The formulation of a product innovation strategy can be divided into five steps, as shown in Fig. 2.3.

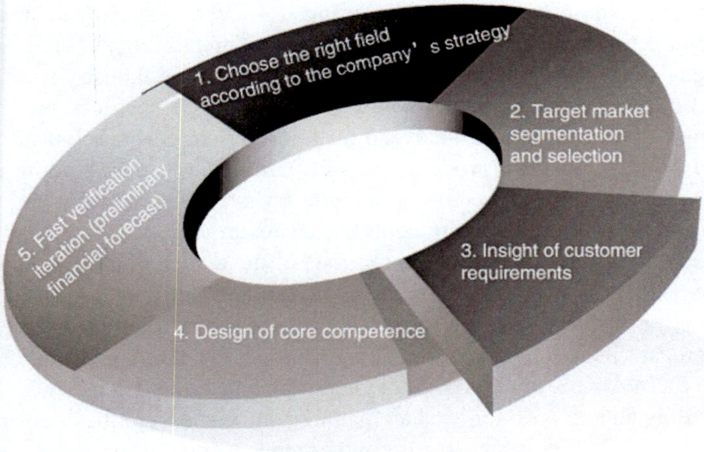

Fig. 2.3 Framework of the process of the formulation of product innovation strategy

First, the product strategy should be in line with the overall development strategy of the enterprise, because the company's strategy has pointed out the direction of product development based on the analysis of the trends of the development of industry, technology development and transfer of value chain trend from the overall perspective.

The second step is to select the specific target market and segment customers after the general determination of the areas.

The third step is to collect, analyze, make judgments and decisions on customers' needs.

The fourth step is to build the differentiated competitive advantage of products after the comparison to the similar products of main competitors on the basis of a deep understanding of customers' needs.

The fifth step is to formulate key marketing strategies and make a preliminary analysis of product profitability. Different from formal product development, the stage should have some flexibility in the design scheme, cost and quality with the highlight on the realization of the key "killer" features of products. It is necessary to quickly iterate to form the final product specification definition upon the verification from the small batch of friendly customers.

From the whole, we can see that comprehensive and profound analysis of the customers' requirement serves as the basis of building the strengths of product differentiation, while before the analysis of customers' requirements, the issue of requirements source should be firstly solved through collecting the customer requirements as much as possible.

2.3.1.1 Comprehensive Collection on Market Requirements

In practice, Huawei has summarized a set of efficient multi-dimensional methods to collect customers' requirements, as shown in Fig. 2.4. When entering an area, the enterprise should first understand the threshold and technical requirements of the industry by analyzing the trend of technology development and industry standards. At the same time, the existing products and roadmap of the competitors, especially benchmarking enterprises need be analyzed for a further understanding of product requirement from benchmarking products. Actively participation in the bidding activities all kinds of customers, especially of the industry's leading customer can help. Fully understand the essence of requirements that customers accumulated over a long period of time through fully learning the requests of the tender. Huawei ensures to 100% comply with the product requirements defined in the bidding documents during the bidding for the business with Telefónica. The reason is that Telefónica serves not only the significant index of sales in Spain and Europe, but also a great influencer on the whole Latin American market, so the requirements defined in its tender have important guiding significance for product planning and can ensure the competence of products in the world. The relevant terms of the tender are defined upon the conclusions formed by leading customers and benchmarking friends after years of research

Fig. 2.4 Comprehensive collections of customer requirements

and analysis of the trend of the development of market and technology and the needs of customers. Even the possible barriers pre-set by friendly competitors can serve as a way to know better about the requirements of the customers as well as the strengths of the friendly competitors, which can make the less-developed enterprises more efficient with less efforts in the future. Face to face communications with customers are the most direct way to obtain the requirements of them. According to the relationship with customers and the significance of customers, the modes of communications can be divided into peak routine strategic discussions and forums for senior level of enterprises, routine communication and professional exchanges for all aspects and all levels of customer, and user conference for the common relationship between the grass-roots and the customer, including the partner meeting and consultation general meeting, exhibition, launching conference and promotion activities jointly held with partners.

The advancement of digital marketing technology provides a new means for collections of requirements. Driven by the Internet economy, enterprises and individuals prefer to collect customer needs, find sales leads and realize sales through online systems such as search engines, social media, enterprise websites and e-malls. More and more enterprises start to adopt the three-dimensional marketing mode through the integration of shops of bricks as well as shops of clicks, and from the perspective of requirements acquisition alone, the cost over online shops is obviously lower than that of offline stores. Therefore, enterprises must adapt to the new market requirements, open up requirement collection channels to get customers involved in enterprise innovation activities. But the establishment of a digital marketing system calls for the upgrading of the IT system of the enterprises and the construction of clear process and system architecture.

2.3.1.2 Methodology of Customer Requirements Analysis

As shown in Table 2.1, the classic $APPEALS for the analysis of the customer requirements comprehensively defines eight dimensions of product requirements. As the basic theory of requirement management, the description of the main dimensions of $APPEALS basically follows the consulting results provided by IBM to Huawei. At present, many books and articles about IPD misinterpreted $APPEALS for not fully understanding the actual meaning of each element, or because of the literal translation upon "mechanically copying" the ideas from English. Here, we update them as follows.

Table 2.1 Eight dimensions of $APPEALS requirements analysis

$ for price	A for availability	P for package	P for performance
Affected by the following factors: Engineering Capacity Technology Raw materials Production Suppliers Manufacturing Components Labor cost Management cost Equipment	What are the customer needs reflected? When, where and how to get it? Marketing Sales Channels Distribution Delivery period Advertising Configuration Optional configuration Pricing Customization	The physical appearance and geometric features before the eyes of customers: Style Size, quantity Geometric design Modularity Architecture Surface Mechanical structure Identification Images Internal and external packaging	Expected functions of the product: Functions Interface Features Power Speed Capacity Adaptability Multi-function
E for ease of use	A for assurance	L for life cycle cost	S for social acceptance
All users, buyers, operators and distributors need be taken into consideration: User friendly Control Display Ergonomics Training Documentation Help system Human factors Interface Operation	Guaranteed performance under foreseeable conditions: Reliability Quality Safety Error bound Integrity Intensity Adaptability Dynamicity Load Redundancy	Life cycle cost includes: Life span Operation time/downtime Safety Reliability Maintainability Services Spare parts (Old products) Path for transformation Standardization Infrastructure Cost for installation and operation	Other factors affecting procurement besides the customers' requirements: Indirect impact Consultants Purchasing agent Standard organization Government Social recognition (environmental protection, green, health, etc.) Politics, laws, regulations Shareholders Management, employees, unions

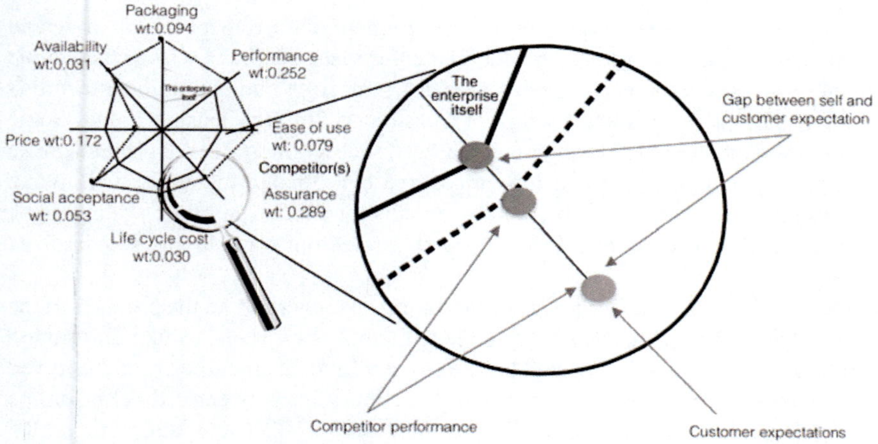

Fig. 2.5 The difference analysis of customer expectation and competitiveness

- Price ($): The traditional definition of $ Price is shown in Fig. 2.5. It is one of the customers' requirements that Chinese enterprises are most ready to meet, and a means of competition that Chinese enterprises are "masterful" of. But with the emergence of new technologies and business models such as "Internet+", "0 payment", equipment leasing and PAYG can meet the needs of customers in many aspects, so the leading supplier needs to focus on meeting the needs of customers without the use of competition strategy through the low price of competitive suppliers. Huawei had ever adopted the strategy of "entering at low price entry, and expansion and upgrading to high price", which not only lowered the entry threshold, but also ensured the goal of overall profit. For example, in the bidding process of telecom operators' equipment, Huawei achieved its overall profitability in the later stage through steady expansion of the board with the increase of users, following equipment entrance at a low price for the small amount of construction in the first phase to bring the whole machine rack into the operator's. In the construction project of the future generation network for Deutsche Telekom, in which the author had ever been personally involved, Huawei formulated the marketing strategy of "occupying the core network at a low price and entering the access network with the largest purchase volume". Although the sales of the core network were not realized due to non-technical reasons, the scale sales of the access network were realized. Product mix and solutions are one of the important methods for leading manufacturers to build market barriers, but with the good care taken about the direct internal benefit distribution of product line. We also need to well understand the customer's mode of decision-making on investment, especially in the economic downturn in that the customer's capital expenditure (CAPEX) will not be very large, which calls for a gradual increase in the investment upon the growth of the users and income through operation, that is, to realize the transformation of equipment investment to operation investment.

Only by fully understanding the real requirement of customers for the price and making a win–win business model, can enterprises keep away from the simple price war. Many large and medium-sized engineering equipment manufacturers solved the price-sensitive problem of customers through leasing mode. Some small and medium-sized equipment markets, such as enterprises of printers, make profits by selling printers at low prices and consumable materials such as ink cartridges at high prices, which however calls for a redesign of the pricing mode in the market of weak intellectual property protection k and highly standardized parts.

- Availability (A): Availability means to inform customers about the products of the enterprises, which are easily accessible to them. For example, availability should take questions like when to get? Where to get it? and whether the products proved "not like described" into consideration. The connection between offline and online operations is essential. especially for the mode of B2B and B2C. Originally, Huawei runs its website as one-way propaganda, just like many enterprises will do. BG enterprises websites designed e-commerce platforms for small and medium-sized customers, while its own internet marketing model such as Huawei mall has been further developed for customer BG. The reason why there would be the so-called "hunger marketing' is mostly that the requirement is not met. Huawei and Xiaomi both acknowledge that they are "unable to do it" for "lack of stores", while the deeper reason for that is the lack of market confidence and insufficient stock.
- Packaging (P): Please note that we use the gerund "packaging, which includes internal and external packages and labeling, the shape of the product, components and instructions. Apple, as a typical representative of B2C, sets a benchmark for the industry, which Samsung and Huawei follow suit one after another, just the same way as German construction machinery serves a typical representative of B2B.
- Performance (P): Performance is one of the focuses of competition, as well as the most obvious manifestation of the competence of the products, for which comparison should be made item by item by making good use of strengths with avoidance of weaknesses, upon a deep understanding of the customers' requirements to highlight the USP.
- Ease of use (E): Ease of use refers to features like a user-friendly graphical interface, foolproof operation and installation through one click. Apple creates the industry first with its smartphone interface easy to operate even for children who know not much English. Exceeding customer expectations in terms of ease of use often becomes a key factor for customers' decisions, which also explained why the "experiential" economy is booming recently. In the field of industrial products manufacturing, ease of use is reflected in the modularization, easy assembly and easy debugging of the equipment, which is particularly suitable for SKD and CKD production modes in the process of internationalization, if accompanied with good ergonomic design and training guidance, the product competence of enterprises will be greatly improved, without any failure to lose he contract like some products for the customers not instructed how to connect to the adapter. To

reduce the service expenditures to small and medium-sized customers, enterprises can help the agents meet the needs of customers in terms of ease of use through videos or online services over websites or mobile APPs.

- Assurance (A): Assurance mainly covers the guarantee in the perspectives of quality, service and safety, such as personal safety, leakage radiation, exchange or return within the period of quality assurance, maintenance services, and so on for mechanical and electronic equipment. Komatsu's intelligent system is of a great reference value. By monitoring the starting status of mechanical products and the wear degree of important parts, Komatsu timely reminds the customers about the maintenance and preparation of spare parts, which greatly improves customer satisfaction and sales of spare parts.
- Life cycle cost (L): IBM's defined this very at a very early time in its IPD process, the significance of which Huawei didn't really understand until 2005 when it became a strategic supplier of BT. Total cost of ownership (TCO) has two meanings, the one is that the products provided by the supplier make the customer's TCO lowest when the customer carries out business; and the other is that the TCO of the products by suppliers themselves is the lowest. TCO serves as one of the key means for leading manufacturers to build competitive barriers, and the key is to let customers understand the difference between the transaction price and TCO. For example, the early free maintenance services by the foreign communication equipment manufacturers posed an important shielding of domestic manufacturers. In addition, in overseas developed markets, TCO, such as the recovery of equipment at the end of its life calls for the attention of enterprises as well.
- Social acceptance (S): No overstatement of the role of the brand doesn't necessarily mean that the brand is not important, but means the brand should not be taken as an excuse for poor expansion of the new markets. The fame of a brand is made, not publicized. In the process of globalization, it is very critical to comply with local standards and legal provisions, among which, words of mouth of the third party (such as consulting company) have far better effects than the "praising your own broth". In addition, it is necessary to identify the real requirements under the current fashionable slogan of "environmental protection, low-carbon economy". When Huawei was communicating with the CTO of DT about the environmental protection of equipment, the other side asked bluntly: considering that the annual electricity cost of DT's equipment is 400 million euro, how much can Huawei's equipment save the expenditures on electricity? The other issue is about green energy. Huawei makes photovoltaic products as well, but not to catch up with the fashion and grasp the so-called opportunity, instead, to help customers reduce operating costs and promote the sales of their own equipment by providing photovoltaic products to Africa and some other areas where the cost of oil-fired generators is high but with abundant solar and wind energy.

Some of these elements define the key elements in the process of product development, and others define the key elements in the process of product launch. Therefore, product planning is a combination of "innovation + creativity", in which these elements are related to each other, for which the important point is to fully grasp the customer requirements, but not with attention paid to the function, performance and price only.

A Case

In the requirement analysis of a leading pump enterprise in China, one of the product lines sets the weight of price requirement as 40%, and the weight of life cycle cost as 5%. The superficial understanding of customer requirements makes the leading enterprise fall into the "whirlpool" of a price war with competitors, and unable to build a competitive threshold upon the high quality and service advantages of its own products. In fact, the product runs in a tough environment, so customers attach great importance to product quality and life cycle cost. While at the same time, the competitor only offers one year free maintenance, while the enterprise provides three years free maintenance, with the quote merely 5% higher than that of the competitor. But they fall into a simple price war just because while marketing, the sales staff failed to show customers the advantage that the average annual price of products is much lower than that of competitors in the whole life cycle.

With the changes of the times, to endow each element of $APPEALS with a new connotation, the mutual transformation relationship between each element and the essence behind the customer requirements must be fully understood as well. The core of requirement management is to balance customer expectation management and competitive differentiation management, as shown in Fig. 2.5. Sometimes it is necessary to achieve the effect of "winning by one move" by offering functions or features exceeding the expectation of customers in some aspects, while for the other time we just need to do better than our competitors, for actually, it is very difficult to fully meet customers' expectations or beat our competitors in an all-round way. Therefore, it needs to be carried out based on the considerations of the priority of customer requirements, difficulties in engineering, the time window of opportunity.

To achieve the "win–win" outcome, in addition to sound management of the customers' expectations, comprehensive judgment needs to be made, which can be considered in the following aspects.

- Significance of requirements: It is necessary to make clear whether the requirements are basic requirements or industry standards, whether it is a necessary option for product competition, and whether it can bring unique value (differentiation advantage) to customers.
- Proposers of the requirements: Priority should be given to meet the needs of key customers, while the needs of general customers are to meet selectively.
- Investment return over requirements: The most direct one can be the profitability analysis of products, but for those products mainly for competition, indirect financial return and market value can be used for the analysis as well.
- Development time and opportunity window for the requirements: For the requirements feature difficulties, call for a long time with the possibility of missing the opportunity windows, careful considerations need be taken, unless the requirements can improve the product competence in the long run.

In the formulation of product innovation strategy, differentiated innovation based on the incremental development of customer needs and competitive requirements turns out to be a realistic choice for Chinese enterprises. To meet the needs of customers, the input–output ratio should be considered, and the needs can be achieved in different stages of the product roadmap. Products with unique value call for more profound customer insights. Especially when customers have raised no obvious requirements on the features of the products but only their pain points, it is time for the enterprises to tap customer requirements. SPI boasts a unique methodology, that is, through efficient questions and interviews, to find the pain points of customers at different levels, to analyze the relevance and transmission of the pain points, to build a preliminary solution and a complex analysis upon repeated verification and confirmation, so as to confirm customer needs and form sales opportunities.

2.3.2 Four Elements of Innovation-Decision Management

Even with clear processes for the formulation of product strategy and for the development of an integrated product, Huawei has still suffered major setbacks in the process of product innovation, including three times of "meeting its Waterloo" for investments of over RMB 100 million, which calls for deep reflection by all enterprises.

2.3.2.1 Lessons From the Failures of Huawei's Innovation

Huawei's three typical failure cases interpret the significance of the decision-making for innovations.

1. **Soft switching system abandoned mercilessly by customers**

Background of the project: The digital program-controlled C&C08 switch, No.1 in the domestic market with a high reputation, serves once as the key cornerstone of Huawei's development from scratch, with an estimated value of more than RMB 10 billion upon the evaluation initiated by Huawei. However, changes are undergoing quietly in the field of telecommunication technology, and influenced by the development of Internet technology, the traditional compact closed structure has evolved to the next generation NGN structure with modularization and separation and opening, which not only facilitates the network upgrade and business innovation of operators with the clearer and more flexible network structure, but also reduces the cost of the network construction for operators through full competition among more manufacturers.

The strategies of Huawei: Pre-research department of Huawei take active initiative in carrying out the research and development of the next-generation network, finally determines the NGN system in line with the future development and the brand of iNet after studying the products and road signs of benchmarking enterprises, and various technical exchanges with the research institutes of the operators.

However, when the product is formally engineered and put into the market, pre-research and product development sees a disagreement between each other, in that the product development and market system wish to continue the leading advantages of C&C08 through, on the one hand, adopting the integrated solutions in product development, and deliberately delaying the realization of full separation architecture, while on the other hand, in the aspect of listing management, taking a negative attitude towards the operator's verification of the fully separated and open structure, and naming the brand "C&C08iNet". Under the repeated requirements of customers, Huawei still insists on being self-centered, consequently, the customer decides to exclude Huawei from the list of NGN Beta manufacturers in the whole network, which buried a "bomb" for the future selection of the commercial model.

It is a mistake easily made by leading manufacturers, that is, they attempt to maintain their leading position with their own market and technological strengths. Enterprises will eventually be abandoned by the market and customers if they do not put the customer at the center, conform to the development trend, or take the initiative to change and innovate.

2. **Wireless 3G system coming belatedly**

Background of the project: Wireless 3G was "hot" in the industry at that time, just like today's so-called projects with the greatest investment potential, such as green energy, lithium batteries and electric vehicles, when the international standards organization has taken frequent actions in the formulation of 3G standards, resulting in the constant updates of the standards. Huawei's wireless product line keeps pace with the industry, with key resources organized upon the focuses of 3G products, with expectations to walk out of the shadow as a latecomer for the 2G era. However, global investment suffered shrank at the burst of the first Internet bubble, when Huawei's wireless products were still in their infancy with its major market still in China, which is also affected by global economic changes, and more importantly, who has put forward the "TD-SCDMA3G" standard with independent property rights. However, the domestic market delayed long in issuing the 3G license, five years later than expected, which puts the development of 3G products in an awkward situation, for the products can not be verified and affirmed by the market until after a long time.

The strategies of Huawei: The company makes a correct decision in taking 3G European standards as the main direction, with the specific product development decided by product line, which adopts the strategy of focusing on and follows international standards closely in developing several versions like 3GR95, R97 and R99. The pre-research department concludes that Huawei needs to conduct leapfrog R & D by directly skipping the RXX phase, with the focus on the R4 Standard Version after comprehensive analysis based on the global investment shrinkage, few 3G terminals and lack of killer services. But compared with RXX network architecture, the network architecture of R4 has changed substantially for its belonging to the next generation network architecture in the wireless field, thus a disagreement emerged between the group addicted to tradition and the one who prefers modernization.

However, the fact has it that, after adopting the R4 next-generation network architecture, even if the issuance of 3G license continues to be delayed in China, the separated architecture also enables Huawei's 3G core network to sell overseas firstly. The product finally came out of the dilemma by "sending fragrance outside the wall though blooming inside the wall". Huawei realized the advanced layout of 3G core network overseas, laying a foundation for the entrance into 3G network access and gained market experience, which in turn greatly improved the competence of the technology in the future China market. Therefore, the grasp of market maturity and technology maturity is one of the key capabilities of innovation management.

3. **The signal system for express railway ended up in vain**

Background of the project: in 2010, Huawei established three BGs, namely, the business for operators, enterprise networks and consumers. The industry market of enterprise network BG includes government institutions, transportation, electric power, energy, finance and other fields, each of which with urgent expectations of a market breakthrough. In the field of transportation, the construction of the express railway was in full swing with huge investments at that time, when Huawei had made some achievements in the supporting communication system for the express railway. Upon analysis, Huawei found that the signal and intelligent control system for the express railway seems to have many similarities with the communication system, and the system is supplied exclusively by CRSC, and the senior management implied the intentions to introduce another company to participate in the competition. Upon this, Huawei began to set up a team to analyze and conduct small-scale research on the signal system for express railway and saw the product R & D team in Hangzhou alone soon exceeding 200 people, with the active introduction of industry experts in express railway. However, with the development of the situation and after Huawei's in-depth research on the signal system for the express railway, Huawei became increasingly aware of its serious insufficiency in the understanding of the business environment and technical difficulties in this field. Finally, Huawei has to make a hard decision to terminate the project, since the prototype developed by Huawei can not meet the industry requirements in a short period, no matter in terms of progress, function, or quality, in addition to the changes in the market.

This lesson made Huawei's decision-makers realize that when they enter a new field, they should not only fully understand the external ecological environment and the market positioning of the enterprise in the new field, but also fully understand the internal competitive advantages and resources of the enterprise. Only when the new direction comes in line with the main strategic channel of the company, can they form a joint force to speed up the pace of breakthrough in new areas.

2.3.2.2 Four Elements of the Decision on Product Innovation

Many enterprises have been trying to avoid losses by fishing out how to make reasonable decisions in the "misty chaos" of innovation. From Huawei's lessons of failure and successful experience, four key elements can be summed up, namely, the consistency between strategies for product innovation and strategies of the enterprise, trend conformity, enterprise resource and capability evaluation, and investment priority evaluation.

1. **The consistency between strategies for product innovation and strategies of the enterprise**

Innovation strategy should conform to the overall strategic direction of the enterprise. Huawei defined the "main channel" of its business in its basic law officially issued in 1997. To make Huawei a world-class equipment supplier, Huawei will never enter the industry offering information service, of which the basic starting point is not to become a competitor of the customers of itself, namely telecom operators. This means Huawei put its focus on the communication industry, with its product innovation concentrating on the research and development of communication equipment. In the process of gradually developing upon survival, most enterprises will adopt business strategies of market-oriented opportunism for a long time, which leads to the diversification of the enterprises in pursuing market hot spots or government-supported industrial hot spots, either passively or actively. Few companies would establish strategic boundaries of enterprises through basic law in their early days, like Huawei, but it is just the strategy of "main channel" that made Huawei's innovation decision-making relatively easy, for any proposal off the main channel would be rejected, which enables Huawei to strengthen and enlarge its resources during its high-speed development.

There are many successful cases of enterprises adopting a diversification strategy. Many entrepreneurs expressed their concerns for they believed that it would be risky to put all the eggs in one basket. But in China, people are more worried about enterprises adopting diversification strategies. In fact, Huawei's main channel itself covers a lot of product areas, but there are some collaborative relationships between these products, such as technology platform and marketing platform, which can give play to the advantages of integrated strengths. GE adopts diversified operation, but still with its strategic requirements for the business unit to be among the top three in the world, so as to be bigger and stronger, or it will be cut resolutely. In fact, the strategic logic remains the same, when the management ability is strong enough, the field span can be large, but not to pursue "opportunities", for otherwise, you may turn out to be a good businessman, but not a good entrepreneur, and consequently, the enterprise will not be running "stable for a long time".

With the continuous integration and development of technology, especially under the push of IP technology and Internet open architecture, ICT integration has become the future development direction with the boundary between communication technology and information technology gradually broken, when Huawei's business strategy with the focus on "communication equipment" was greatly challenged. After many internal conflicts among innovation concept, investment decision-making and organization management of IT products such as data communication and server, and even the painful process of high-level break, Huawei's main business strategy channel has entered the era of 2.0, when it became the provider of ICT equipment, with Tencent and Alibaba as its customers. The rapid rise of Internet enterprises like Tencent enriched the definition of information service while greatly eaten the traditional business of operators, and rewritten the extension and connotation of the "information service industry". Huawei saw substantial business income after its quiet entrance into the business operation field through the back-end application platform after its terminal comprehensively learned the successful model of Apple's success. And this marked that Huawei's main channel entered the 3.0 era at a position as an equipment and platform provider of "terminals, pipeline and cloud services". With the establishment of BG cloud service and the cloud service joint venture with China Mobile and Deutsche Telekom, Huawei, on the one hand, continued to work hand in hand with operators, on the other hand, was burning to find a path for a breakthrough of cloud service based on operators' network and customer base. However, the question is whether to take IaaS as the main strategic direction to make Tencent and Alibaba its target customers, or to get PaaS and SaaS included to compete directly with Alibaba and Tencent. At that time, Huawei's strategy was not very clear, besides, the "limitation" on "neither to touch business upward nor to touch data downward" and Huawei's own gene and system problems in business operation, they still needed time to test and revise the main channel strategy 3.0, though actually the main channel strategy 3.0 still has a clear business boundary.

From the evolution process of Huawei's main channel of business development (as shown in Fig. 2.6), it can be seen that the definition of enterprise strategy and the main channel has a strong guiding significance for innovation decision-making, and the enterprise needs to have market insight and be flexible to adapt to circumstances.

2. **Trend compliance and maturity assessment**

It is the key factor to ensure the success of innovation that not only conforms to the development trend, but also grasp the pace of innovation based on maturity. It can be analyzed and evaluated from the two dimensions of market and technology.

- Market trend: Saw mainly from the change of value chain and market requirement, as shown in Fig. 2.7. First of all, insight should penetrate into the changes of the industry value chain, and innovation projects should be positioned at the high end of the value chain or the area approaching to the high end of the value chain. Secondly, close attention should be paid to the growth of customer requirements and the degree of implementation of the requirements in the selected region, instead of just the heat of academic discussion of the technical experts. At the same time, by analyzing the investment growth and supporting policies in the innovation field, especially when the market share is basically clear and the market application growth is obvious, we can basically judge that this field belongs to the project of investment potential.

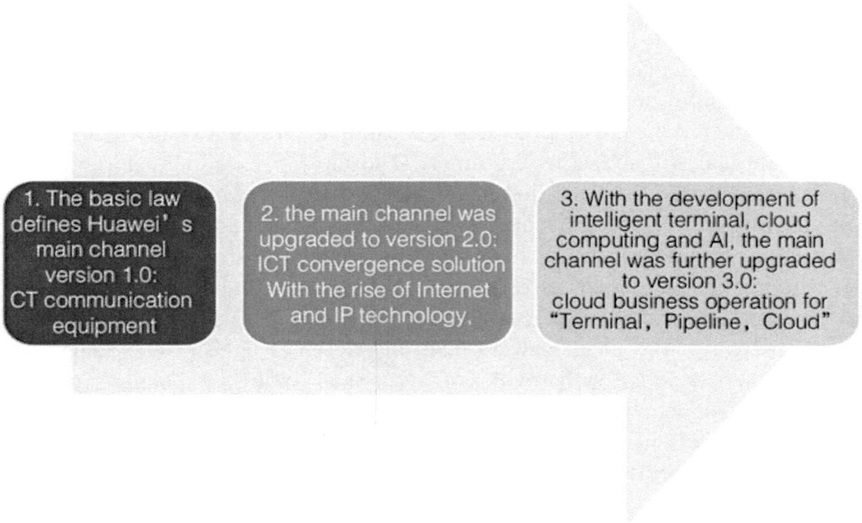

Fig. 2.6 The evolution of Huawei's main channel strategy from version 1.0 to version 3.0

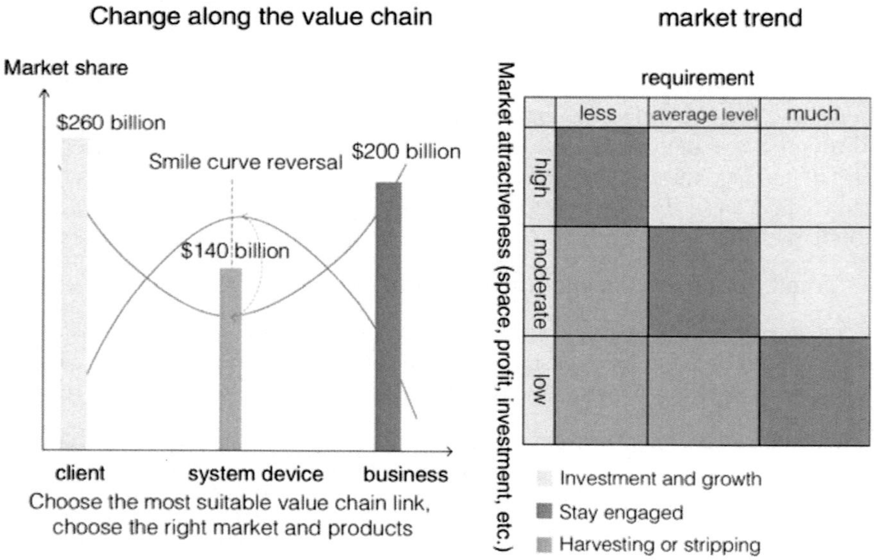

Fig. 2.7 Analysis of changes along the value chain and market trend

- Technology trend and maturity: Technology maturity in the field of innovation is often the key to the success of innovation, often means "one step ahead to sacrifice". In the field of TMT, Gartner releases ten new technology trends every year, involving virtual reality, artificial intelligence, robot, the Internet of Things and other new development fields, with its speculation cycle curve of high reference values, as shown in Fig. 2.8.

Generally speaking, venture capital will pursue the technology and projects near the peak of speculation, while Huawei basically will not get involved in these fields in its internal product development system. It mainly tracks through funding scientific research institutions, participating in innovative companies of schools, with a small scale for pre-research in 2012 Laboratory. Only about 5% of innovative technologies can pass through the death trough, and be applied on a large scale and accepted by the market. The projects that can enter Huawei's R & D pipeline are basically the 5% technologies and products that have crossed the trough. With its increasing investment in basic research, Huawei's focus on innovation will gradually move forward, with its basic principles remain unchanged.

3. **Resources and capabilities**

Even if the external conditions are basically mature, enterprises still need to choose innovation mode and innovation project according to their own reality, because different levels of innovation call for different abilities, as shown in Fig. 2.9.

For enterprises, such as traditional manufacturing enterprises, that gain market position through mass production, their core competence is cost control and market competence. Therefore, the focus of innovation should be on value engineering innovation and marketing innovation. To improve the company's position and realize the transformation from mass production to product differentiation, market-oriented R & D investment need to be increased, with the product differentiation advantage

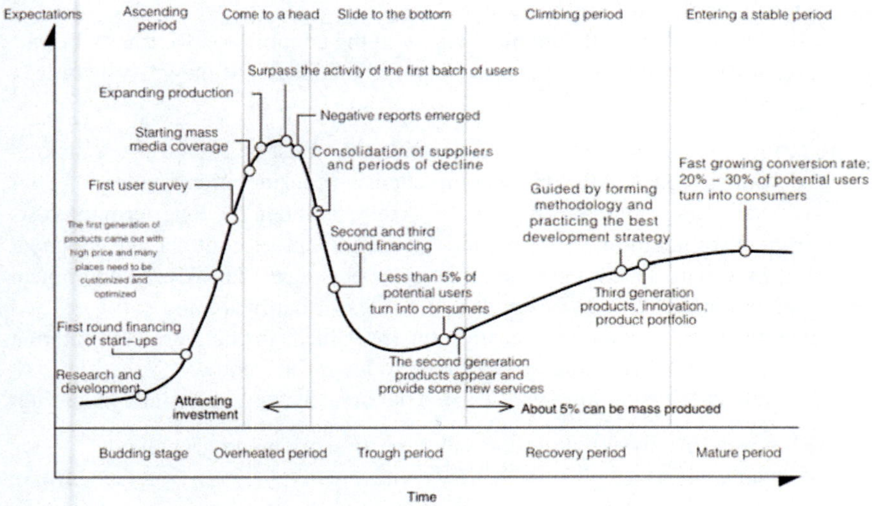

Fig. 2.8 Gartner new technology speculation curve

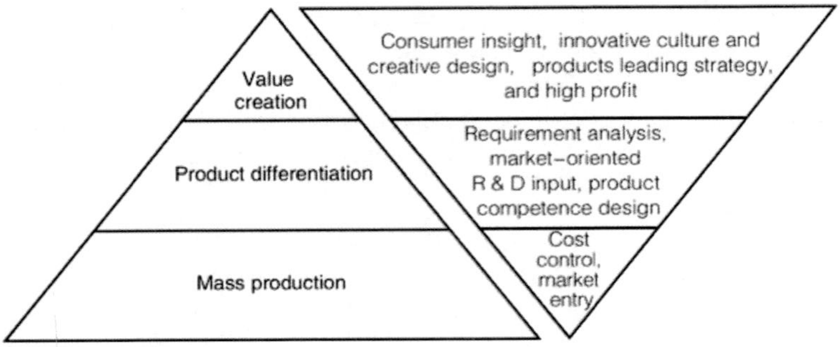

Fig. 2.9 Resource and capability requirements for innovation

built upon customer requirements. In addition to the investment of funds, substantive changes should be made in innovative mindsets, innovative processes, incentive mechanisms and management of human recourses. To become a product leading enterprise, maintain long-term strategic investment should be made in customer insight, especially in the discovery and stimulation of customers' potential needs, the establishment of innovation culture and innovation mechanism.

Foxconn's strategies of innovations concerning its brand and solutions still need to be tested over time. Based on its own advantages, with its focus on the intelligent manufacturing innovation of the whole industrial chain, and controls over the key links (screen, memory, etc.) of the industrial chain, Foxconn sees the enterprise developing more healthily.

4. **Product profitability/business model and financial evaluation**

The product profit model includes:

- Sales of hardware;
- Charges for application services;
- Free of charge for the software platform, with the commission for transaction;
- Charges for high value-added service (such as the results of the analysis of user big data), etc.

The profit model of the product is a question that must be solved when making product decisions, which calls for the comprehensive consideration on how to better adapt to the tax policy, increase customer viscosity, maintain the long-term interests of the product, in addition to the mode of management of contract and payment collection, as well as the competence of the sales personnel. The overall equipment sales mode is gradually replaced by separate sales of hardware and software, and high value-added services are increasingly more valued. In the era of the Internet economy, to cash the flow is the focus of the product profit model.

Product financial evaluation can be carried out in many ways, generally including:

- FAN(Financial Analysis) of product sales, profit margin and growth rate;
- Break-even analysis;

- ROI analysis, etc.

The case in Fig. 2.10 is the breakeven point that can be reached when the sales volume of the product is estimated according to the product life cycle cost (fixed cost + variable cost), sales forecast, etc. (according to the sales ability, it can also be estimated how long it will take to sell), and the estimated total rate of return on investment, for the leaders' reference in making decisions.

Product profit model and financial evaluations are one of important bases for product planning and decision-making, which have great value as a reference for investment, arrangement of sales target and pricing.

Among the four main decision-making points, the principle of keeping in line with the company's main channel strategy generally has the power of one vote veto, while the other three generally need to be comprehensively analyzed, if one of which is not satisfied at all, it is necessary to further collect evidence and make a decision again.

Case of Decision-making: "PHS" product decision

(1) Basis for the decision

  I. communication equipment come in line with the company's main channel
  II. Trend conformity

  - Market trend: GSM pattern has been set, with 3G as the direction, though the license has not been issued yet;
  - Technology trend: PHS technology is about to be eliminated, and it is limited to Japan but not the global mainstream

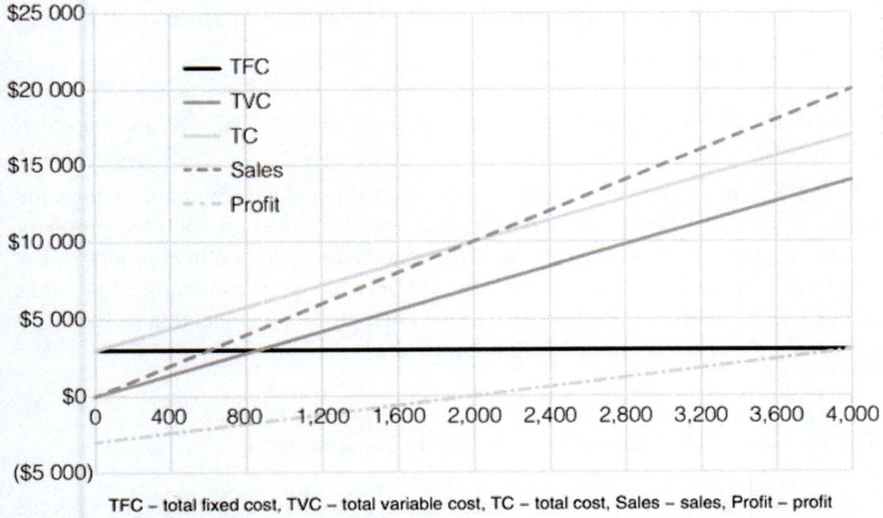

Fig. 2.10 Product profitability analysis

III. Return on investment and competitive intensity

- The customers are only China Telecom, who has no mobile experience, and unknown investment intensity and investment period;
- The main players are UT Starcom and ZTE

IV. Construction of core competence

- The main components of the equipment from mobile phone chips are all controlled by manufacturers like Kyocera from Japan, leaving little room for Chinese manufacturers

(2) Conclusion of the decision

Focus on mainstream standards and technologies, reject opportunism, "NO GO!"

(3) The market is changing quietly

- As the 3G license has not delayed in its issuing for five years, PHS has invested continuously for four years, with an average annual equipment investment of RMB 20 billion yuan, and the scale of the mobile terminal market is equivalent to that of the equipment market;
- With the profits earned by PHS used in the R & D and joint venture acquisition of mainstream technology WCDMA, UT Starcom displayed its 3G equipment in a high profile
- Due to the development of soft switch technology, the core switch and mobile base station are gradually decoupled. PHS manufacturers gradually occupy the commanding height of the mobile network with the mobile soft switch, and advanced the layout for the future 3G market
- Their competence in human resources is becoming stronger with a large number of mobile personnel with practical work experience cultivated
- The mobile value chain from the chip, business, channel agent to production, especially the relationship with customers, was strengthened and improved

(4) Adjustment of decision

PHS shook Huawei's leading position in 3G technology and can be developed as a competitive product, "GO!"

In decision management, the basis for the decision and the key point of decision-making is different for business development products and competitive products. The above smart decision-making cases illustrated typical competitive products. The analysis of its return on investment is done not only on the investment income of the product itself, but also on the decrease of the competitor's income, that is, the effect of "burning grain warehouse of your competitors".

2.3.2.3 Keys of the Management of "Inclusive Innovation"

- In the construction of an innovation organization, the way of "applying new people to new things" should be avoided, instead, the leading group with entrepreneurial spirit should be arranged while strengthening the introduction and cultivation of experts in various technical fields. Huawei adopts the "three-wave attack" mode in the organization and construction of its new enterprise network BG and consumer BG, with the first wave to explore the law of the new business and establish basic teams based on the consideration of the law of the new business, and the second wave to rapidly expand the team for the establishment of a key system with the important leaders of the Group as the heads of the business divisions, while the third wave to achieve the business objectives under the leadership of those who dare to challenge themselves and have strong ability to solve the problem. During this period, industry experts and professionals would be actively introduced and trained, with the resource globally distributed to improve the overall organizational innovation ability.

- In terms of innovation investment, the proportion of research and innovation investment would be increased, with 5 ~ 10% of its revenue used as funds for R & D, and the investment in the pre-research system increased from 10 to 20%. Different industries have standards of input for different innovations, and the average investment of the traditional manufacturing industry is usually less than 4%. However, to achieve transformation and innovation, it is necessary to take the industry benchmark as the standard to ensure continuous innovation investment. Huawei inaugurated the Strategy Research Institute in September 2019, with the goal of "moving from technological innovation to technological invention", which indicates that Huawei will have a qualitative improvement in basic theory breakthrough, open innovation and investment intensity, and is expected to realize the strategic deployment "up to the sky".
- In terms of innovation management, especially in terms of evaluation mechanism, Huawei adopted a more tolerant attitude towards failure within generally a 2–3-year exploration period. "In uncertain fields, there are heroes in failed projects. It's a success as well to know that this road is blocked".

Improving the insight and decisiveness of decision-makers is a crucial part of decision-making management. Under the guidance of innovation culture, enterprises need to strengthen the formulation and implementation of the innovation system, especially the leadership training and assessment of leaders. Managers should set an example by taking the initiative in updating their knowledge and enhancing their leadership, which includes insight and decision-making. In addition to training, in practice, it is an important means for Huawei to quickly cultivate and identify the leadership of cadres by formulating the strategy of the business unit and organizing forces to implement it. Therefore, Mr. Ren Zhengfei required that strategy formulation, identification and management of the strategic opportunity should be implemented at the level of the representative office, with the head of the office personally reporting the strategy, which was taken as an important indicator of the assessment of the leadership of cadres.

Chapter 3
Key Choice of Enterprise Internationalization Strategy

3.1 The Summary and Reference of the Internationalization Mode of Chinese Enterprises

In the late 1990s, China's TMT[1] and manufacturing enterprises, represented by Huawei, Lenovo and Sany Heavy Industry, summed up many experiences and lessons through their repeated defeats and hard-won breakthroughs overseas. Now under the Belt and Road Initiative, Chinese enterprises see a new wave of internationalization with the emergence of new modes for internationalization, among which, cross-border M&A has served as a shortcut for rapid development and internationalization of enterprises. *Blue Book on the Internationalization of Enterprises: Report on the Globalization of Chinese Enterprises (2015)* jointly issued by CCG[2] and the Academy of Social Sciences pointing out that the total success rate of cross-border M&A of Chinese enterprises is 40%, higher than the global average of 25%. According to the data from the Ministry of Commerce, only about 30% of China's enterprises invested overseas saw profits within the stern global economic atmosphere, among which the average success rate of overseas M&A is only 14%. From the perspective of the data, Chinese enterprises have made huge progress in recent years, with some effective methods drawn from past lessons and experience. However, the failure rate of more than 60% still deserves the vigilance of Chinese enterprises! A global study shows that overseas projects saw 30% of the total failures at the pre-negotiation stage, while 17% of the total failures during, comparing to the possibility of failure in the implementation and integration phase as high as 53%, which presents a shred of strong evidence that the signing of the agreement does not necessarily mean the success of the project.

The lessons of TCL's selection and implementation of strategies for internationalization are worth learning for Chinese enterprises. Li Dongsheng never shies away from talking about the dilemma that TCL had fallen in during its internationalization,

[1] TMT: The acronym of Technology, Media and Telecom.

[2] CCG: Center for China and Globalization.

L. Tao, *Huawei Wisdom*,
https://doi.org/10.1007/978-981-19-1169-9_3

with the expectation that Chinese enterprises can learn from its lessons and avoid detours. The main lessons are as follows.

Lesson 1: Choices of strategies. TCL hopes to become the number one TV company in the world by distancing its domestic competitors through acquiring Thomson, the originator of picture tube enterprises, while at that time, the technology and market were experiencing great changes, with LED technology advancing by leaps and bounds and Thomson's patents gradually losing their value with the rapid technological innovation.

Lesson 2: Management of localization. TCL has invited top professional institutions in both mergers and acquisitions, such as Morgan Stanley as the investment bank is, First Boston as the investment consultant, and Ernst & Young as the accounting firm. However, they only mentioned laws and regulations, but non-written-rules, which brought a lot of troubles, for example, for the trade union is very strong in protecting the interests of the employees, so TCL can only lay off workers who can find jobs, at the same time, he differences in cultural management, channel management and salary system after M&A lead to a large number of brain drain, which trapped the company in a state of chaos out of control. TCL cast 314.9 million euros on M&A, but to see the failure of the reconstruction in 2010, before it had to pay RMB 500 million in compensation as ordered by the French court.

Lesson 3: Focus on strategies. TCL was originally very strategic and far-sighted in the acquisition of Alcatel's mobile phone business, but because the acquisition was carried out at the same time as that of Thomson, resulting in a serious shortage of human resources in acquisition and management, which made the process of integration and management seriously impacted.

Upon the experience summing up, TCL shifted to focus on the core technology in the period of the transformation of products and market, and extended to both ends of the value chain. In addition to continuing to integrate the rapidly developing mobile business, it also invested in CSOT (China Star Optoelectronics Technology) project and vertically integrated the core component LCD, which pushed the development of TCL to a new height.

It can be found from the case of TCL that the Chinese enterprises that take the lead in going overseas are generally the top ones in the industry. So why do these enterprises, as the pioneers thriving at home, will falter overseas? From the general perspective of Chinese enterprises as a whole, through a large number of questionnaire surveys and statistics, in addition to the consulting reports of Accenture and KPMG, the management of Chinese enterprises (including the person in charge of internationalization) believe that the major reasons for the failure of internationalization of Chinese enterprises can be summarized into eight factors, as shown in Fig. 3.1.

Generally speaking, people tend to put their eyes on the objective reasons, but are less aware of their ability to resist risks, or the truth that the problems may be directly caused by the management or overseas leaders. In the same global economic environment, why do some enterprises succeed in internationalization, while others fail? The three most prominent issues of Chinese enterprises in the process of internationalization as shown in Fig. 3.2 may give some clues.

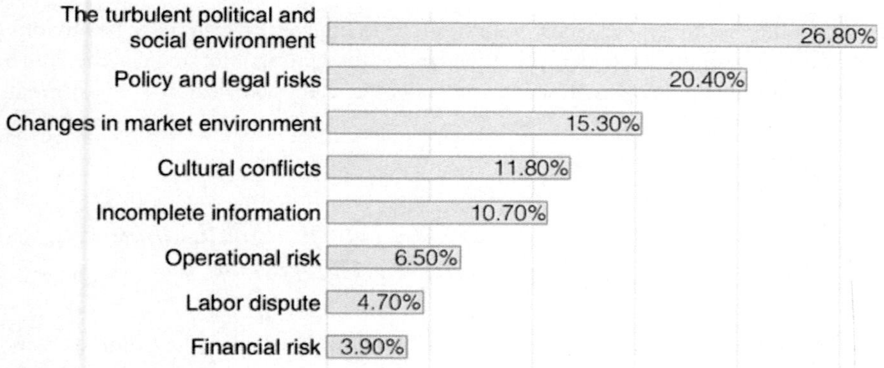

Fig. 3.1 The major reasons given by top managers of Chinese enterprises for the failure of the internationalization of the enterprises

Fig. 3.2 Three key issues of the internationalization of Chinese enterprises

Most enterprises failed to make a clear strategy for internationalization, but stuck to opportunism and traditional mindset for trade, due to which, the short-sighted strategy, enterprises go to the overseas market merely with the purposes of "clearing up the inventory". It is never rare to see that Chinese enterprises are fighting each other instead of "huddling together for warmth" overseas, but engaged in an extended domestic price war abroad, which disrupted industry rules, hurt the quality, and consequently injured Chinese brands. Sometimes, some other enterprises failed to make a long-term plan but take internalization as a "try". As mentioned above, the overseas projects saw 30% failures of the total before the negotiation and 17% failures of the total during the negotiation, while the possibility of failure in the phases of integration and implementation can be as high as 53%, so it can be obvious that in addition to the strategies, the organization mode, operation management and execution ability of overseas projects, especially the talent pool, are also of very great importance.

3.1.1 Summary and Reference of the Internationalization Mode of China's Manufacturing Enterprises

Through continuous follow-up research, it is found that in the past, the Chinese enterprises realize internationalization mainly through the modes like endogenous development, merger and acquisition, upgrading and transformation from OEM/ODM to PB (private brand), plant construction overseas, PE equity investment, or innovation and technology. Whatever mode is adopted, the essence of management remains the same. The formulation of its internationalization strategy, the selection and implementation of key paths, the internationalization governance and the localization strategy of the company will directly affect the process of internationalization and whether the enterprise will succeed in internationalization.

3.1.1.1 Mode of Internationalization Through Endogenous Development

Huawei takes a stable approach towards global transformation gradually until it made the final break through establishing its own marketing platform in key markets selected after understanding the overseas environment through agents and expatriates. This mode is called the mode of internationalization through endogenous development, which is adopted by Huawei, ZTE, BYD and many other enterprises, with features as follows.

Advantages: The organizational system extends overseas mainly through internal growth, supplemented by investment merger and joint venture cooperation, with overseas leaders mainly appointed domestically, supplemented by those who recruited outside the enterprises. This is a mode for gradual internationalization with strong controllability, small impact on enterprise management, resulting in stable but long-term financial growth.

Requirements: Clear strategy should be made, as well as a practical and feasible path for the internationalization paved, for the establishment the market-driven rapid response mechanism of R&D and service through the phased focus on key markets and main products and the close collaborative organization of front line and headquarters. In the initial stage, the focuses should be put on main businesses and key products, before product portfolio and network-level solution sales gradually being carried out, and finally the overall solutions from project financing, consulting, planning and design, special services to products provided to realize the transformation from production-oriented to service-oriented. At the same time, internationalization forces enterprises to change and realize the second leap of management. Today, Huawei's global operation has surpassed internationalization in the ordinary sense.

Risks: Internationalization through endogenous development takes a long cycle of investment and development, during which it is necessary to continuously build and optimize the core competence of overseas organization systems and human resources.

3.1.1.2 The Mode of Internationalization Through Investment and Merger

The representative enterprise internationalized through this mode is Lenovo, the financial changes of which in the process of M&A are shown in Fig. 3.3. In 2004, Lenovo realized the financial merger after the completion of the acquisition of IBM's PC business like "a snake swallowing an elephant", and saw its sales increased significantly. Lenovo got the brand and product of IBM's PC business but not brand, product, R&D capability and market capability as it was initially expected. After the acquisition, Lenovo needs to expand the market all by itself, as well as the R&D capability of the other side, which is not left behind. As a result, the PC business of Lenovo, not seeing any convincing innovations, has long been living off its past achievements. Lenovo saw a financial deficit for the first time because the drop in its overall profit fell due to the careless prediction of the financial black hole, especially upon the financial crisis in 2008 and the expenditure on the integration of IBM's

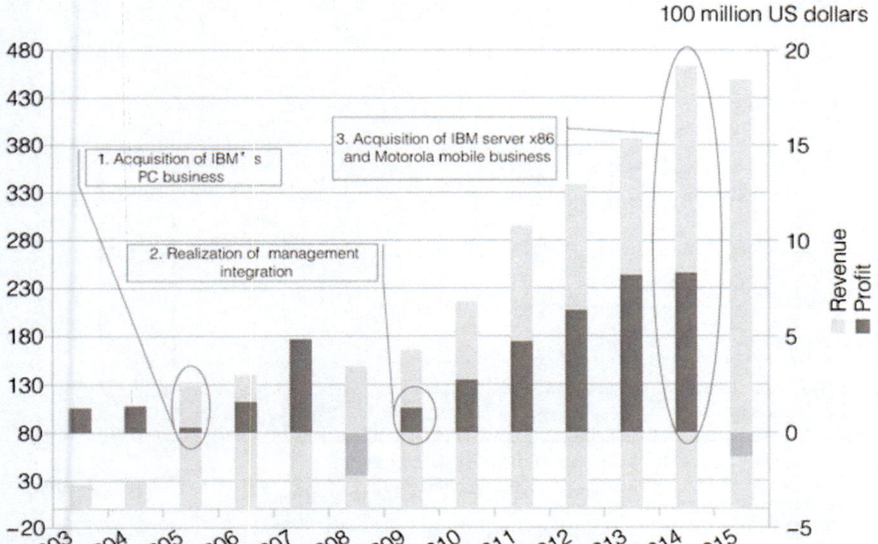

Fig. 3.3 Financial changes in the process of Lenovo's M&A

PC business. In 2009, the newly acquired business and traditional business Lenovo saw their management integration, and in 2011, through the acquisition of NEC PC business, Lenovo PC R&D center was established in Japan. With the advancement of its R&D capability, Lenovo's global status was consolidated and enhanced upon the improved overall performance.

Lenovo enjoyed growth in its revenue thanks to the merger of IBM X86 and Motorola mobile businesses. Lenovo Group acquired Motorola mobile from Google for $2.9 billion, but with a large number of core patents acquired by Google, leaving Lenovo patents with minor values. Motorola of no brand influence on smartphones, in addition to the rapid development of mobile technology, left Lenovo not such a long integration window period as PC business, which made Lenovo's position even threatened in the domestic market in China, not to mention to achieve the goal of the globalization of its Mobile business. The IBM X86 server business including SystemX, BladeCenter, FlexSystem blade server and converter acquired by Lenovo, and Flex integration system based on X86, NeXtscale and iDataPlex server and related software, make Lenovo the third-largest supplier in the X86 server market, only after HP and Dell. From the strategic point of view, mobilization and cloud are the future development direction that would be important for Lenovo in its business layout and globalization in the future. Lenovo's capability layout through acquisition and merger is shown in Fig. 3.4.

Lenovo attaches great importance to acquiring current products and markets through M&A, and improves its international management ability through M&A. In particular, its experience in appointing top leaders after M&A is worth learning from by Chinese enterprises. The CEO of Lenovo used to be Stephen Ward, former vice president of IBM PC, and Yang Yuanqing was the chairman. However, due to

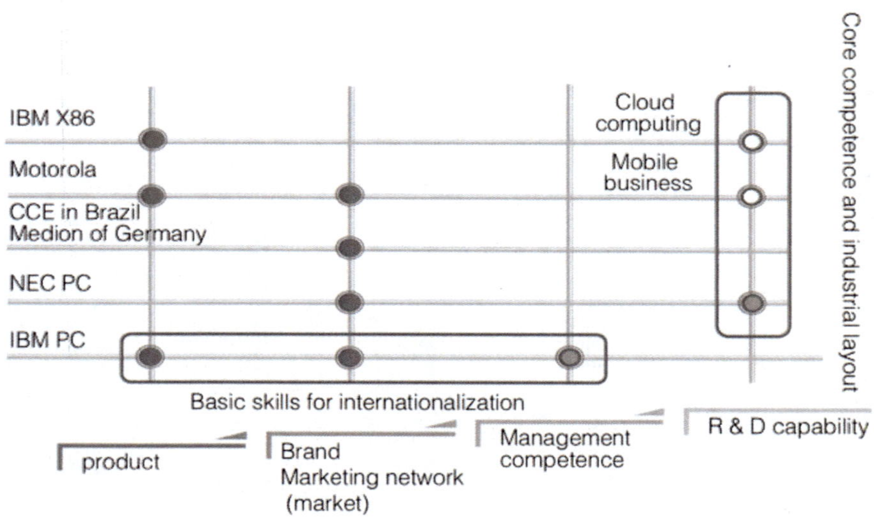

Fig. 3.4 Lenovo's capability improved through M&A

the different business philosophies and strategic thinking of the two sides, after a painful lesson, Liu Chuanzhi believes that the top leader of the enterprise should be the Chinese.

The biggest problem that emerged in Lenovo's M&A is not enough attention to the innovative capacity of the research and development, which may happen under the influence of Lenovo's overall "trade-engineering-technology" strategy. Compared with Huawei's endogenous mode, Lenovo's overseas sales accounted for more than 60% in 2014 and overseas profits accounted for 50%; Huawei saw its overseas sales accounting for more than 65% and over 60% of overseas profits in the same period.

Many companies, like CIMC, Geely, and TCL, all favored the made of internationalization through merger and acquisition. Upon learning from each other's experience, more and more enterprises succeeded in doing the same. The characteristics of internationalization mainly through investment and merger are as follows.

Advantages: The mode of internationalization through investment and merger can see an obvious increase in the scale of income, be conducive to the rapid improvement of R&D capability and process flow, and can quickly form market complementary and enrich the categories of the products.

Requirements: The mode of internationalization through investment and merger calls for a clear purpose for the acquisition and merger, as well as accurate strategic judgment on the direction of development, specifically, the sufficient fund support, strong cross-cultural organization integration ability and leadership control ability. The management mode of localization will be led by financial target assessment, with managers mainly recruited outside the enterprises. This mode is more suitable for enterprises with highly standard products that are relatively independent and focused.

Risks: Financial traps, intellectual property rights and labor legal barriers, as well as differences in language, culture, governance structure, and salary system, may present as major risks. The short-term financial combination has an obvious effect, and the actual benefit can be seen only after the real integration is successfully made.

3.1.1.3 The Mode of Internationalization from OEM/ODM to Self-Owned Brand

Wanxiang Group serves as a typical representative of this mode. Earlier Wangxiang had ever been cooperating with Universal Automotive Industries, Inc. (UAI) to provide products overseas as OEM or ODM. As one of the three major suppliers of universal joint in the American automobile maintenance market, UAI used to be the enterprise with the most patents of universal joint in the world, which offered a wide range of products of high quality to the global market, with its branches founded in Europe, Asia, North America and Oceania. UAI often handed over the products of small amount, urgent supply and great difficulty in processing to Wanxiang Group, which greatly improved the engineering of special mold, and gradually established a flexible manufacturing and supply chain system in line with the high-quality standards of the United States, thanks to this cooperation. In 2000, Wanxiang

Group acquired UAI through the cooperation with LSB, in which LSB accepted UAI's workers and factories while Wanxiang Group took UAI's brand, patents, special equipment and marketing network for only US $420,000. This acquisition rapidly resulted in two high-end brands of UAI and Wanxiang, which achieve rapid globalization upon its self-owned strong engineering and manufacturing platform.

Opportunities are always reserved for those who are prepared. Aucma refrigerators and Skyworth TV are all kings of OEM in their respective fields, which pave their own way of globalization upon export, OEM and self-owned brand. The emerging companies, such as AAC Technologies (AAC) and Goertek, as the designated OEM or ODM suppliers of acoustic products for brands of mobile phones like Apple and Huawei, have rapidly occupied the global market and achieved more than RMB 10 billion in revenue with their small products under the light of Apple. The characteristics of the mode of internationalization through OEM or ODM are as follows.

Advantages: With the manufacturing advantages of China full played, enterprises follow this mode risk little when initially entering the overseas market, so it is easy for the enterprises in the development period to realize the transformation and upgrading with their own international brands established by constantly deepening the understanding of overseas markets and gradually establishing their own marketing system upon the requirements of the market. To serve overseas developed markets as OEMs or ODMs, enterprises can establish international high standard product quality and production systems quickly, which is one of the key paths to drive enterprises to build high-end manufacturing capacity and maintain core competence.

Requirements: With global strategic vision and long-term deployment, enterprises should take servings as OEMs or ODMs as a means rather than a goal of globalization, and they should always remain sensitive to the requirements of the market and look for enterprises with excellent brands and wide marketing networks as targets of acquisition or cooperation, so as to accelerate the process of internationalization.

Another kind of OEM or ODM enterprise also has a global vision of strategic development. But what is different from the former is that they take the path of Intel's "Intel inside" by not handling the whole machine brand, but the technology brand of parts. This is also a very suitable path for Chinese parts manufacturers to go globalized.

Risks: This mode also calls for the enhanced ability of cross-cultural integration, especially a good job in self-owned brand and cooperative brand regional division or product grade division. And for companies of technology brand, they need to further their investment in core technology to keep themselves pioneering.

3.1.1.4 The Mode of Internationalization Through the Construction of Overseas Factories

This mode is commonly followed by enterprises of industrial machinery and automobiles, of which Sany Heavy Industry can be a typical example. Sany Heavy Industry has gone through three stages of internationalization from international trade to the establishment of factories overseas, and then to the construction of core competence.

In 2006, Sany Heavy Industry put $60 million, the largest direct investment of Chinese enterprises, in construction of the machinery production base in India, while a low-cost competitor stands there as TATA. In 2007, Sany Heavy Industry invested $60 million in the United States for the construction of a new machinery manufacturing plant, as the first Chinese enterprise of machinery manufacturing to build a factory in the United States, posed as an immediate competitor against Caterpillar (CAT) of USA, the largest machinery enterprise in the world. In 2009, Sany Heavy Industry put 100 million euros to build a European Machinery Manufacturing Base in Cologne. In the early stage, due to the problems in the selected market, the purpose of the factory construction is to sell and remove the capacity. Sany Heavy Industry built very high-end factories in the United States and Germany. Compared with TATA, the factories built by Sany in India are "neither good nor bad", for which Sany Heavy Industry was gradually forced into the third stage. In 2012, Sany Heavy Industry acquired the "elephant"[3] at 360 million euros. As the core R&D capability is fully preserved, the acquired brand image is intact (dual brands to meet different markets in the world), Sany saw its revenue increasing by one third, as well as the growth in the sales of core parts, in addition to more parts supplied by Sany Heavy Industry to "elephant". But the problem with this approach is it takes time to integrate and all the benefits of consolidation need to be further developed.

The construction of factories is mainly meant to break trade barriers, avoid high tariffs (save overall cost) and shorten supply time, such as Brazil's tariffs on imported equipment of complete machines can be more than 25%. One of the key factors for CRRC to construct factories in the United States is that, under the Buy American Act (BAA), 60% of the parts purchased through Government Procurement must be manufactured within the territory of the United States. From the case of Sany Heavy Industry, it can be seen that the strategic intention and market selection of the factory construction are particularly important, and only by cooperating with the construction of core competence can enterprises achieve international success. The characteristics of the internationalization through overseas factory construction are as follows.

Advantages: This mode can reduce trade barriers (such as tariffs, foreign exchange control, etc.), improve supply speed and reduce logistics costs, etc.

Requirements: Enterprises need to select proper plant sites with clear objectives and investment returns upon a deep understanding of the local market and customer

[3] On January 31, 2012, Sany announced the acquisition of German construction machinery manufacturing giant Putzmeister, which is known as "elephant".

requirements. The selected products should be highly standardized with mature engineering to meet the requirements of local standards. In addition, enterprises also need to be familiar with the local policies concerning tariff, land, employment and the local requirements to further reduce the comprehensive cost of TCO. When Fuyao Glass just built its factory in the United States, after careful comparison between the TCO in China and that in the United States. To reduce the risk of capital and management, the mode of SKD or CKD can be adopted in the initial stage.

Risks: Overseas plant construction takes a long time and large investment, so whether the political and economic environment is stable, whether the market space and comprehensive cost can guarantee a reasonable return on investment, and whether the local skilled industrial workers are rich in resources are the risks that need to be focused on.

3.1.1.5 New Modes of Internationalization for Enterprises of Scientific and Technological Innovations

This mode is represented by emerging technology companies such as DAJ and Royole, whose main operators and capital are strongly international for they are born with the gene of internationalization. Its characteristics are as follows.

Advantages: Boasting advanced technologies, this mode belongs to the seller's market, with a low threshold of entering the international market as the products are mainly oriented overseas.

Requirements: This mode s a clear product strategy to maintain sufficient focus and R&D pressure, and the R&D base needs to be located in the birthplace of technologies to synchronize and catch up with the latest advancement of the technologies.

Risks: This mode poses tests for the multinational management ability of the start-up enterprises, for even the birth, its products need to meet the high standard quality requirements of the international market, especially the developed market. This mode also presents challenges of the industrialization level of the company. At the same time, the enterprises' strategy should stay clear of too much interference of capital.

The above-summarized are the five main modes of internationalization for manufacturing enterprises, and sometimes enterprises will adopt means of mixed modes to realize internationalization. However, no matter what mode is adopted, the formulation of a clear strategy for internationalization, the construction of the core competence (R&D, marketing, supply chain) and the management of an international team remain the three pillars of successful internationalization for enterprises.

3.1.2 The Path of Internationalization of Service Enterprises Represented by BAT (Baidu, Alibaba and Tencent) and the Enlightenment upon It

In today's open Internet era, no entrepreneur will only set their eyes on the Chinese market only. BAT, as the pioneer of China's Internet, was born with the gene of internationalization. So what's the actual situation of BAT? Compared with Huawei, Lenovo, TCL and other manufacturing enterprises, what common lessons, and what different experiences can be drawn from the experience of BAT?

3.1.2.1 BAT's Ambition of Going International and the Harsh Reality

From the beginning of the company, Jack Ma (Ma Yun) has been bearing a great strategic goal of internationalization: the marriage of the wisdom of the East and the management of the west is sure to win the world market.

While Robin Li (Li Yanhong), with great passion, believes that our generation is ushering in the best opportunity for the great rejuvenation of the Chinese nation, so we are not only to export the best Made in China to the world, but also the most cutting-edge technologies and innovations to the world.

Among the Internet upstarts, Tencent takes a most peculiar path for internationalization. It doesn't seem to care much about internationalization, neither does it seem to have the self-confidence for that. It was not until WeChat became popular that Pony Ma (Ma Huateng) cemented his determination to join the game: Success or failure, this is the only opportunity for (Tencent's internationalization) all its life, though he also once said that the chance is half to half, a shred of evidence that Tencent is absolutely sure about the game.

Theoretically, boasting an inborn international pedigree, international capital, international team and the mode of open global Internet business, BAT will find it easy and swift to realize their overseas expansion. After ten years of effort, BAT's overseas business achievements in recent years are shown in Fig. 3.5.

In terms of internationalization capability matrix, BAT's overseas business only reaches the level of primary international trade stage. After 2017, due to the poor overseas performance, Alibaba simply stops listing the overseas income in the financial report. In this level of overseas business, only Tencent sees its growth at a normal trend. It's quite fair to say that BAT can only "live off China's market" at present. So, what's the reason for that? Now, let's find out why from the process of their internationalization.

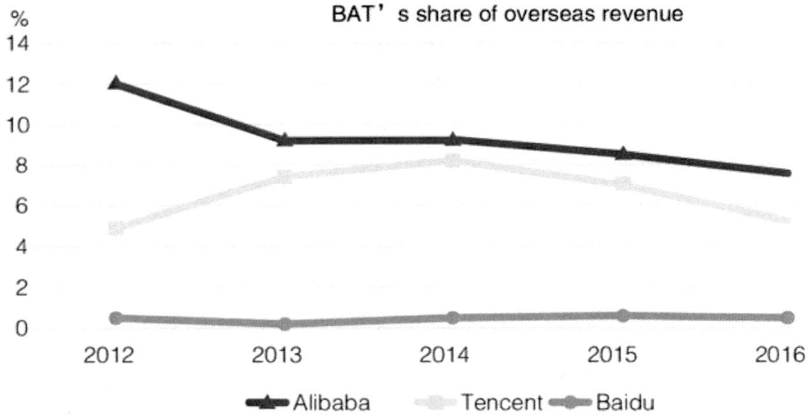

Fig. 3.5 Proportion of BAT's overseas revenue over the years

3.1.2.2 BAT's Overseas Business Development and the Problems Encountered

1. The Development, Layout and Major Problems of Alibaba's Overseas Business

The development of Alibaba's overseas business can be divided into three stages.

The first stage: The most essential mistakes in the internationalization and even the survival for an enterprise were made in that "enterprises with not enjoy stability without prosperity in the domestic market, either will they accumulate their strength without expansion in the international markets". Alibaba set the year 2000, the second year of its initial business, as the key year to expand its overseas market. At this time, the domestic market has yet to be developed, but in order to meet the requirements of internationalization, Alibaba put its headquarters in Hong Kong, China, and set up an American R&D center, followed by offices in the United Kingdom and South Korea successively established to speed up the development of overseas business, in addition to the eager preparation of the websites in Japan, Oceania and other countries and regions. However, the Internet bubble burst and less than a year later, Alibaba lost more than 90% of its international talents. Looking back now, even if the Internet bubble did not burst, without a strong market as the "base" and a definite user base for the sound financial income, Alibaba will fail to grow into an international enterprise as well if it only favors hot money.

The second stage: Alibaba's internationalization set sail for the second time through investment and acquisition in addition to the integration of overseas high-quality resources and expansion of the overseas capabilities of the core platform. After years of dormancy, the core business B2B trading platforms Alibaba, Taobao and Alipay firmly occupied the No.1 place in e-commerce in the domestic market, and Alibaba grew into the representative internet enterprises of China.

Marked by its cooperation with India's largest B2B media Infomedia in 2008, Alibaba launched a new round of overseas expansion through frequent investments and acquisitions in the international market. After years of layout, a relatively complete global business system was established for Alibaba.

In January 2014, Alibaba announced its internationalization strategy: first, Aliexpress.com, a foreign language website, mainly engaged in overseas retailing, the second is world.taobao.com for international consumers who can read Chinese, while the third, T-mall, provides the authentic imported goods for China market. Alibaba fully copied the domestic core business platform to the international market, with its market layout gradually moved from 2B to 2C. Especially in the US market, Alibaba became an immediate competitor of Amazon and eBay by launching 11 Main, the US version of T-mall.

The third stage: the adjustments of its strategies. In June 2015, Ali sold its one-year-old US subsidiary 11 Main, marking the failure of its first large-scale self-established international business. Jack Ma's ambition to increase the share of the company's overseas revenue from 4 to 50% within five years, that is, by 2020, suffered a major setback. The major problems in its internationalization are as follows.

- **A clear strategy for internationalization, as well as the path of its implementation, are needed**. If Alibaba's strategy for internationalization is to develop transnational e-commerce upon its platform to enable China's 600 million Internet users to buy goods from any corner of the world, then it is still a mode to take the money from Chinese consumers before giving it to foreign enterprises, consequently its overseas business income target will never be realized for it is not truly internationalized. According to BDO UK accounting firm To the U.S. market, where Alibaba chose to get listed, the withdraw of Alibaba is undoubtedly an important statement, which makes people doubt the development of Alibaba if it is to rely only on the Chinese market. If it chooses the strategy of internationalization to fight "tit-for-tat" against the "local leaders" in the overseas market through its self-established shopping malls, is it appropriate for Alibaba to choose the United States as a battlefield? As localized application innovations based on the imitation of American Internet companies and growing up under the wings of domestic policies, what's the odds of success if BAT go directly challenging the home field of their "teachers"? At present, Alibaba seems to have chosen the former as its strategy for internationalization. In fact, it should be a more sensible choice to adopt different strategies in different markets and feel flexible in taking these two ways.
- **Build core competence, so that enterprises can "feel secured inside" when "competing outside"**. The cross-domain operation may trigger a new round of reshuffle when the three giants are heavily invested as the domestic mobile Internet competition intensifies. Therefore, Alibaba must slow down its pace of overseas expansion with the focus shifted on mobile Internet to improve the revenue of the mobile business. Though being second to none in China in learning and practicing big data application, digital marketing, customer behavior analysis based on business intelligence (BI) and business opportunity capture, what unique core ability

can Alibaba be equipped with to win the game in the face of global giants overseas? Domestic Internet companies generally lack investment in core technology and core competence construction, so the emergence of new business models such as mobile Internet often shakes the foundation of their domestic market and gets them into the state of paying attention to one thing and losing the other between the domestic market and overseas business, and consequently disabled in achieving the goal of becoming bigger and stronger through internationalization.

2. The Development, Layout and Major Problems of Baidu's Overseas Business

The overseas business development of Baidu can be divided into two stages.

The first stage: Another taboo of internationalization touched for "pulling out the lion's beard". In 2006, Baidu embarked on its international journey, with Japan as its first stop. In March 2007, Baidu Japan station began its debugging, before Baidu Japan search engine was officially launched in January 2008. But from 2008 to 2011, Baidu lost RMB 680 million in the Japanese market, with baidu.jp only ranked 940 in Japan in terms of its flow. In 2015, Baidu search quietly withdrew from the Japanese market. Although Baidu first chose its searching engine, its sharpest products, to attack overseas, but overlooking the fact Japan embracing not only the world giant Google, but also the local international giant Yahoo, which will make it is extremely difficult for Baidu to enter the Japanese market. Ren Zhengfei once warned his underlings "not to pluck the lion's beard", meaning that choice of the market presents the first obstacle on the path of internationalization for Chinese enterprises.

The second stage: The strategy of "encircling the city from the countryside" in the market with hard practice in technology. Since 2011, Baidu started from emerging countries to restart its journey of internationalization. Upon its strategies of internationalization featured "attentions in a great area with focuses on some key regions", Baidu laid the foundation for the launch of its search engine in Vietnam, Thailand, Indonesia, Malaysia, Brazil and other countries, upon the strengths of a series of application s such as hao123, Baidu Post Bar, Baidu Zhidao (knows), Baidu antivirus and Baidu browser to and Baidu's overseas, the overseas layout has begun to take shape.

As one of the world's earliest batch of experts on the search engine, Robin Li knows well how the core technology account in competitions. In July 2012, Baidu Singapore laboratory was inaugurated, followed by the establishment of Baidu US R&D center in May 2014, before a world-class technology R&D center by Baidu in Brazil in July 2014. According to public data, in 2014, Baidu invested more than RMB 7 billion in technology R&D, accounting for nearly 15% of its revenue, which is not only much higher than the average investment level of 4% in the industry, but also higher than the average investment proportion of 7% for leading technology enterprises in Silicon Valley. In 2014, Baidu not only stayed first in terms of the number of patent applications in its traditional field of searching, but made great achievements in such internet frontiers as cloud computing, artificial intelligence and big data.

The strategy for internationalization of Baidu is growing more like that of Huawei, of which lies the high uncertainty of whether the core technology can lead to breakthroughs as leaders, so this road is destined to be of extreme difficulties. Baidu's overseas business has been at a loss for a long time, with losses of RMB 572 million, RMB 1.63 billion and RMB 3.31 billion respectively in 2012, 2013 and 2014. Upon the huge differences between the products of Baidu and that of Huawei, Can Baidu find a more suitable path for its internationalization? In February 2015, Baidu made some adjustments to the company's organizational structure with the establishment of the mobile service group, emerging business group and search business group. The overall strategy focuses on the consolidation of mobile business in the domestic market and the development of O2O, with the international business department merged with new business groups and consumer business groups to form emerging business groups, and the international business department to prove itself with facts. It is nothing bad for Baidu to consolidate the domestic market, break through the basic search technologies (including image/video search, artificial intelligence, etc.) and build the strongest mobile search and mobile Internet business as a sharp tool for international breakthrough.

3. The Development, Layout and Major Problems of Tencent's Overseas Business

Tencent's overseas business development can be roughly divided into two stages.

The first stage: A modest try. In fact, Tencent started its internationalization comparatively earlier. In 2005, it set up its internationalization division in addition to the branches set up in the United States, India, Vietnam, and Italy. Tencent invested US $300 million in DST, a Russian Internet company, in 2009, but with little success. Tencent did not push QQ to the international market after it occupied the PC end. Perhaps Tencent was fully aware that QQ happens to succeed only when it takes root in China on the basis of "reference + micro innovation + luck", and it is not qualified to go abroad, or perhaps Tencent knows that compared with Baidu's human–computer interaction and Ali's human–material interaction, QQ's human–computer interaction involves more cultural, national, legal and regulatory issues, and there will be more obstacles on the road of its globalization.

The second stage: the internationalization strategy and steps more clarified—to gradually internationalized with core products as weapons, starting from countries and regions with more people speaking Chinese. In April 2011, with Weixin entered the international market with the English name of "WeChat", the second stage of internationalization was officially started. In terms of the overall strategy for internationalization, Tencent hopes to follow the international standards in technology, products, company structure, underlying database and layout. In terms of the selection of products, Tencent chose two No. 1 products in the world as weapons for international breakthrough. The one is WeChat, which, as the first of its kind in the world, appealed to 500 million active users upon the integration of communication, social networking and platform, in addition to the platform like Moments and Public Account. The other is the games with a revenue of US $7.5 billion, which tops the global game industry. Tencent sells the two as a combo with WeChat as the channel of distribution and payment for Tencent games, so as to increase the social interaction of the game, and promote the internationalization of WeChat through the game. In terms of the choice of market, starting from Southeast Asia, Tencent advances to India, the United States, Spain and other regions. In 2013, Tencent saw the establishment of WeChat US office, as the "special force" of Tencent's internationalization strategy, being responsible for the development and research of WeChat users, the establishment and expansion of customer relationships and cooperation in the United States. In the overseas market promotion, Tencent began to be aggressive in international stars as product spokesmen through joining hands with Facebook, Google and other giants.

However, in the face of strong competition from products such as WhatsApp, Line and Facebook Messenger, the global market structure of WeChat still needs to be further improved.

- Developed markets: The major English-speaking countries and France, showing no strong requirements, are not keen on the virtual network world. Many tools are available in the markets that are not concentrated, where even WhatsApp, the one with the highest user coverage as the "dominator of the world" in Europe, accounts for less than 50% of the market. Although Tencent bears a goal of internationalization rather than Asianization, it is not necessarily a wise move to focus its main propaganda on the U.S. market prematurely before the Asian market has formed an advantage. According to the market data of Onavo and other research institutions, Tencent's user coverage in the United States is only about 1%, even which is basically confined to the Chinese circle.
- Developing markets serve as Tencent's main target markets, while among which Latin America is dominated by WhatsApp, accounting for more than 90%, so Tencent's main advantage markets are in Southeast Asia and other places with more Chinese.

Instant messengers feature high viscosity of users and distinctive local cultural characteristics, so adopting differentiated solutions to adapt to the markets in different regions remains the key to gain a competitive advantage, which requires a lot of resources. Although Tencent has made great achievements in many regions of Asia in just four years, much faster than Huawei in its internationalization process, from the perspective of development, the search volume of WeChat in emerging markets is still significantly less than that of WhatsApp.

This has sounded an alarm for Tencent in showcasing that the main target markets still have low recognition of WeChat, so Tencent needs to consolidate and develop its existing market for greater development in a more stable strategic pace.

3.1.2.3 The Key Path for BAT to Break Through the Obstacles of Globalization

Growing up under the special protective policy and economic environment, the Internet upstarts have never fought with international giants at home, so their core competence construction, the formulation level of internationalization strategy and key measures, internal management ability and external competition skills need to be improved. The huge revenue and high-profit level covered up the problems of internal strife, waste in engineering, low efficiency and insufficient international control ability, which will define BAT's bump road to overseas. Therefore, some measures and means are needed to make up for the key short board quickly.

1. Develop Strengths and Avoid Weaknesses to Build Core Competence

Most of the early products of BAT are applied innovation and mode innovation according to the characteristics of China market based on the reference of American products. For example, Taobao put forward the concept of a unique platform for business and supermarkets upon the analysis of Amazon as an example, the same goes with Alipay's mode of the third-party credit guarantee, and WeChat red envelope. Therefore, in the next step, we a breakthrough in the basic mode or core technology is called for to ensure the long-term development of the enterprise.

- Upon the full play of the advantages of overseas listed companies, as well as full use of international capital, the global layout of the market, core technology and industrial chain, can be advanced. The core technology has become a prominent short board hindering the internationalized development of Chinese enterprises, especially for Internet enterprises. Xiaomi's cost-effective strategy completely failed in overseas developed markets, in that Xiaomi's price advantage was totally offset for the patent license fee, which accounts for 30% of the total cost, with Achilles' heel in intellectual property rights standing out prominently. At present, BAT have established R&D and investment centers in the United States, the birthplace of the Internet, to provide sharp weapons for the enterprises' globalization upon the use of the most advanced technology, talents and capital. Baidu and Tencent have similar investment methods overseas, with each investment being not large and no representatives to the board of directors of the company which they invested, but play more as consultants and partners. On the one hand, they were tracking the latest technology for future development opportunities, on the other hand, they were exploring and how to carry out business overseas. Baidu attended more to the acquisition of underlying core technology and the balance between investment and private research. Tencent's overseas investment accounted for 70% in 2013 and 49.4% in 2014 with almost all the companies invested being social-related. Alibaba is the most enterprising, with its overseas investment and M&A projects centering around its core business being rarely less than 10 million US dollars, accounting for more than 10% of the shares in most projects. On the premise of the consistency of the strategies, the enterprises can also take the similar way that Lenovo has ever taken at the right time, to accelerate the process of internationalization through investment, holding or wholly-owned acquisition of related enterprises, so as to realize the leaping growth of the overseas revenue.
- Enterprises can give full play to the advantages of China's human resources, through low-cost and efficient research and development tactics upon "sea of people", so at to "open cooperation" to cooperation with the local forces to meet

the requirements of different regions. BAT's products, all service products based on a deep understanding of local culture and human nature, are different from the standardized hardware products of the manufacturing industry, so it is difficult to replicate in scale in other regions, which affected and the efficiency of the development and cycle of products. When all global Internet companies are facing the same problem, Chinese companies can make use of the advantage of China's "tactics upon the sea of people". Take the Southeast Asian market as an example, where WhatsApp used to stand with absolute advantage, but with the development team of fewer than 100 people in the United States who were unwilling and unable to carry out customized improvement for the local market, it was quickly surpassed by Line in many Southeast Asian countries and regions. If Chinese companies are to give full play to the advantages of "tactics upon the sea of people", the prerequisite is to establish an efficient coordination mechanism between the headquarters and the front line, which has a keen market feeler for a deep understanding of the local cultural characteristics and market requirement, in addition, the headquarters' ability of rapid response to overall planning.

In addition, some functions of overseas products can be opened up for cooperation with local enterprises for complementary advantages. Especially for some regions of minority languages, it can reduce the consumption of R&D, market and human resources for services. This puts forward higher requirements for the architecture design and open ability of the product. For example, through the mode of joint development, Tencent game NBA2KOnline formed its own core competitiveness in the international market upon the large-scale replication of its mode of "product + operation" overseas with its partners after the user base established over the Online version upon the introduction of foreign IP into China at the initial stage.

Enterprises can find their own path for internationalization in the process of global layout upon their core competence developed through self-developed products, mergers and acquisitions and joint development.

2. Problems that Internet Enterprises Must Seriously Consider Are the Reasonable and Clear Strategies for Internationalization and the Right Path and Suitable Markets

BAT preferred to "pluck the lion's beard" and directly attack the commanding heights of the global market, but with not many desirable effects. Reasonable overseas development should take steps as follows.

The first step: Enterprises should take the Southeast Asian countries and regions with more Chinese as the first battlefield to occupy a certain market share and cultivate the circle of overseas users to enhance the competence of overseas products and enhance the international management.

The second step: Enterprises should go deeper into developing countries and regions with large populations and large language families, such as French-speaking countries in Africa, Arabic-speaking countries in the Middle East and North Africa, etc. BRICS, with huge development potential, can be considered as places for key breakthroughs, considering that Internet products, being different from manufacturing products, are almost not affected by tariff barriers. For the emerging markets such as Africa, the Middle East and Southeast Asia, where fixed networks are far less popular than mobile networks, mobile Internet will be an important market opportunity.

The third step: Enterprises can choose developed countries without strong local competitors.

After the completion of the above three steps, expansion in the U.S. market can be made possible.

In terms of the strategy for their expansion, the following ways should be considered.

The way of "going global by the leased boat": In areas with the brands established by Huawei, ZTE, Lenovo and other ICT manufacturers, enterprises can choose to cooperate with local operators. For example, through cooperation with Orange in Egypt, Baidu quickly launched its business online. Enterprises can also cooperate with many overseas mobile phone manufacturers to pre-install relevant business and reduce the threshold of overseas expansion.

The way of "subduing foreigners with foreigners": Enterprises can learn from the foreign enterprises to break through domestic regulatory policies through investment, to obtain huge revenue from the domestic market through agents to, and to invest or merge local enterprises in the target market to occupy the market quickly.

3. Formulate Strategies for Information Security, Improve Privacy Protection Ability, and Accelerate the Accumulation of Intellectual Property Rights

This is a difficult problem that Chinese enterprises have to face in the process of internationalization, while the communication and Internet industry is usually regarded as one of the industries involving national security. Huawei, even just as an enterprise "manufacturing iron boxes and pipes", will receive "special" attention from local media, congress, military and industry when entering a new market, especially in the United States, Australia, India and other countries that are greatly influenced by geopolitics. Though compared with the communication industry, Internet enterprises will suffer a greater impact, there are still some methods worth learning.

- Huawei has done a lot of practical attempts in this respect, either passively or actively, which has made a significant effect on opening the European developed market. Its methods include open-source code and trust security verification to a neutral authority. The UK security certification center was established and opened to the relevant departments around the world, in addition to the former local government security officials employed as chief security officers for Huawei.
- As listed enterprises, the transparency of corporate governance and foreign investment background of BAT made them more international and neutral. Therefore, the enterprises should increase investments in technology, strengthen the construction of local R&D centers and other institutions, increase local employment through joint development and other ways, improve product transparency,

and further avoid the local government's doubts about information security and intellectual property rights.

- Enterprises should try to reduce the security concerns caused by the modes of their operations. Technically, in order to provide better global services, BAT have deployed or rented data centers all over the world, and improved their operation through cloud computing, big data mining, business intelligence and other technical means. More and more countries and regional organizations, especially in the United States and the European Union, paid close attention to digital assets including customer information, which can be exemplified by the incident of leakage of the information of the customers by German telecom, which caused a great disturbance in the European Union. Based on the consideration of the security of information and the protection of privacy, in addition to stronger security technology, the European Union requires that digital assets must be kept within the European Union, besides, individual countries even require or have started legislation that their digital assets must be physically within their own territory. However, when it comes to domestic Internet companies, including Xiaomi, almost all of their core data such as customer information and operators are in China, which has aroused the concern of many countries. Therefore, the planning and construction of cloud computing infrastructure, information security strategy and privacy protection technology of BAT must better meet the requirements of globalization if they want to see their overseas market expanded, so as to distinguish between the international version and domestic version of the product, and make the data centers physically and geographically isolated from each other. For example, the international version of WeChat should be different from its domestic twins, with each using a separate server and maintained by different teams.

From a non-technical point of view, the content filtering, public opinion monitoring and customer regulating by BAT in cooperation with regulatory policies are bound to arouse doubts from the outside world, thus affecting its global image and market expansion. In addition to complying with local laws, BAT must also face the issues of establishing the relationship between its brand and high-level political and business fields.

For Internet companies and even the whole high-end service industry, the process of internationalization is always mixed with heavenly moments and heavy moments. The rapid development of Internet technology and open business model are disintegrating the traditional boundaries, with "globalized operation", "open platform", "differentiated products" and "localized services" as irreversible trends.

3.2 Clear and Reasonable Internationalization Strategy as the Premise of Successful Internationalization

Ren Zhengfei believes the enterprise can afford to wait to go until there are no problems, instead, the enterprise needs to get familiar with the market, win the market, train the team of cadres in the process of its expansion of the overseas markets… If the enterprise failed to build an international team in three to five years, Huawei can wait only for its bankruptcy once the Chinese market is saturated. Upon the release of *Vision and Actions on Jointly Building Silk Road Economic Belt and 21st-Century Maritime Silk Road*, Chinese enterprises ushered in the Era of Internationalization 4.0. "Belt and Road" runs through the active East Asian economic circle and the developed European economic circle, where the investment in the next three years is estimated to be 1.6–6 trillion dollars. How can the enterprise speed up its internationalization in a favorable environment thanks to "Belt and Road Initiative"? The strategy of internationalization that is suitable for the current situation of the enterprise according to its internationalization ability (or maturity) needs be formulated at the beginning.

3.2.1 Suit the Remedy to the Case—Evaluation of Enterprises' Internationalization Ability

As shown in Table 3.1, the evaluation index system of an enterprise's internationalization capability adopts the following three major categories (a total of eight indicators).

- Evaluation on the capability in formulating strategies for internationalization: The evaluation is mainly done from the following aspects: whether the international strategy is clear, whether the objectives are specific, whether the annual/semi-annual update and routine management are carried out, whether the implementation is effective, whether the key measures are closely related to the strategic objectives, whether the key measures are executable, and whether the strategic objectives are linked with the assessment.
- Evaluation on the standard of the international operation: For this, the enterprises will be comprehensively examined from the aspects of marketing, R&D, service, supply chain and other organizational systems, as well as the internationalization level of talents, and the characteristics of the internationalization.

Table 3.1 Evaluation index system of enterprise's internationalization capability

Orientation of the internationalization	Operation of the international	Performance of the internationalization
• Strategies for the internationalization of the enterprise	• Organization internationalization • Supply chain internationalization • Assets internationalization • Talents internationalization • Brand internationalization • R&D internationalization	• Overseas operation effect (including overseas income and profits)

- Evaluation on the performance of the internationalization: The evaluation will mainly be done upon the absolute value and relative value of overseas revenue, payment, profit and other financial indicators.

These three items can be weighted to get the internationalization capability index of enterprises, so as to evaluate the internationalization level of enterprises. After a lot of comparative studies, this book creatively puts forward the concept of internationalization maturity matrix, as shown in Fig. 3.6, which takes the formulation of international strategy and operational level as the abscissa, and the performance weighted index of overseas revenue and profit as the ordinate. According to the position in the internationalization maturity matrix, enterprises can choose a better strategy for their internationalization and a suitable path for the development of their own capabilities.

In the four-quadrant division of the internationalization maturity matrix, the adjustment should be made on whether the overseas performance composite index should be divided by 30% according to the characteristics of the industry. This principle is basically applicable to the pan-manufacturing industry. The low proportion of overseas revenue is not enough to change the operation of enterprises. The comprehensive evaluation of the internationalization strategy and operation carries on quantitatively and qualitatively, with the industry benchmark as the reference.

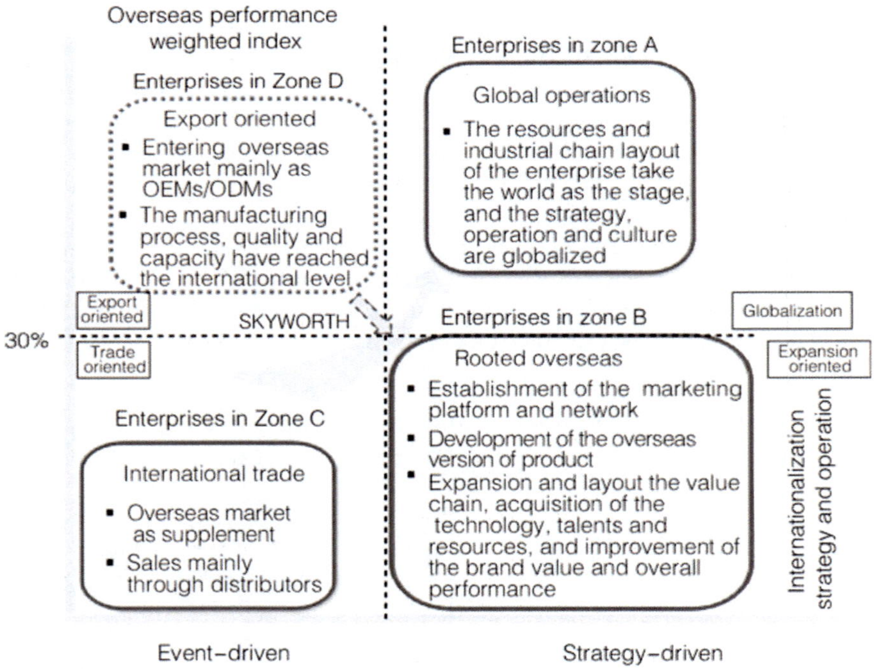

Fig. 3.6 Internationalization maturity matrix

After summarizing and analyzing the internationalization modes and cases of many enterprises, we can find the following characteristics.

Enterprises in Zone C: Enterprises in Zone C see not high proportion of overseas sales, for, being in the primary stage of international trade, their ability is not strong in international operation. Enterprises in this stage mainly sell through overseas distributors, with customers' requirements mainly coming from channels. In this stage, it is most important for the enterprises to discover and develop good channels, at the same time, they should be aware that it is easy for them to be "kidnapped" by the channel as well. Therefore, internationalization can be upgraded through two paths, of which one is to develop to zone B to achieve a gradual breakthrough in the international market by establishing its own overseas marketing system step by step to take the initiative to understand the needs of the international markets and customers, and independently develop or acquire products that meet the needs of overseas customers of the selected markets, while the other way is to develop to Zone D to make the manufacturing process, quality and capacity of enterprises meet the international level by seeking large OEM/ODM partners through channels with the focus on meeting the product manufacturing capacity of overseas markets.

Enterprises in Zone D: Enterprises in Zone D are those whose overseas sales have reached a considerable scale, and whose design and manufacturing capacity has reached the international level, while the overall organization of which is still in China. As they enter the overseas market through partners, they do not have a deep understanding of the global market and end-users, therefore, they are mainly driven by events, but less by strategies. There are also two ways for such enterprises to realize global operations. One way is to establish its own overseas marketing system and independent brand, and build the ability of international strategy formulation and operation through self-development or merger and acquisition. The other way is to establish its own technology brand to realize the development into Zone A upon the global layout of their technology, capital, government business relationship and production capacity through the cooperation with their partners, but not the dependence upon them.

Enterprises in Zone B: the international marketing system and management mode of the enterprises in Zone B are relatively mature, but the proportion of their overseas performance is not high. Therefore, globally competitive products and solutions come as the urgent needs of such enterprises, of which the ones with strong R&D strength can realize product internationalization by establishing their own global R&D organization and product internationalization development process system to meet the needs of the international markets for the increasing the proportion of overseas performance, while the ones with strong financial strength can quickly realize the internationalization of products and develop to jump into Zone A upon the global layout of innovative technology through investment, or through mergers and acquisitions of core resources and key products.

Enterprises in Zone A: The formulation of international strategy and operation ability of enterprises in Zone A is relatively mature, with the proportion of their overseas performance playing an important role in the enterprises. From a global perspective, such enterprises need to make a global layout of their administrative center, financial center, R&D center, manufacturing center, supply chain center, service and training center, so as to maximize their global resource advantages and realize global operation.

3.2.2 The Formulation of the Strategies for Internationalization and the Selection of Its Path

Strategies equal to choices. The selections of the markets, products and the focuses of each stage are the key considerations for the formulation of the strategies for internationalization. Different countries are in different stages of development, so enterprises need to make the right international layout in the right place to meet the needs of local customers with the right products and solutions. Based on the research over the years, the author has the following findings.

Developed countries: Developed countries are attracting a lot of investments in capital-intensive new technology innovation and product R&D, high-end technology service industry, intelligent manufacturing, and precision manufacturing industry.

Emerging market countries: Emerging market countries see their industries and infrastructures in a period of rapid development, with strong requirements for basic production and manufacturing, industrial machinery production and manufacturing, infrastructure construction, food deep processing, medical equipment production and manufacturing, etc.

Developing countries: Boasting a large amount of less costly labor force, there are many opportunities in the developing for industries such as assembly, consumer goods and food processing, just as the "three-plus-one" trading-mix (custom manufacturing with materials, designs or samples supplied and compensation trade) in the early stage of China's reform and opening-up.

Therefore, according to the situations of different countries, the internationalization process of enterprises will experience a smoother journey if they are to provide more products matching the requirements of the markets. Many products and services are generally needed in every country, despite of some differences, and are constantly upgraded with the development of these countries. Enterprises can provide products of different grades and standards for different countries according to their own industry and technical standards.

3.2.2.1 How to Make Swift Dive into Overseas Market

Enterprises that are new to overseas markets often suffer from the mistakes of "acting on impulse" or "planting more than they can get", which consumes resources, as well as undermines their self-confidence. In the early stage of internationalization, Huawei, following suit upon no clear awareness of the overseas markets, chose the countries with a large population and large area as the market breakthroughs, where

Huawei has to invest in local factories to meet the local government's requirements in terms of tariff and localization. However, the slow market development finally resulted in a waste of investment. After repeated failures in Russia, South Africa and other markets, Huawei eventually returned to the international strategy of "encircling the city from the rural areas".

At the beginning of "going global", the biggest problem for the enterprises is the choice of the markets. In the absence of necessary and real data and information of the overseas markets, it presents a difficult problem for enterprises to "tear open" in the overseas markets. Though Huawei determined on the overseas development strategy of "encircling the cities from the rural areas", it still experienced a shift from the perceptual judgment of "acting on impulses" to the rational analysis of "go where they mean to".

In the early days of its development in the African market, Huawei experienced the process of choosing its markets during which it chose South Africa as its first choice before its "giant force" move to Nigeria and Egypt, and finally ended up settling down in the "grain barn" in Africa. As an "action upon impulses", it still got some internal logic. Huawei's screening of African markets is shown in Fig. 3.7. In the early days of market development, there was a lack of personnel in Africa and even the whole overseas market, so Huawei had to choose countries where English is spoken, and the ones of diplomatic relations with China with no disturbance from any war, for which reason, options have been reduced from 54 African countries to 18. To ensure the market development potential and payment capacity of the target countries, and in line with the national strategies of "going global", starting from the countries of "oil

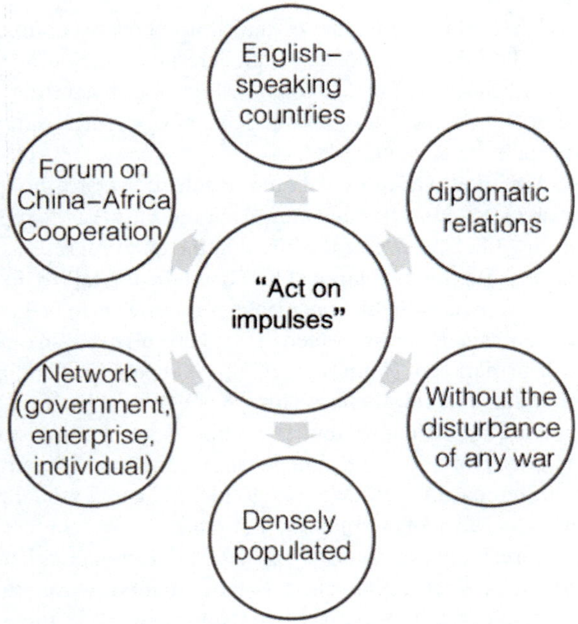

Fig. 3.7 Screening process of the African market

dollar" and "mineral dollar" and African countries with a large population, Huawei screened out four key expansion countries quickly, namely Nigeria, Egypt, Tanzania and Kenya. With the policy support of "double favorable policies and dual loans" from China Development Bank and the Export–Import Bank of China, Huawei quickly broke through the African market through its own efforts in expansion, supplemented by equipment gifts to member countries of Forum on China–Africa Cooperation. Huawei achieved sales of over US $100 million in Nigeria, which became Huawei's stable and sustainable cash cow and its largest representative office in Africa. Under the guidance of the Belt and Road construction, China's enterprises feeling ready to go global can make breakthroughs in overseas markets along the route of the Belt and Road Initiative upon the assistance of the new financing channels such as New Development Bank (NDB), Silk Road Fund and Asian Infrastructure Investment Bank (AIIB).

In the middle and later stage of its internationalization, Huawei has accumulated a lot of market data with an in-depth understanding of overseas markets. In the process of its overseas expansion, Huawei continues to sum up experience, and makes rational analysis and choice of the markets with the help of appropriate methods and external brain, which greatly increases the rationality of Huawei's internationalization strategy. The specific method is to analyze the target country's market in the region from the two dimensions of market attraction and enterprise comprehensive competitiveness, so as to determine the priority of market expansion.

The evaluation factors of market attractiveness are: first, market-scale, including market room and growth potential; Second, profitability, including strategic value, competition intensity and profit margin, as well as cooperative resources and even locations.

The evaluation factors of the comprehensive competence of the enterprises are: first, the market influence of the enterprise, including the quality of the company's brand, the network of relationship and marketing platform; Second, product competence, including product cost performance, service ability and differentiated competitive advantage.

A market was drawn about the selection portfolio analysis chart Take Huawei's main target countries and regions in the East Pacific region as an example, as shown in Fig. 3.8. The size of the circle in the chart represents the overall size of the target market. Taking the diagonal line from the top left to the bottom right as the dividing line, the market in the upper right corner needs to be given priority, while the market in the lower-left corner needs to be carefully considered.

The market of Hong Kong, China: Due to its lack of international experience in the early stage, Huawei chose Hong Kong, China because it was adjacent to Shenzhen, which made it convenient to communicate with customers and provide technical support. Hong Kong, China, located at the top of the upper right corner, has become a springboard for Huawei to "go global" and a model point for internationalization though it presents a small market scale.

Korean market: In terms of scale, the Korean market is the second-largest market in the East Pacific region after that of Japan. However, the Korean market has a strong national complex and insufficient competition, so there is a lack of competition, for

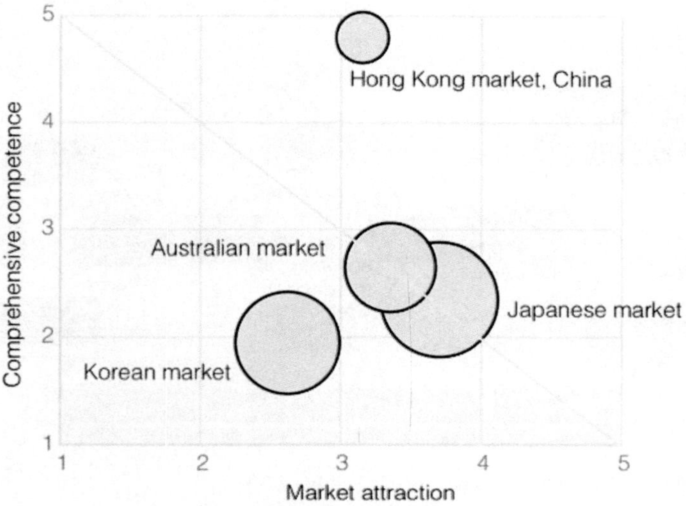

Fig. 3.8 Market selection portfolio analysis

as long as there are local products, customers generally will not choose the foreign one, unless the foreign equivalence shows a high differentiation advantage, so the entry threshold of the Korean market is very high. Located in the lower-left corner, the Korean market belongs to the problem market. From the perspective of the actual effect of the expansion, Huawei's market in South Korea has been lukewarm for a long time, with sales of about US $30 million, which was later taken over by the Japanese representative office.

The other two markets are close to the diagonal and need careful analysis.

Australian market: Australia belongs to the Commonwealth. With Huawei's continuous breakthrough in the UK, Singapore and Malaysia markets, its brand won a high international reputation. In Australia, Huawei soon made breakthroughs with two or three types of customers. However, when dealing the largest customer, Huawei has been strongly hindered from many aspects, so the largest customer remained undone for a long time. In 2019, Australia even announced its rejection of Huawei's 5G technology, which made the Australian market one of Huawei's difficult markets globally.

Japanese market: Japanese market is the one with the largest potential in the Far East Pacific region, in that it is not only a large market, but also be full of competition and high strategic value. One of the reasons for Huawei's low comprehensive competence evaluation in the Japanese market at that time was that Japan had its own industry standards, which were different from those of Europe and the United States. At that time, Huawei did not have products that met Japanese standards, and it was difficult for the front line to promote the headquarters to develop products that met Japanese standards; Secondly, at that time, the customer relationship was mainly established through the agency, leaving the direct customer relationship weak. Upon

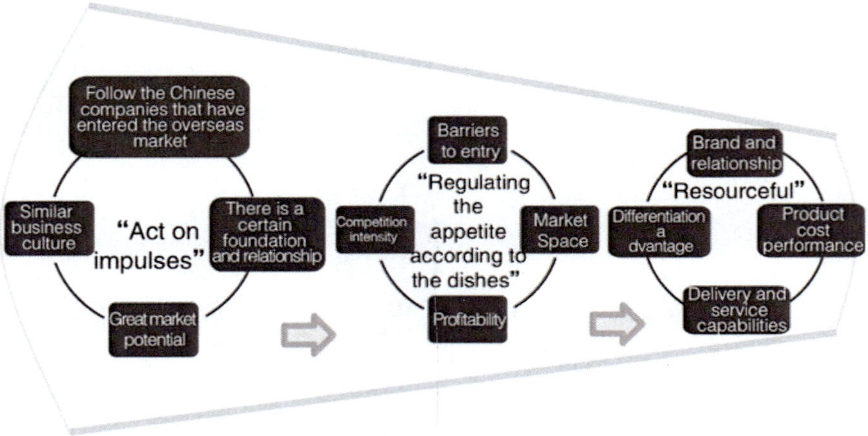

Fig. 3.9 Evolution of overseas market selection ability

determining the strategic position of the Japanese market, Huawei's R&D department actively carried out the product R&D of Japanese standards, with the East Pacific Region Department moved its headquarters to Japan to increase its efforts in developing the Japanese market. "The 3· · · 11" earthquake marked a turning point for Huawei in the Japanese market, will made Japan soon a high-quality market with sales of more than 2 billion US dollars for Huawei in a single country.

After years of experience, Huawei's ability of strategic choice in overseas markets has been evolving, as shown in Fig. 3.9. Huawei has gradually changed from the early perceptual choice of "acting on impulses" to the rational choice of overseas markets according to the difficulty of market access, its own competitive advantage and the profitability of the market.

Enterprises should focus on different stages, and adopt different methods to break through the target markets with different products and solutions for different target markets. Once mastering this effective method, Chinese enterprises can realize the qualitative change from "accepting the results passively" to "following the purpose actively".

3.2.2.2 Insights into Customers to Grasp Global Strategic Opportunities

1. Find Opportunities

A comprehensive insight into customers in the target market is the key behavior to discover market opportunities. First of all, customers should be divided, through the similar method of market classification, into strategic customers, value customers, customers to be maintained and potential customers from the two dimensions of customer attraction and enterprise comprehensive competitiveness, before making different customer development plans and optimizing customer resource management accordingly.

Customer relationship is the first productivity, so a detailed customer development plan and customer relationship development plan need to be formulated. In the customer development plan, enterprises should first understand whether the customer's strategy on the selection of suppliers had changed. Whether it's for the need to improve financial performance, the need to balance suppliers, or technological innovation, chances can only be brought by changes. It is necessary to conduct a comprehensive analysis of customers' purchase tendency, value orientation and decision-making chain, so as to establish targeted high-level and middle-level customer relationships, as well as general customer relationships for middle and lower-level customers. The focus should be put on the understanding of three key points: understanding customer development strategy, interpreting customer KPI, identifying customer needs and pain points, and establishing two major relationships, namely, customer relationship platform and customer relationship network.

Customer insight is commonly done through a "5 × 5" analysis method, as shown in Fig. 3.10, to analyze the challenges and strategic pain points faced by customers in detail from the five aspects of customer's operation and financial status, organization and management system, business status and future development, technical ability and competition and cooperation relationship, so as to understand customer development strategy and business design logic, master customer investment plan, and find sales leads and opportunities, so as to develop the customer marketing strategy and key measures.

2. Management of Opportunities

With the gradual deepening of the understanding of the market and the gradual improvement of the ability of overseas organizations, enterprises will find more and more opportunities, just like "when arriving the African prairie, they would find animals everywhere, but failed in hunting them". Ren Zhengfei once warned everyone that any opportunity from the company's strategic sand table can bring tens of billions if seized, but if trapped in short-term interests, enterprises will lose strategic opportunities because of wasting time on non-strategic opportunities. Therefore,

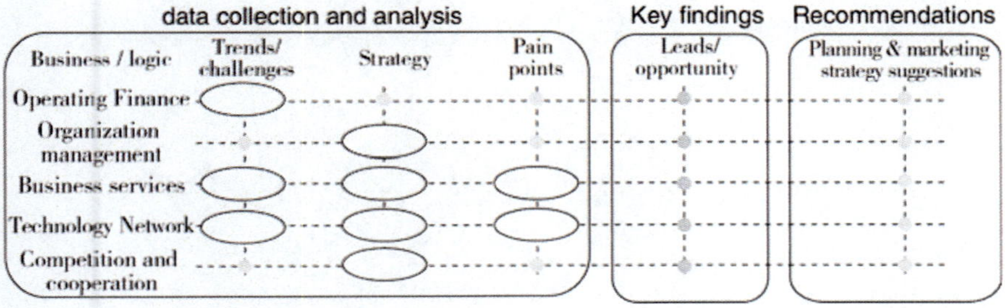

Fig. 3.10 "5 × 5" method for customer insight

Huawei's "stupidity" is also reflected in not being lured by opportunities of short-term profit, being not eager for quick success and instant benefits, not being moved by a single scale growth, but daring to give up non-strategic opportunities to gamble on the future. Here the "gamble" means to have a strategic vision, to focus on big strategic opportunities, to focus on the allocation of resources on key success factors.

Therefore, first of all, enterprises need to sort the priority of opportunity and identify strategic opportunity. According to the market and its own characteristics, Huawei has adjusted and optimized the applicability of many templates and tools. From the perspective of market positioning, competitive position and financial analysis, Huawei has analyzed different opportunities in different markets, focused on strategic opportunities, incubated potential opportunities, and adopted different methods for investments upon different opportunities. Secondly, through the development of a strategic opportunity sand table, the opportunity are managed hierarchically, linked up and down, and implemented layer by layer through strategic decoding, as shown in Fig. 3.11. Especially for the strategic opportunity at the company level, it is necessary to invest the company's resources for key guarantees, with the company's senior leaders taking the lead to implement them. Instead of looking at strategic commanding heights in general terms, enterprises should divide them into many positions for the plans and specific measures after analyzing them one by one. All sectors of the company should focus on the windows of opportunity. We should not only benchmark the strategic commanding point in sales, but also allow the representative offices to plan the strategic opportunity by themselves.

Through the multi-level and hierarchical decoding of strategic opportunity, combined with the closed-loop management of planning and assessment, the

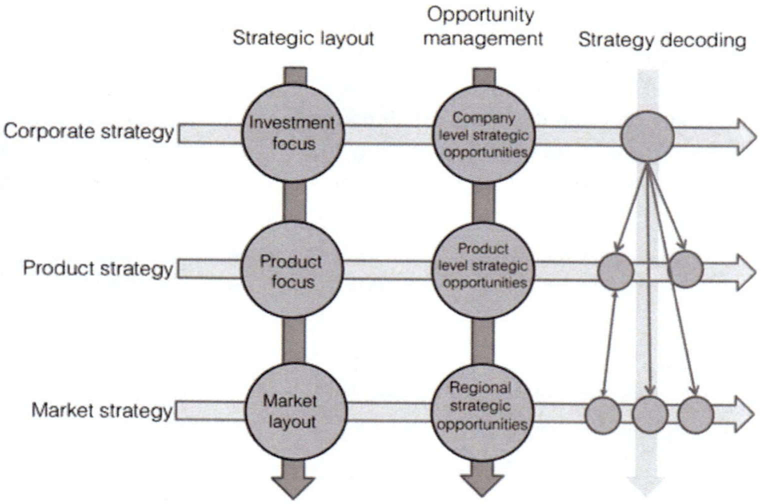

Fig. 3.11 Hierarchical management of strategic opportunity

company's complete strategic sand table and action plan are formed, which lays the foundation for the subsequent establishment of the MTL/LTC process system.

3. How to Grasp the Opportunities

To grasp the opportunity, enterprises need a strong background system for support. In the early stage of going global, it is generally impossible for an enterprise to build a strong back office system first, instead, the leadership will run through the relevant departments of the enterprise and give support to the front line according to the market opportunities captured by the front line. With the increase of market opportunities, business lines will impact the existing management system continuously, resulting in low efficiency of the collaboration between the frontline and the backstage. Some enterprises even hope to use domestic products all over the world, without even attention on the overseas market requirement, let alone coordination between the frontline and the backstage. Two or three hundred strategic opportunity should not just turn out as the results of Strategic Benchmarking, but the focus of the whole team of the enterprise, with the weapons of the R&D team adaptable to the combat structure of the opportunity. At this stage, enterprises should have such abilities.

Under the guidance of this strategic mindset, a collaborative organization with core processes such as IPD and ISC (integrated supply chain) as the main body was gradually established between the front-line and headquarters of Huawei, with minor success as a major one, striving for good management in the overseas end-to-end project management themed "requirements—landmark planning—product development—delivery" to grasp the market opportunities. Especially for the market opportunities of strategic key customers, the company is required to fully comply with the requirements of the tender. This is because strategic customers not only lead the future development direction, but also influence and cover global market opportunities, such as Vodafone's wide coverage of the European market, African market and even North American market, as well as Telefónica's extensive subnet opportunities in Latin America.

Through the "needle tip" strategy and years of continuous investment, Huawei has entered the world's leading ranks in 5G and other technology fields and enterprise management. According to the strategic requirements of globalization, Huawei must turn these "leading fields" into actual "territory", that is, to turn its "advantage" into "success", and to turn strategic opportunities into real market acquisition. Huawei's lawsuit against Samsung and T-Mobile of the US is a concrete embodiment of the main battlefield of seizing strategic opportunities and converting technological advantages into market share and revenue. Therefore, to grasp the strategic opportunity and realize efficient collaborative operation are the key guidelines for the formulation of strategies for internationalization.

3.2.2.3 The Choice of the Path for Internationalization

Upon the comprehensive analysis of the path for the internationalization of many Chinese enterprises, the following internationalization paths can be preliminarily drawn.

- **The way of "going global by the leased boat" for small and medium-sized enterprises**. HH international sales company saw its overseas profits at 4 times that of the listed parent company through differentiated service solutions in its maintenance serves for a large project on behalf of the other enterprises along the route of the Belt and Road Initiative, through the cooperation with large enterprises of EPC[4] construction like China State Construction Engineering Group Co., Ltd. (CSCEC) and China Power. The small but strong overseas service enterprise, like HH international sales company, is not only a contributor to the Belt and Road Initiative, but also a model of overseas "China Service".
- **The way of "going global together" for private enterprises**. In important areas along the route of the Belt and Road Initiative, such as Indonesia, the joint private enterprises and capital, represented by China Minsheng Investment Group (CMIG) have adopted the ecological cooperation mode of "Finance + industry + service" similar to that of Japan syndicate, and invested in the construction of industrial parks and other complexes, realizing the sharing of resources and experience to the maximum extent, and improving the anti-risk ability of Chinese enterprises overseas.
- **The way of "going global with courage" for benchmarking enterprises**. BYD's strategy for its internationalization is worth learning from by Chinese enterprises. On the one hand, BYD continues to expand its territory with North America and Europe as the key high-end brand markets for its innovative new energy vehicles and energy storage products. On the other hand, BYD, as the world's leading supplier of energy storage solutions, laid the foundation for the promotion and use of the application in the countries and regions along the routes of Belt and Road Initiative by promoting the commercial application of energy storage power station and photovoltaic power station in the industrial park in the national circular economy education demonstration base and the national urban mineral demonstration base through the cooperation with Grammy. It is the key to the success of internationalization of enterprises to develop quickly upon the opportunities and steadily in seeking the opportunities upon the strategy of internationalization "within self-control" upon the characteristics of their own industries.

[4] EPC (engineering procurement construction) refers to the whole process or several stages of contracting for the design, procurement, construction and trial operation of engineering construction project entrusted by the owner in accordance with the contract.

3.2.2.4 Strategic Confidence in Going Global

- **Lack of international brand awareness**: The lack of awareness is a common problem for Chinese enterprises to "go global". I remembered once in Huawei's brand department, after a leader reported his work to Ren Zhengfei, Ren Zhengfei said that the brand was made, not publicized. Without core competence (technology/product/service/supply chain/management), the once popularity will always die out soon, just like the "I'm happy to be here in China" by Lei Jun, which made Indian MI-fans heartbroken. The patent license fee, which accounts for 30% of the terminal, is more like the sword of Damocles. The key to Sany's successful brand marketing in the Fukushima nuclear disaster is that it has excavators with the longest arms in the world. Therefore, there are skills to establish an international brand, but not shortcuts.
- **Strategic self-confidence**: The foundation of building strategic self-confidence is the construction of self-power and the ability in the utilization of third-party authoritative competence. With its core competence, Huawei achieved an out-of-court settlement after suing Cisco. With its core competence, Sany dared to win the lawsuit against former US President Obama. Another important manifestation of strategic self-confidence is to dare to manage "foreigners" and "foreign affairs" and avoid the recurrence of the lessons of SAIC's acquisition of SSANG YONG Motor Company and TCL's acquisition of Alcatel. I have personally experienced the experience of recruiting a regional CTO. When I first went overseas, with insufficient English, I would only focus on their resumes and ask a few questions when I saw the tall white candidates before then pushing them to the leadership for decision. Later, when at the time to dismiss the foreign employees, many local legal issues occurred.

Huawei's internationalization strategy has been continuously sublimated by comprehensively promoting to developed markets. Ren Zhengfei's philosophic and popular ideas of "land for peace" and "never pluck the lion's beard" often make overseas leaders promoted at emergency felt quite in the cloud, leaving the clarity of internationalization strategy and the enforceability of key measures imminent. For this reason, Huawei introduced the world's top consulting companies, such as Accenture, Mercer and IBM, however, whose advanced theories, templates and methods are greatly challenged by Huawei's international strategy makers' separation from the front line, lack of market data as support, and rigid application of methodology.

To enhance the formulation of international strategy, especially the ability of overseas front-line strategic planning and the strategic mindset of cultivating front-line leading talents, Huawei improved the methodology and extended the authority of strategy formulation from headquarters to overseas regional markets, which marks that Huawei's international strategy has officially entered routine management. With the accumulation of experience and data, tools and methods play an important role in market analysis. At the same time, the internationalization strategy and objectives, resource planning and performance appraisal have formed a benign interaction and closed-loop management, making the internationalization strategic layout and key measures the guide of the business program of the overseas front-line.

Chapter 4
An Iron Army for International Marketing

4.1 Huawei's Customer-Centered International Organization System

The promulgation of *Buy American Act* by the United States and the *Localization and Economic Rights Act* of Zimbabwe has once again sounded an alarm for the "going abroad" of Chinese enterprises. After years of guidance, warning, training and practice by the government, enterprises and third-party consulting service companies, the risks of "going global" for Chinese enterprises have finally won full attention. However, the analysis reports of several consulting agencies pointed out that Chinese enterprises would put more emphasis on external factors, while the ability to prevent internal risks, especially the implementation of the internationalization strategy, is seriously insufficient.

It is time to bid farewell to the extensive mode of "going global", either for the government or for the enterprises. In addition to formulating clearer strategies for internationalization, the key is to build a stronger executive force, which in turn calls for the guarantee from the international organization system, ability and talents.

4.1.1 Frontline "Iron Triangle" Pioneering Team

The customer-centered "iron triangle" organization has been proved to be a highly market-sensitive and responsible organizational structure.

With their internationalization strategy starting at seeking overseas market opportunities based on the sensitivity of the endings of their overseas nerves, enterprises should carefully analyze the objective needs of the market in terms of both business and technology. Chinese enterprises often experience disabilities in effective communication with their customers at the initial stage of going overseas, in that the technical personnel can not fully communicate with customers for their poor competence in languages or interpersonal communications, while those customer managers who

L. Tao, *Huawei Wisdom*,
https://doi.org/10.1007/978-981-19-1169-9_4

are masterful in languages and background knowledge of the foreign trade are but less aware of the company and the product. In 2006, Huawei's North Africa division first proposed the front-line "iron triangle" work mode according to the situation of overseas expansion at that time, which effectively solved the organizational problems of identifying customer needs and discovering opportunities.

4.1.1.1 Before the Construction of the "Iron Triangle"

In the early stage of market development, enterprises will generally assign a sales manager to each region, or expand the market through development agents, to find opportunities by establishing relationships with customers, and then sign contracts, urge for goods and perform contracts. There are few projects in the initial stage, so the sales managers can cope with them. But when there are more projects, the sales managers will fail in shouldering the responsibilities. Such a phenomenon will happen in two ways. The one is for there too many responsibilities to carry, while the sales manager still put his the focus mainly on the completion of the sales task, who, due to the limitation of energy, sense of responsibility or knowledge, has no energy or even unwillingness to pay attention to other things such as requirement management and maintenance ability. In the end, the enterprise mainly assesses the short-term sales of the sales manager. The other situation has something to do with the ability. The sales manager is generally assumed by the customer manager. With the development of the enterprises, more products of greater complexity present greater challenges for the sales managers to understand the products and technology. As a result, the front line of the market will turn to the R & D, technical service, supply chain and other departments of the headquarters for help when it encounters problems. However, due to the imperfection of the consulting mechanism, problems often occur, such as the repeated requirements fail to be implemented, and sometimes they need to travel by air for replacement of the boards for the equipment, which leads to high costs and low customer satisfaction. Especially in the poor areas of Africa, it is very difficult to get on-site support due to the problems of cumbersome visa procedures, long journeys and poor living conditions. Therefore, Huawei developed its first "iron triangle" in Sudan of Africa. In extreme cases, when some enterprises go overseas, many sales managers are recruited directly from the Institute of foreign trade, who only know foreign languages, but lack the basic skills of customer managers, and little knowledge about the enterprise and its products and no internal interpersonal resources and channels for help. Therefore, "three pats" offer occurs in the front line of the markets, that is, "patting the chest" when making a promise to customers, "patting the head" to show their concerns when not knowing whether the R & D ability can meet the product requirement, and "patting the bottom" and go away when failing to fulfill on time.

4.1.1.2 Running-in in the Construction of "Iron Triangle"

The market "iron triangle" is a sales project team established according to the characteristics and needs of the market development of the industry, as shown in Fig. 4.1.

The definition of "iron triangle" by Huawei is an AR (Account Responsibility) in charge of customer interface, SR (Solution Responsibility) in takes care of products and solutions, and FR (Fulfillment Responsibility) sees to the fulfillment, whose responsibilities together cover the three core business systems. How to set up an efficient marketing team according to the characteristics of the industry is the key to the success or failure of the construction of an enterprise's marketing system.

According to the characteristics of different industries, the operation mode of the "iron triangle" needs to be adjusted appropriately and transformed into "two iron points" or "iron quadrangle", for the core of which is to identify the most important roles of the enterprise in the market, and collaborate these roles efficiently. Upon the investigation and consultation of many industries, the concept of the "iron triangle" is found to be universally appliable. The mode of the "iron triangle" for some industries is shown in Fig. 4.2.

The construction of the "iron triangle" also well matches the mode of customer's decision-making. Especially for the decision-making of large contracts, the customer decision-making team generally includes the customer leader, purchasing department, user department, maintenance department, engineering department, etc. The "iron triangle" can help build a solid and in-depth customer relationship upon the understanding of the customer's pain points and needs at different levels through the extensive and fixed communication interface with the customer's top decision-making, middle-level management and professional and technical sectors by corresponding to the customer's organization and matching

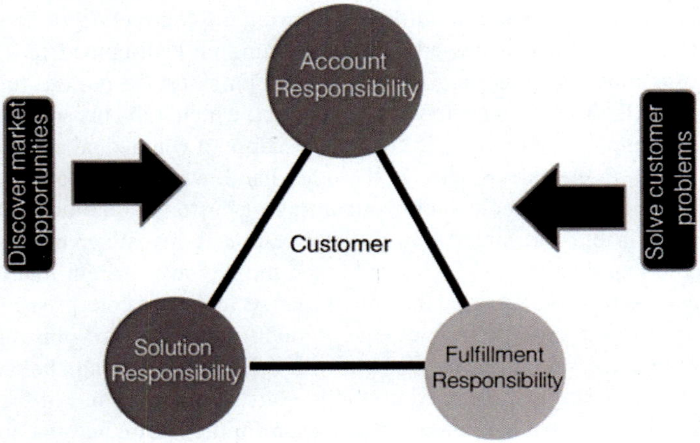

Fig. 4.1 The organization mode of the market "iron triangle"

	Simple products →	Complex products
Distribution (B2C)	• Channel + franchise • Technology and service • Supply chain Reference industry: Chain business	• Channel + franchise / high touch • Marketing and technical support • Supply chain and fulfillment Reference industry: intelligent terminal
Direct selling (B2b)	• Channel + key customer direct sales • Technology and service • Financing, fulfillment and collection Reference industry: small and medium equipment, aquaculture	• Channel + key customer direct sales • Technical support and marketing • Service and fulfillment (supply chain) Reference industry: enterprise ICT
Direct selling (B2B)	• Customer line + channel • Technology and service • Fulfillment, financing / collection Reference industry: medium and large equipment, such as electric power	• Account Manager • Technology marketing • Service and fulfillment Reference industry: TMT industries like the industry of communication

Fig. 4.2 Mode of "iron triangle" for markets of different industries

the customer's decision-making chain, while internally, the establishment of the customer relationship, the understanding of the customer needs and the consistency of commitment can be maintained through the integration and complementation of skills with improved customer satisfaction and lower risks by the flow of personnel.

The operation mechanism featuring "iron triangle" was initially established in Huawei, but without a clear definition of responsibilities and rights, resulting in many problems in the operation with the effects like "the railway police who just care about the affairs in each section of their own authority". When encountering a dominating customer manager, the customer interface and project leader often expect that the Solution Responsibilities just takes care of configuration quotation and but not to meet the customer, while the fulfillment responsibilityfulfillment responsibility just needs to take care of the back-end fulfillment. During the contract negotiation, when the key terms are not fully discussed within the team, not well-considered commitments, such as those on price, requirements, ultra-long service period, fulfillment period, etc., are likely to be made to win the contract, which will bury a lot of hidden dangers for the implementation of the contract, because of which dual contracts have even been signed in the early stage. On the other hand, when the account responsibility stands in a minor position, apart from arranging customer communication, the project manager is totally disabled in bearing the responsibility. When the author was in Australia to expand the market, he witnessed the vicious incident that different Solution Responsibilities slandered the other products their own enterprise in front of the same customers in order to promote the products within their responsibility, but the customer managers found no way to deal with it. Peng Zhongyang, the proponent of Huawei's "iron triangle", summed up the lessons from the failure of the project operation. He believed that the fundamental reason for the failure was that the enterprise's organization was still operating in the traditional mode even when it did not match that of the customers, resulting in that the customer line did not understand fulfillment, while the fulfillment line did not understand customers, and the product line only focused on the quotation. All parties are only concerned about the businesses of their own concerns in a very "me-centered" manner, but being very passive in responding to the needs of customers, no wonder why it failed! Therefore, it is of great significance to clearly define the responsibilities, rights and collaborative operation mode of the "iron triangle".

4.1.1.3 The Operation of the "Iron Triangle" with Both form and Spirit

Through continuous practice, Huawei has gradually clarified the roles, responsibilities and management authorities of the different parties of the "iron triangle".

- **Account Responsibility**: As the first person responsible for the operation, overall planning, customer platform construction, customer satisfaction, achievement of business indicators and market competition of relevant customers/projects (groups), for the enterprises which mainly sell through channels, the account responsibility is mainly responsible for the development and management of agents, the planning of the target for the regional market and the achievement of business indicators. At the same time, for key customers and strategic customers, the account responsibility needs to collaborate with agents to deepen the relationship with them. The overseas representative promoted from the account responsibility is no longer the big account responsibility who gets a commission for every order sold, but as the local CEO, who should not only achieve the short-term goal, but serve as a local representative of the enterprise to well manage the local operation, competition and long-term development.
- **Solution Responsibility**: As the first person responsible for product brand and solution, the solution responsibility sees to pre-bid guidance, technical exchange and scheme design, and quotation disclosure to customer manager, in addition to the responsibility for the business objectives of customer group solutions, including the targets of the sales of the product for a short-term and the targets of the market in a medium or long term. For the enterprises which mainly sell through channels, Solution Responsibilities need to carry out marketing empowerment, technical support and co-branding activities in the consideration of the characteristics of different agents. At the same time, they need to have an in-depth understanding and analysis of key customer needs to provide input for product planning upon their responsibilities not only to achieve the current product sales target but to satisfy the future requirement in a medium or long term.
- **Fulfillment Responsibility**: As the first person responsible for the overall fulfillment and service of the customer/project (group), the fulfillment responsibility-fulfillment responsibility sees to the key links of payment collection (acceptance report), as well as the target of the sales of services. For the enterprises which mainly sell through channels, the fulfillment responsibilityfulfillment responsibility should not only open up the channels between the supply chain of the enterprise and the partner to empower and support the partner, but also provide

direct technical services to the key customers who definitely need the technical services from the original factory. The fulfillment responsibility is responsible for customer satisfaction, because the final acceptance report is related to the payment collection. And one step further, the service also leads to sales. fulfillment responsibilityFulfillment responsibilitys play increasingly important roles in solution transformation and sales as well. In addition to traditional technical support, fulfillment responsibilitys also play an important role in network planning, consulting, professional services, integration, etc.

Although the main responsibilities of each role are clearly defined, the responsibility subject and key points of the "iron triangle" should be dynamically adjusted according to the different stages of project operation in order to prevent the managers from minding their own business in operation like "the railway police who just care about the affairs in each section of their own authority". The transformation of responsibility subject of the "iron triangle' in the sales process is shown in Fig. 4.3. Traditional sales pay more attention to the opportunities in front of them. Therefore, it is often the case that large and small suppliers flock to the market after the customers' issue bids. Some enterprises even have the mindset of "developing on requirement". At this time, the customer manager is generally the first person responsible for managing opportunities and the operation of the "iron triangle". After entering the bid answering stage, it is mainly to guide the technology and clarify the scheme. At this time, the solution responsibility is the first responsible person, with the fulfillment responsibility participating in the discussion of the scheme. Huawei's solution responsibility is also responsible for the commercial quotation of products to balance the rights of customer managers. In the stage of negotiating and signing the contract, the responsible subject is again transferred to the customer manager, with the solution responsibility and the fulfillment responsibility assisting in the clarification of relevant technical terms, and the solution responsibility assisting in the price negotiation. In the process of contract execution and fulfillment, the fulfillment responsibility becomes the main body carrying responsibility, with the solution responsibility carrying out the handover of technical solutions, the solution of R & D problems, and assisting in the testing of solutions. After the contract is executed and the fulfillment responsibility obtains the customer's acceptance report, the customer

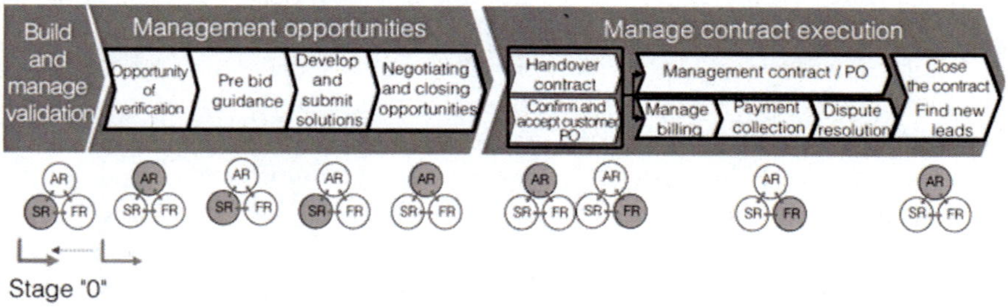

Fig. 4.3 The shift of the responsibility subject of "iron triangle" in sales process

manager becomes the main body of responsibility again, responsible for payment collection and contract closure.

In the whole process, although the responsibility subjects of different stages are different, the customer manager is generally responsible for the management throughout the whole process as the project manager; In addition to the responsibilities specified in the role, the solution responsibility should also help maintain and deepen the customer relationship of the technology line, change the role positioning of traditional technology sales waiting for customers to issue bids, understand customers' needs by analyzing customers' pain points, takes the initiative to find sales leads and new business opportunities by advancing guidance and incubating leads. The "0" stage has been added in the sales process, which opens the 2.0 era of Huawei marketing. In addition to the responsibilities specified in the role, the fulfillment responsibility should also help maintain and deepen the customer relationship of the service line, upon a deep understanding of the problems encountered by customers in the service, so as to ensure the success of customers and find new market opportunities in the service; The end of the contract is just the beginning of a new opportunity. Many successful sales cases have proved that market opportunities are often found and broken through from the back-end service stage.

The case of Huawei in the overseas high-end data communication equipment market fully shows the role of fulfillment responsibilitys in discovering opportunities. Due to the fact that Huawei's high-end data communication products are rarely used overseas, the brand awareness is not high, and the customers' general channel agents, integrators and main equipment suppliers are Huawei's competitors. Huawei has been playing the role as a co-bidder in many biddings, because of the customers' senior managers' trying hard to securing their "black gauze cap (a kind of cap worn by ancient Chineses officials, thus it is a symbol of position and power)", the customers' middle and basic managers' weak confidence in China's technology, in addition to the joint containment of the competitors to Huawei. However, with the rapid growth of customer business, the original main equipment supplier's supply cycle can not meet customer requirements, and customers are eager to get the business into operation. So Huawei seized the chance and offered to solve this difficult problem in the shortest time. Upon the customer's permission, Huawei's technical support department immediately mobilized all the warehouse equipment, organized the strength and made every effort to complete the delivery and installation of the equipment on the same day, opened the customer's business, alleviated their urgent need, and realized the "zero" breakthrough from the original corner of the customer's last technical service. In the later stage, Huawei comprehensive replaced the customers' core backbone network equipment with the help of the front and rear cooperation through seizing the mistakes and weaknesses of its competitors again and again, while giving full play to the role of the "iron triangle" team in the front line.

From the case, we can see that service and fulfillment play important roles in the marketing process of industrial products. The concept of service marketing integration advocated by Huawei plays an important supporting role in the establishment of the company's brand and the success or failure of the project. Project operation is not only in the front end of the bidding, nor can it be completed by the single role of sales personnel. The overall competitive forces of the team need to be given full play to seize the weakness of the enemy, find the pain points of the customers, and launch a comprehensive attack on them for a greater effect. Huawei's "iron triangle", that is, the customer line responsible for customer relationships, the product line responsible for technical exchange and the fulfillment line responsible for service fulfillment, has manifested huge power again.

The "iron triangle" market model of Huawei has been gradually promoted all over the world from Africa. This model not only greatly improves the ability of each role, cultivates a large number of cadres with "one specialty and multiple abilities", and realizes the efficient collaborative operation on the front line. More importantly, it constructs the "iron triangle" model of Huawei, which maintains a high sensitivity to the market and plays an effective supporting role of the platform.

4.1.1.4 The Evaluation Mechanism of "Common Profits Through Collaborative Efforts" Serves as the Guarantee for the Efficient Cooperation of the "Iron Triangle"

The core idea of the operation of the "iron triangle" is to encourage individual heroism upon collaborative teamwork, with attention on the realization of current goals and discovery of future opportunities, the implementation of which must be guaranteed with a sound incentive mechanism.

Immediately after Huawei secured its survival, the system of "sales commission", which was a common practice for many enterprises, was abolished in its sales system. The commission system may have a certain effect on stimulating the enthusiasm of sales personnel, but for the sales of complex products, especially the sales that call for team cooperation, its side effect can be very huge, which often leads to the information blockade, internal excessive competition, and even mutual poaching, which is particularly obvious in the second-hand real estate market.

One of the key reasons for difficulties in the implementation of the "iron triangle" in many enterprises is the assessment and bonus distribution for each role. Huawei improved the cooperative combat capability of the "iron triangle" by improving the assessment method. We can often see that even in areas where the market and human resources are weak, the "iron triangle" still enables Huawei to maintain a "three against one" advantage against its competitors. Therefore, the relevant practices of Huawei can be a significant reference for many enterprises, which can be shown in the following points.

- **Balance between the interests of individuals and that of the team**

The bonus distribution at the front line changed from "sales commission" to a bonus package allocated upon the rate of the target achievement. Hey designed the reform for Huawei's salary system, based on the statistical law of most enterprises, that is, only 10% of the employees can achieve 100% of the target when they work hard. Otherwise, the target setting may be unreasonable. Therefore, Huawei generally adopts the way of overall proportion control of performance evaluation results for bonus distribution. The specific methods are as follows.

First of all, the market of different departments/regions will be evaluated based on the completion of the target, ranked for the decision on the bonus package coefficient determined according to the reference proportion of 10, 40, 45 and 5%, for which the "horse racing" culture is formed between different regions, so each employee will give priority to ensure the collective's leading position and enlarge the collective's total bonus package, thus promoting the company's overall sales at the same time.

Secondly, for the teams in the same region and the members of the same team, similar methods are used to determine the bonus coefficient on the ranking of the performance. In this way, employees will understand that individual bonus is not only related to individual efforts, but also to the overall performance of the team, therefore, everyone in the team will be willing to help each other. In Huawei's regular sales management meetings, including the annual market meeting, half of the time is often used for the discussions upon the completion of sales targets, and the other half for sharing project experience and helping other departments/colleagues achieve the targets, with the spirit of win–win cooperation and passion to make the team bonus package bigger alive in the team. At the same time, in order to praise projects and individuals with outstanding contributions, special awards and individual awards were set up to achieve the balance of collective and individual interests. The wolf-like culture for team cooperation, together with the "iron triangle" and the highly matched evaluation and incentives ensured the collaborative power of Huawei's "iron triangle".

This way of reference proportion realizes the expected value management theory well in human resource management, and provides the basis for the elimination of the backward personnel, which is also in line with the provisions of the newly-updated Labor Law of the People's Republic of China. With 10% of people achieving the goal while most people understanding that they have not completed the task, the expectations of whom will gradually become reasonable. In fact, upon everyone's efforts, the company's overall performance will continue to improve, and consequently, the effects of positive incentive actual will be realized with bonus far more than that of the competitors, and even more than personally expected.

- **Balance between benefits in short-terms and that in long-terms**

To achieve sustainable growth, enterprises should not only focus on immediate interests but also balance short-term and medium and long-term interests in investment.

For the project team for the development of new products and strategic markets, due to the instability of new products or the uncertainty of new markets, the people who try in the hard markets like "cultivating in the saline-alkali soils" suffer losses if the absolute value of financial indicators is used in assessment, resulting in unwillingness to develop new products and new markets, thus affecting the long-term interests of enterprises. For the sales of new products, a combination of process indicators and financial indicators should be adopted, such as sales revenue (the weight should often be greater than the sales of existing products), sales growth rate and test access, while for the development of the new markets, the quantitative and qualitative indicators such as sales revenue, market target completion rate, new customer/key customer relationship establishment should be used for a comprehensive assessment. By reasonably designing the assessment method, combining with the strength of the "iron triangle", and based on the consideration of the maturity of the market opportunity, different resources, roles and authority can be defined to achieve the balance between the short-term interests and the medium and long-term interests of the enterprise, and achieve the goal of steady and sustainable development like "eating what is in the bowl, with eyes on what is in the pot and expectations about what is in the field".

- **The customer life cycle management through the optimization of the assessment index for the performance of the "iron triangle" of the project**

The assessment indicators should be constantly optimized from the body to the soul of the "iron triangle", as shown in Fig. 4.4. From the index of minding each own business like "the railway police who just care about the affairs in each section of their own authority" to the operation of the customer's whole life cycle, the financial index is interlocked. In addition to assessing those for the customer manager, business indicators should also be broken down to the solution responsibility and fulfillment responsibility. Solution responsibilitys should be evaluated upon the sales indicators of solutions/products, and fulfillment responsibilitys should also be evaluated for the sales indicators of service products (such as agent maintenance, professional services, training, maintenance, etc.), such as for Huawei's service products (agent maintenance, network planning, network optimization, training, etc.) with annual sales revenue of more than 16 billion US dollars. When the back-end is to integrate with the front-end, the front-end should consider the ability of the back-end, such as the requirement of financing sales makes the traditional market financial manager not only perform the responsibility of "Bean Counter", but also the responsibility

Iron triangle	Basic responsibilities	Optimize responsibilities
Account responsibility	• Sales indicators • Customer relationship	• Customer management • Financial indicators (including payment collection) • Customer satisfaction
Solution Responsibilities	• Product promotion • Technical bid response and quotation	• Pre-bid guidance (technical level relationship) • Financial indicators of product sales • Requirement management and market objectives
Fulfillment responsibility	• Fulfillment • Engineering installation • After sales support	• Financial indicators of service sales • Customer satisfaction • Payment collection (acceptance report)

Fig. 4.4 The optimization of assessment of "iron triangle"

in promoting sales through financing means. In the past, payment collection was only the responsibility of the customer manager, but now it has become an important assessment indicator of the fulfillment responsibility. The three roles should bear their own corresponding customer satisfaction indicators, so as to form an efficient cooperation mode of "common profits through collaborative efforts".

The evaluation indicators include short-term financial indicators and medium and long-term market objectives, which not only reflect the requirement management indicators of "the first line calls for support", but also reflect the customer satisfaction "customer-centered" indicators, and reduce the excellent operation indicators of TCO, to realize the win–win between enterprises and customers.

- **Expansion of the administrative power of the person in charge of the "iron triangle" project**

The right of bonus distribution was added to the right of performance evaluation for the evaluation of project members by the project "iron triangle" leader. In the pilot and transition period, the representative office and the system department can allocate 50% of the bonus in the traditional way, with the rest 50% of the bonus directly managed by the "iron triangle" project manager according to the performance of the project members. In 2016, Huawei generated more than 13,000 project reports, from which the project profit and loss can be used to determine project bonuses. In addition, the expansion of the project manager's power to evaluate the project members' professional ability and comprehensive evaluation throughout the year determines the salary and promotion of employees. It is often necessary for employees to provide evidence when evaluating their competence, while as employees usually participate in multiple projects at various time, the evaluation experts find it impossible to confirm the authenticity and objectivity of the evidence one by one. Huawei's project management system can clearly record the role and performance evaluation of employees in different projects, automatically provide evidence based on its system for the comprehensive evaluation of multiple projects throughout the year. Through continuous improvement of project management and powerful financial and human resources IT management platform, Huawei is constantly expanding its front-line administrative power and implementing the organizational and operational transformation with the front-line commanding the back end.

4.1.1.5 The Principle for the Construction of the "Iron Triangle"

Many enterprises think highly of the mode of "iron triangle", but they encounter many problems in practical application, which are mainly reflected as follows.

- Companies with complex product structures can directly follow Huawei's practice, and make clear the key roles and functional requirements according to the characteristics of their own industry. The main problem of such companies is the shortage of human resources, which makes the construction of the "iron triangle"

difficult, in addition to the other problem like that they lack clear methods for the management and assessment of the "iron triangle".
- For enterprises with relatively simple product structure, such as industries of small and medium-sized equipment and feed, the "iron triangle" is often unable to land in the basic combat unit of the market, the main reasons for which are that the value of the "iron triangle" is not obviously reflected, in addition to the problems in the construction cost and assessment.

In fact, the core issue here is how to present the value of the "iron triangle". With the change of market, the value of marketing will gather greater significance. The development and evolution of Huawei's "iron triangle" have also gone through three stages.

The initial stage of development: Huawei found itself lack of personnel, lack of ability and process support.

- The marketing technology department was set up in R & D department acting the role of solution manager.

Medium-term development: The first-line "iron triangle" and market-driven development process were basically formed.

- With resources shared, the counterpart relationship is relatively fixed.
- The customer representative of the key account was fixed, and the Solution Responsibilities and fulfillment responsibility offered shared support.

The later stage of development: The headquarters and regional platforms were formed, and the core process established.

- The "iron triangle" was built according to customer levels, with exclusive resources for key customers.
- Regional "heavy brigade" established.

To learn from Huawei's practice, first, enterprises must set up an "iron triangle" according to their needs business, with the responsibility and operation mode of each role clearly defined. Secondly, a two-step landing can be applied with test first and promotion later, especially for the role of solution responsibility (more technically).

- Landing in the key account department: Here is the department with many customer needs, and difficulties in marketing.
- Landing in the area/representative office: To be shared within the area/representative office to ensure work saturation.

In this way, technical marketing experts can be constantly found and trained to lay a foundation for the construction of an enterprise marketing system.

4.1.2 *Efficient Collaboration System Between the Front Line and the Back End*

In order to support the large projects in the first line of the market, the vice president of the company often would act as the sponsor of the project, taking on the backstage resource coordination and other work of support, to win the project by integrating the company's resources. This kind of project management mode of "major victories upon the accumulation of small ones" is critical in building up the confidence for the overseas market and accumulation of experience on overseas development at the initial stage. However, with the increase of overseas projects, this operation mode of the project is no longer efficient, but causes serious impacts on the existing management system of enterprises. To go from the success of individual projects to the success of group projects, and achieve the goal of overall internationalization from quantitative change to qualitative change, it is necessary to build a mechanism for the coordination between the front line and the back end with high execution during the process through continuous promotion of the establishment of international organization system and the improvement of overseas operation ability through projects, so as to realize the qualitative change of the organization system and the operation mode for the internalization. After continuous practice and accumulation during the globalization of the enterprise, Huawei has established an efficient collaborative organization mode and collaborative management mechanism between the front line and the back end, as shown in Fig. 4.5.

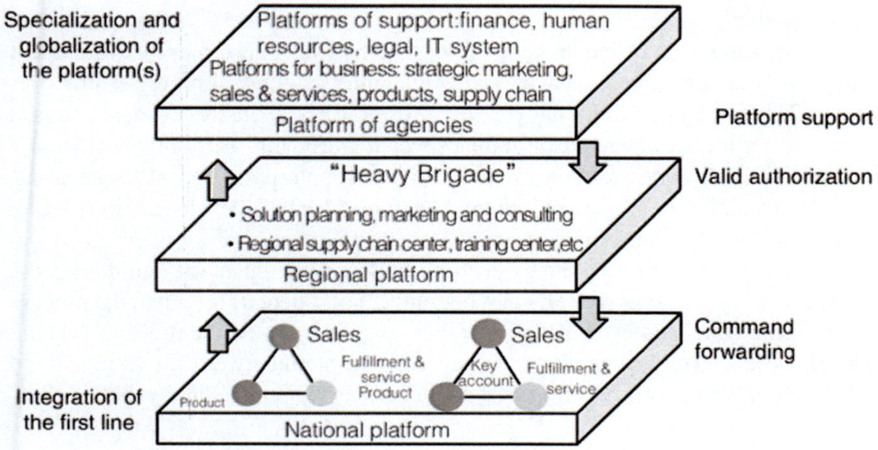

Fig. 4.5 The efficient collaboration mechanism between front line and the back end

4.1.2.1 The Organizational Structure of the "Iron Triangle" with the Support of a Large Platform for the Front Line

Under this organizational structure, the first line was equipped with keen market expansion ability upon "one specialty with many abilities" in the form of "iron triangle", which in turn laid higher professional requirements for platform departments. Huawei's early platform departments were mainly set up in the headquarters, while with the continuous expansion of the market, Huawei established eight areas in the world. Due to the great differences in market requirements, product standards and customer characteristics in many areas, the response to "the front line's requirements of support from the headquarters" turned out to be slower.

Therefore, the institutional platforms, especially the platforms close to the work at the front-line such as product planning, solution design, fulfillment and supply chain, should move down to the regional platform for the quick response to the needs of the front-line. The "Heavy Brigade" mentioned again and another time by Ren Zhengfei in his speech just referred to these "mobile forces" and the resource pools of the reserved cadres. Some enterprises have similar organizations, because, in the initial stage of expansion, these enterprises have no permanent staff in some market areas. At this time, the "mobile forces" can be used to expand the market, before the permanent organization is established after the market is basically mature. Sometimes, due to the scarcity of high-end expert resources in enterprises, it is necessary to set up expert "Heavy Brigade" in the headquarters or regional platform, in addition to the ensured resource sharing in the regional or global scope.

To better serve strategic key customers, Huawei established a unique key account marketing and support system, namely the key account system department, to meet the requirements of independent management of key customers' development strategy, product information, business planning information and supply chain information. The front-line "iron triangle" organization has exclusive resources and a higher service level. Huawei also set up a special "mirroring" team of key customer solutions in the headquarters to provide efficient counterpart support to the front-line "iron triangle" in marketing, product customer version development, solution verification, supply chain, etc.

In short, we should refine the essence of the front-line business, summarize the working steps of the front-line efficient operation, sort out and formulate the process from the front-line, and establish a processing organization on the process. It is the core principle to establish an efficient cooperation system between the front and the back to cut down the process links and organizations that cannot add value.

4.1.2.2 Collaborative Management Mechanism Between the Front Line and Back End

In addition to the organizational structure, to ensure the flexible operation mechanism of the front line, with a full play of the efficiency and resource sharing of the large platform support, enterprises need to establish an effective authorization management mechanism.

First, price authorization mechanism. Huawei has a three-level price authorization system, with different authorities for representative offices, regional departments and sales headquarters. The front line makes decisions directly within the scope of authorization, and the product marketing is responsible for quoting. When it is beyond the scope of authorization, the product marketing and the representative office start the authorization application. In the later stage, the quotation has been fully authorized to the districts, which can decide the quotation according to the strategic needs, as long as it meets the company's requirements for the assessment of the profit center of the district, while the headquarters only manages the pricing, Different enterprises have various authorization mechanisms, which must be implemented, however different they can be from each.

Second, requirements commitment management mechanism. The mechanism is also a three-tier management system, which includes the regional requirement management team, the product line requirement management team and the company's investment decision committee. The front-line requirement management team needs to collect customer requirements regularly, verify the authenticity of requirements carefully and analyze the impact of requirements on market development. Especially for major requirements, the front-line requirements decision-making team needs to discuss and submit a written application to the authority. The product line requirement management and planning team needs to analyze technology, development cost, market ROI and other aspects on a global scale, and give feedback to the front line within a time limit. When there is a dispute for which no agreement can be reached, the regional department can give feedback to the higher decision-making team IRB. The development commitment is made by the agency headquarters, with the front line having the right to propose and appeal, as well as a clear commitment to the market development after the requirement is met. The front line should be made fully aware that "there should be a cost for the support".

Third, S & OP (sales and operation planning) coordination mechanism (as shown in Fig. 4.6). In the face of the future market requirements, the sales department should complete the sales forecast as accurately as possible in the marketing planning, complete the supply and requirement matching at the company level together with the production planning department and the supply chain department, and output the *Executable Fulfillment Plan*, which, on the one hand, serves as a programmatic plan for the overall operation of the company to ensure that the pace of each department is coordinated, and on the other hand, make sales clearly understand the company's supply capability in the front operations, and avoid the back-end supply chaos caused by the blind commitment to fulfillment.

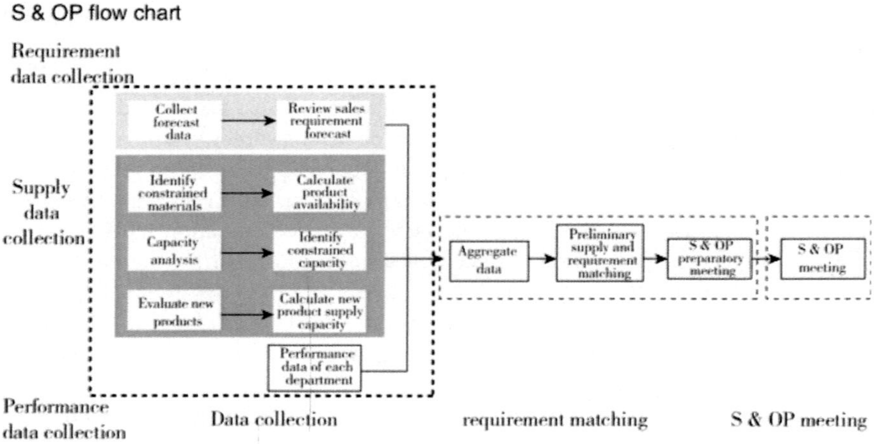

Fig. 4.6 The coordination between sales forecast and fulfillment plan

4.1.2.3 "Human" as the Key Factor of the Efficiency of the Collaborative Mechanism

The middle and high-level leaders of the headquarters, controlling the resources with the power of organization setting, process design and formulations of rules, should take the customer-centered and market-driven actions, but not only in their mindset, for which requires cadres deeply understand the business and needs of the front line. For this reason, Huawei selects cadres with working experience in the front line, and requires them to go deep into the front line, and introduce a large number of cadres returned from the front line to the posts of management. Through this two-way flow, it lays the foundation of "human" for the collaborative mechanism of "the support reaching the first line whenever it is in the need".

To better implement the reform of "veteran salespersons with the expertise at the front line" and equip the front line with a greater voice, Huawei gave stronger power to the person who is in charge of the project "iron triangle", so that the project manager can directly assess the project members (including headquarters personnel) and decide the allocation of the bonus. This requires a sound project virtual settlement method and a powerful IT system as support, and so Huawei's financial department has been able to form and manage more than 13,000 financial statements in tune with the front-line projects. Through its IT system, Huawei can also provide accurate and objective evidence for the evaluation of the qualification of its employees upon the accurate evaluation on the role, working time and actual contribution of employees in the project. In addition to scientific mindset and able cadres, the establishment of an efficient mechanism requires support from a sound process, organization, mechanism, and IT system.

Upon lessons from the previous successful experience and the characteristics of the enterprise itself, the project management mode, organizational framework and management and control mode adapted to the development of globalization are constructed in the early stage of internationalization, which will play a multiplier effect on the continuous enrichment and development of the enterprise in the process of overseas expansion.

4.2 Go Out of the "Green Gauze"—Qualitative Change of Overseas Marketing Ability

After more than three decades of development, China's market economy saw great changes in the markets and users, mainly as follows.

- In view of the market changes and the expansion of big customers when the mode of customer management gradually developed from individual business to intensive business, enterprises should pay attention to how to change from individual operation to team cooperation, optimize marketing organization and build new competence;
- With increasingly higher requirements, the customers are gradually changing from buying simple products to buying solutions including training and service consultation, which calls for the front line marketing organizations of enterprises to pay attention to how to actively grasp the deep-seated requirement changes of customers
- When the market expansion mode of horse racing enclosure basically ended, the industry has begun to shuffle, with the focus shifting from competition centering on price (cost performance) to competition over value, for which enterprises should pay attention to how to balance the relationship between centralized control and appropriate authorization, through the establishment of the cooperative organization between the front line and the back end to answer the "the front line's requirements of support from the headquarters", and make quick decisions and respond to customers' needs.

Enterprises should carry out marketing through the relationship, when the type of marketing where "every potter praises his own pots" has become increasingly disabled in meeting the needs of the market. As in the growth process of many enterprises, Huawei has run for quite a long time without an independent marketing department when the related functions of marketing were developed and shared in the marketing department of the sales system, the marketing technology department in the early stage and in the R & D system and the product planning system in the later stage. Even after the founding of the marketing department in 2003, it was still groping for its position in chaos. With the continuous development of the IPD process, especially the front-end MM process, the essence of IPD management has gradually penetrated into all aspects of the organization, the responsible departments of product planning and listing process, and the connection between processes urgently needed to be clarified. Especially after 2004, Huawei's market layout in Asia, Africa and

Latin America has basically taken shape. After starting to "walk out of the green gauze" and comprehensively marched into the overseas developed market, the role of marketing became more and more important, and the requirement for marketing was also higher and higher. Upon its powerful sales platform, Huawei began to build its own "operational" capability.

4.2.1 *Evaluation of Enterprise Marketing Ability to "Suit the Remedy to the Case"*

Enterprise marketing ability evaluation is the premise of diagnosing enterprise marketing problems and finding solutions, which can be evaluated from eight dimensions, as shown in Fig. 4.7.

Element 1: Assessment of Strategies

This element refers to the evaluation of the enterprise's ability in making the strategies for marketing, which can be seen from the following aspects.

- Is the marketing strategy and annual marketing plan formulated routinely? Is reflection and update of the marketing and annual marketing plan carried out regularly?
- Is there a reasonable marketing budget? Is there a clear method for the evaluation of the marketing effect? Is it equivalent to the industry benchmark?

Fig. 4.7 The dimensions for the evaluation of enterprise marketing capability

- Analysis and decision support—the corresponding analysis software, database, analysis ability are available, and decision support is made upon business data, such as revenue forecast and reasonable priority of all project requirements.
- Marketing and sales collaboration—The sales and marketing departments share a collaborative process to continuously optimize the effect in improving marketing ROI and sales output for the common business purpose.
- A marketing evaluation tool is available, which defines the dashboards, scorecards and measurement standards of various implementation activities, in addition to the process of collecting reports and evaluating.
- Process documents—all key marketing processes, such as market insight, marketing activity execution, and marketing evaluation, can be standardized and documented.
- The significance of marketing in the business—Marketing has a place in the board of directors and plays a forward-looking and strategic role, not just the marketing services and support to fulfill the business needs.

Element 2: Marketing Communication Strategy

- Is there a clear brand strategy?
- Is there a formal marketing communication plan and strategy?
- Content marketing—There is a department responsible for producing marketing content. In order to improve brand perception, affinity and promote new business promotion, traditional methods, such as cases and white papers, can be used, besides the modern methods, such as infographics.
- The rationality of outbound marketing plan, such as public relations, media and analyst coverage, offline activity plan, etc.

Element 3: Market Management

- Market orientation—The enterprise's positioning and value proposition, such as leading, following, cost-effective, and low-cost strategic positioning are elaborately designed and refined.
- Market insight: The market trend analysis is regularly carried out to find the impact of political, economic, social and technological changes on the market, in addition to the market space analysis, market segmentation and market segmentation priority regularly carried out. There are definite methods and processes of market insight in the process of strategy review and formulation.
- Market requirements—The marketing plan is based on the collection, analysis and insight of the real data and information of the market. There are formal market requirement documents to promote product and company decisions.
- Product management process—The standard new product development and launch process are available.
- Pricing system—Marketing conducts a formal pricing analysis to evaluate price adjustment factors based on market requirement.

Element 4: Business opportunity management

- Advertising and sponsorship—Tools to evaluate the effectiveness of advertising and sponsorship are available for enough sales leads through various marketing activities.
- Event marketing such as exhibitions and forums—The effect of event marketing activities can be enhanced through ROI, activity plan and other management methods.
- The application ability of digital marketing, such as website, search engine, social media, mobile marketing (with definite mobile marketing plan), video, etc.
- The collaborative ability of online marketing and offline marketing.
- Marketing automation: It is an automatic management process with lead scoring and lead incubation. It has different management methods and judgment standards for hot/warm/cold business opportunities.

Element 5: Customer-centered customer management

- Customer evaluation—Routine tracking of customer churn rate, customer life cycle value (CLV), customer acquisition cost and other evaluation parameters are carried out, upon a set of procedures and methods to measure and improve customer loyalty.
- Customer satisfaction—The customer satisfaction surveys are carried out through the entrusted survey companies or enterprises, using NPC (Net Promoter Score) score measurement.
- Customer support—The customer support and response time are managed upon service level agreements (SLAs) system.
- Customer communication mode: The routine communication, like the annual strategic communication and interaction of senior management upon the joint innovation communication and innovation center construction of middle and senior management, the establishment of the general customer relationship, as well as the daily visit and annual user conference, should be conducted with customers at different levels to establish organizational customer relationship. The new communication methods, such as the technical support provided by the online customer community and collecting innovative concepts can be used to increase customer viscosity, Xiaomi's Mi fans community and Huawei's user community have collected a large number of mobile phone improvements suggestions. Huawei has extended its scope to the operator's customer requirement collection platform, with an incentive fund of RMB 2 million provided, and the operator's customers who provide significant and effective product requirement can receive a reward of RMB 100,000.
- Customer relationship management—The enterprise should have a written customer development plan, and set up customer files (architecture, roles, responsibilities, etc.) and a customer relationship database management system (CRM).
- Customer recommendation program—The enterprise should have a formal customer recommendation program to bring more new business, such as customer

model point construction, customer marketing activities support, joint marketing activities, etc.

Element 6: Sales enabling and support

- Marketing materials—all marketing materials and recourses should be timely updated and accurate.
- Sales enabling—The enterprise should have an online sales platform, which includes all sales support materials and specifies which content can be downloaded and browsed by the sales team and channel partners. There should be a clear level of authority management, such as product disclosure, quotation authorization, generally only open to the enterprise's own sales team.
- Sales training—The sales training procedures should be updated on time to follow "industry best practices". Different training for different industries can follow different methods. For example, Huawei's "spring breeze action" and "autumn harvest action" are to send courses of training to the countryside in line with sales targets. With the development of the Internet, online training, mobile APPs and video training are gaining greater popularity.
- Sales tools—The development of sales tools, such as typical scenario solutions, competitive reference cases, proposals, configuration tools, automatic quotation tools, should be carried out regularly. Huawei's "one page Zen" in marketing competition is a "one-page report" to tell the salesmen how to highlight the differentiation advantages of its products, enlarge the weaknesses of competitors, aim at the pain points and requirements of customers, and win by means of technology and commerce.
- Sales process—There should be a sales process matching with the industry customer procurement process.
- Partners—The enterprise should know how to manage partners efficiently, whose new business sales project pipeline is visible.

Element 7: Organization system and management

- Organizational structure: There should be a clear marketing organization structure, responsibilities and job description, clear, coordinated and smooth interface with other systems.
- Qualifications for the posts and career planning—Through skill analysis, all skill requirements and qualifications for the posts of each department are formed, with a post-qualification assessment conducted routinely and improvement made over the gaps. The career planning can be provided for marketing staff, to help them to make professional development plans, offer off-job training to them, establish career development channels for them and carry out related activities, etc.
- Training mechanism—There should be a complete set of marketing training and skill development mechanism, through which, for example, the new marketing personnel can quickly get familiar with various marketing processes and use basic effective marketing methods. If the sales of the enterprise are done through agents, it also includes an agent training mechanism.

- Best practice library—The template, process and case library of "marketing best practice" should be established and well maintained.
- Selection of the agent—A set of strict decision-making tools should be available to be used in the selection/replacement of the agents.
- Performance evaluation—There should be a process to evaluate the performance of marketing personnel, in addition to a mechanism to encourage employees to be active, through which excellent employees can be rewarded, low performers can be identified.

Element 8: System and technology

- CRM system—Huawei has the global customer relationship management system CRM, with the introduction of which in 2005 upon the application of LTC (leads to cash) process, Huawei began its reform on the process. Based on CRM, enterprise network BG adjusted to PRM system for the pilot in 2012 according to the characteristics of non-communication market, trying to bring prospect into the scope of management, and cooperating with the pilot and implementation of LTC/MTL (from marketing to lead) process.
- Marketing content management system (CMS)—The enterprise has a global marketing content management system, so that it is easy to update marketing on the website in time.
- Marketing automation—The marketing automation IT system can automatically log in to the web page, track the behavior of website visitors, capture leads, score leads, incubate leads, etc.
- Event planning—The enterprise has a global event planning or marketing resource management (MRM) system.
- Project management—The enterprise has a set of easy-to-use and timely updated project management systems.
- Digital asset management—The enterprise has a system for managing creative assets and selling enabling resources.

This is a complete set of enterprise marketing ability evaluation models.

The eight dimensions of the evaluation method, involving marketing strategy, business, process, organization, assessment and IT system, provide a panorama of the enterprise to improve marketing work. But enterprises can't expect to achieve it overnight, for the idea of comprehensive improvement will bring disastrous results. Different enterprises should set weights on relevant dimensions according to their own industry characteristics, development stages and customer groups, and find the weakest link in current marketing through evaluation, so as to determine the most suitable improvement plan. From the practice of many enterprises, it can be divided into three types.

Type I: The marketing ability stays in the primary stage, and the "operation" and "marketing" organizations have not been separated. At this time, customer management, marketing activities management to create business opportunities, marketing content production, etc. are generally the focus of the work. For 2C business, basic digital marketing channels (websites, mobile apps, etc.) also need to be built in advance.

Type II: The basic marketing ability is already available, while the ability of "operation" still needs to be improved. The key work of this type includes marketing organization construction, marketing strategy and annual marketing plan, market management, etc.

Type III: With the marketing ability and output comprehensively promoted, the key work of this type is generally marketing process system, marketing enabling and linkage, marketing database and marketing automation IT system construction.

4.2.2 *The Construction of Marketing Ability*

Many enterprises have just set up marketing organizations. At this time, the most urgent task is to have some basic marketing personnel in place and determine the focus of stages. In practice, we should start from the basic behavior management, time management, plan management and project operation to improve the basic ability of marketing personnel. Behavior management requires running management. That is to say, Huawei requires front-line staff to be with customers or solving customers' problems. In terms of time management, Huawei requires to allocate different time to different customers, especially for key customers and difficult customers. It needs to invest more time and energy instead of being limited to customers that are familiar with and congenial to itself. In terms of project operation and plan management, the operation efficiency and quality of the project can be improved through basic PDCA (plan, do, check and act) management.

With the basic quality and skills, the key is to improve the professional ability of marketing. Generally speaking, we need to improve the ability of the enterprise in the collection and analysis of customer needs, the formulation of marketing content and the planning of marketing activities through various levels of training, scenario and action learning. The core of professional marketing is to "do the right thing at the right time for the right people".

4.2.2.1 Content-Based Targeted Marketing

Traditional advertising and exhibition feature "bombing" marketing, while targeted marketing is the ultimate embodiment of professional ability, the key of which is that all marketing activities must conform to the customer's purchasing process and decision-making mode. The targeted marketing method matching the customer purchasing process is generally shown in Fig. 4.8.

In the beginning, customers may encounter problems with their existing systems, or they may start to consider upgrading or even building new systems. At this time, the customer stays in the learning stage, and will collect information from various

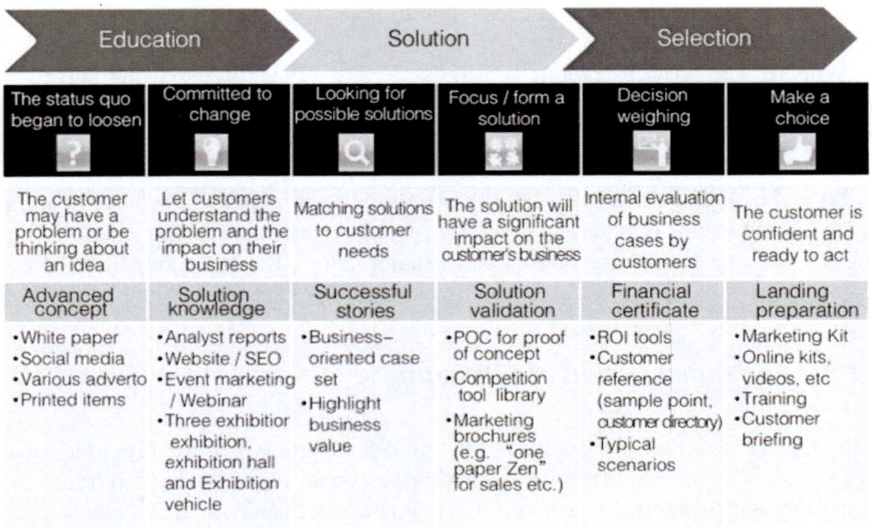

Fig. 4.8 The targeted marketing mode matching the customer purchasing process

channels to master the industry development status, technology development trend and competitor dynamics.

At this stage, suppliers should not rush to promote their own products and solutions, but should, according to the characteristics of the industry, instill into the industry and customers the advanced ideas of the enterprise, the understanding of the key points of the industry development, and the comprehensive differentiation advantages. Enterprises usually use patents, technical white papers, standard organization proposals and other means to establish the leading image and market position of enterprises. At this time, it is best to indoctrinate the advanced concept from a neutral point of view, and do not let potential customers think that you are "crying to sell your pots". The more popular way is to use the endorsement of the third-party authoritative organizations in the industry, such as market research and consulting organizations. The effect of their promotion in helping enterprises to carry out marketing is far better than that of boasting by yourselves. Among ranking in TMT industry like the Gartner's magic four quadrants, IDC's supplier industry status matrix, Frost & Sullivan ranking in TMT industry, Gartner's magic four-quadrant analysis is the most representative, which directly affects the enterprise's brand, market positioning, and even employee recruitment. In Australia, the author once had an exchange with an employee who was working for Cisco at that time. He asked if Huawei's products had entered the Magic Quadrant, and I said not yet. "How can I sell them?" he said disappointedly. Until now, a very important indicator of Huawei's product line marketing work is to strive to enter the magic quadrant. Figure 4.9 shows the position change of Huawei's storage products in Gartner's Magic Quadrant. Every year, Huawei takes the promotion of product status as one of the assessment objectives of

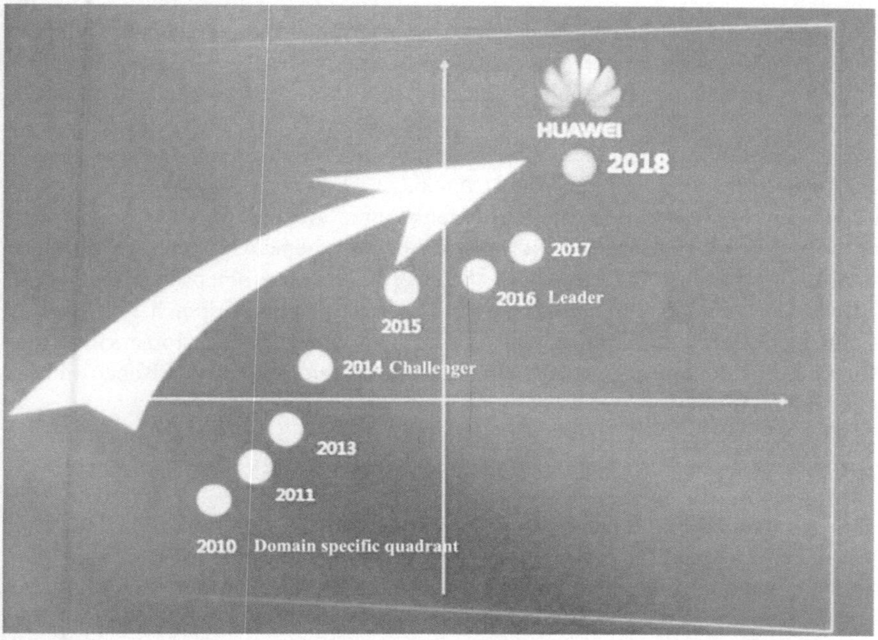

Fig. 4.9 The improvement of Huawei's storage products in Gartner's Magic Quadrant

its marketing work. Huawei hosts the analysts' conference every year, for the propaganda of authoritative third party plays a great role in promoting the brand promotion and sales of products in the world, which can often achieve twice the result with half the effort.

Gartner universal storage Magic Quadrant Huawei storage 2010–2018.

The Wood MAC Kenzie evaluation of the energy, metals and minerals industry and the IMS evaluation of the medical and health industry have similar effects.

The customers will start to think and analyze their own problems, conceive the future development path, and find solutions after they have a deep understanding of the overall development of the industry. Therefore, suppliers should adopt the most effective method in the industry to deliver the enterprise's overall solutions to customers, such as common product launches, exhibitions, etc. Among them, Huawei's unique way of communication is the exhibition vehicles. In the early years, Huawei was not well-known overseas, and many account responsibilitys could not even get into customers' doors or meet customers. By learning from the practices in the industry, Huawei integrates the most mainstream products and solutions into a container, drives the "caravan" to the door of customers to shows Huawei products to past customers and establishes customer relationships through physical demonstrations, videos and pictures. This way is more targeted and timely than the exhibition, and Huawei has 8 exhibition vehicles on the global tour at the peak. With the development of Internet technology, network marketing is more widely used, especially for overseas markets, small and medium-sized enterprises and individuals. The brand name of the video conference system of Huawei enterprise network BG is "Zhizhen". To help more small and medium-sized customers quickly find Huawei's Zhizhen conference system when using network search, Huawei optimizes the search engine to make the "Zhizhen system" rank first in the main search engines such as Google and Baidu, surpassing Monk Zhizhen from the *Outlaws of the Marsh*, and improving the efficiency of enterprise solution dissemination. At this time, customers often feel only pain points but fail to put forward clear requirements. Therefore, suppliers should work with customers to analyze the root cause of the problem and its impact on customer business development. In particular, leading suppliers often help customers in making business development plans at this stage, or even help customers in formulating bidding documents, so as to embed their own advantages in advance and lay a foundation for the bidding work in the next stage.

After the customers have identified their own problems and collected a variety of solutions, the next step is to compare and optimize the solutions. Generally, it is through the form of bidding to compare multiple suppliers. At this point, the solution provided by the supplier must be aimed at the pain points and needs of customers to help customers develop business and create value for customers. For the manufacturers who only participate in the bidding stage, such as Huawei, when expanding overseas markets in the early stage, they should not only emphasize that their products are cheap and the quality can meet the requirements, but also fully reflect their late development advantages. For example, R & D strength can ensure the satisfaction of the product requirements in the bidding document, especially the rapid response to future requirement changes, as well as the advantages of product differentiation; Clear and long-term strategy can ensure long-term cooperation and common growth with customers in system construction, operation and maintenance. Here, we need to further build up the confidence of customers through the actual cases of commercial success. For example, the case of Huawei's intelligent network helping Thai operator AIS's business leap from the second to the first in China has greatly promoted the market expansion of Huawei's intelligent network.

For complex systems, in the process of bid evaluation, customers often build a simplified system for proof of concept (POC) to ensure that the scheme is feasible. In the bidding process of the next generation network NGF of Deutsche Telekom (DT), DT selected four leading suppliers in the world at that time Huawei, Ericsson, Nokia and Siemens to form four project teams, with each project team leader from a different manufacturer, and the team members representatives from the other three manufacturers, who integrate the equipment of other manufacturers for system concept verification according to the plan of the team leader. This way not only tests the project management and integration ability of the team leader, but also the product interoperability and cooperation ability of the team members, and reduces the risk of the future next-generation system construction of Deutsche Telekom to the minimum, while the four manufacturers form an interesting scene of both competition and cooperation. At this time, enterprises should not only fully show the advantages of their products and solutions, but also the ability of continuous support for customers. This is because in the process of proof of concept, many requirements will change, when the problem-solving ability and rapid response of R & D turn out particularly critical. At this stage, we can spread the "favorable material" to customers, focusing on the business value brought to customers in the past, and it is also necessary to provide competitors' "unfavorable accounts" at an appropriate time, so as to influence customers' decisions when they compare different solutions. For example, in the case of the explosion of its mobile phone Note7, to reduce the impact of the event on the Chinese market, Samsung (China) declared that the Note7 used battery suppliers different in the Chinese market from those of the explosion mobile phone. However, the industry has revealed that this explosion is a deep-seated mobile phone design problem, not a battery problem. Therefore, there are still potential explosion hazards for Note7 mobile phones in the Chinese market. This conclusion not only further magnifies the battery problem, but also involves the integrity of the enterprise and the disrespect for Chinese customers, which has become one of the key reasons for the collapse of Samsung mobile phones in the Chinese market. Huawei set up a major project department (How to Beat and X Office) in the sales system to help major projects win in the fierce competition. Through the competitive tool library, case reference and on-site guidance, Huawei provides method guidance for the front line to formulate competitive strategies. In the process of communication and interaction with customers at all levels, marketing materials (marketing brochures) must ensure the consistency of information, and disseminate targeted key information (KM) to senior managers, middle managers and technical levels. As mentioned earlier, Huawei has widely used the sales guidance book, which is known as "one paper Zen", to present the differentiation advantages of products, the value brought to customers and the key points of competition on a single piece of paper, so as to provide a simple and practical weapon for front-line operations to win through only one attack.

After the verification of technology and scheme, the customer will generally conduct a commercial bid evaluation. At this time, many enterprises will fall into the quagmire of the price war, killing 1,000 enemies and losing 800. Many enterprises take it for granted that customers only care about the transaction price of products, and some customers often take the lowest bidder as the bid evaluation standard on the premise of meeting the technical requirements in bid evaluation, which contributes to the price war. However, this often leads to the result of double losses, where the successful bidder feels unable to guarantee the quality and later development and upgrading, and the project often becomes a "fishing project". What's more, our understanding of "price to customers" and "cost borne by customers" is not the same concept, for customers often focus on the cost of the product life cycle, that is, TCO. When Huawei carried out IPD reform in 1998, it introduced the customer requirement $APPEALS model, which detailed the product price comprehensively. In 2005, when BT's purchasing director went to Shenzhen to evaluate Huawei, he asked what Huawei's biggest advantage was, and got the answer from Huawei that the product quality was reliable and the price was cheap, which could help BT reduce the construction cost. However, when the purchasing director asked how much the TCO would be if it chose Huawei, from the chairman of Huawei to all kinds of experts, they were all at a loss.

When a customer introduces a new product, it will evaluate not only the quotation of the product, but also the annual average price in the product life cycle, namely CAPEX and the annual operating costs of the product operation process, such as training costs, power consumption, product maintenance costs, namely OPEX, which constitute TCO together with the cost of capital occupation. Therefore, it is particularly important to deeply understand the business needs of customers and prove the business value of enterprises to customers through financial analysis tools such as input–output ROI. For leading enterprises in the industry, they need to master TCO tools to build value barriers and get rid of the low-level price war of competitors through comprehensive advantages such as R & D strength, product quality, service ability and financing ability. As for relatively standard goods, for small and medium-sized customers, more and more enterprises provide product portfolio, configuration and quotation tools for typical scenarios on their websites, which can facilitate channels and customers to quickly complete portfolio configuration, scheme design and price estimation according to their own situation, so that they can make quick decisions and make financial preparations. For example, on the websites of Dell, BMW, Cisco, Huawei enterprise network BG and those of other enterprises, similar configuration quotation tools will be provided for customers. With the gradual development of the market economy, enterprises will realize the importance of maintaining the healthy growth of the industry value chain. Therefore, more enterprises are no longer just lowering the price for their own interests, so as to leave room for the survival of their suppliers.

After the customer has made the final choice, the supplier needs to show his professional contract performance ability to the customer through clear workflow, complete product package and marketing materials, online and offline training plan, so as to make the customer full of confidence in the completion of the task. Even in this seemingly simple final stage, there is still the possibility of losing the project. During my consulting work, I once served a leading pump enterprise. When the enterprise opened up a certain rural market, the customer had already chosen the product of the enterprise, but because the customer, being a woman, was afraid of connecting the high-voltage cable, for which the product description was not clear enough, so it was not put into use. At this time, the local small competitive enterprises took advantage of this and sent special personnel to deliver the goods to the door and assisted in the installation. Finally, the customer chose a new supplier. Although the enterprise is the industry leader and has a good brand, if it adopts the same service model as the local supplier, it will be unable to develop well because of the high cost. But why not use the current popular marketing model? With a piece of video of the installation for about 1 min, you can easily guide customers to install through the mobile phone, which not only meets the requirements of customers, but also saves the service cost. Therefore, concise and clear product package information, the use of more extensive online and offline marketing and service tools, is an important part of the successful completion of sales which deserves our attention.

Therefore, from the perspective of the whole procurement decision-making process, the most critical link is the customer interface, which needs to be targeted at the right customers and their concerns. For example, in the senior leadership of the customer, CEO pays more attention to the consistency of the two sides' strategy and the achievement of the operation index, and CFO has more of his attention attached to the improvement of the financial indicators, while CTO focuses more to the advanced nature, effectiveness and sustainable development of the technology. Middle-level department directors care more about the improvement of department performance and personal promotion channel, while the executive level is concerned about the solution of work problems and the improvement of their own ability. The other is to provide the right content at the right time, that is, content marketing based on customer value orientation. Therefore, the design and dissemination of Key Messages in content marketing carry a lot of weight, and KM reflects the commercial value of products/solutions. Here a simple and practical syllogism of content design will be introduced.

"Disease": the common problems in the industry development and the main problems of customers.

"Remedy": characteristics and differentiation advantages of supplier's products or solutions.

"Effect": The value that may be brought to other customers, with cases attached, that is, the expected benefits to customers.

The marketing content designed by this method is obviously different from the content designed from the technical point of view, as shown in Fig. 4.10.

In the early stage, KM was designed from the perspective of technology

- Support the access of Wi-Fi/CDMA/WCDMA/LTE wireless technology;
- Support telephone, ADSL/LAN broadband and video access;
- The hardware system is compact and highly integrated, with comprehensive business management software provided;

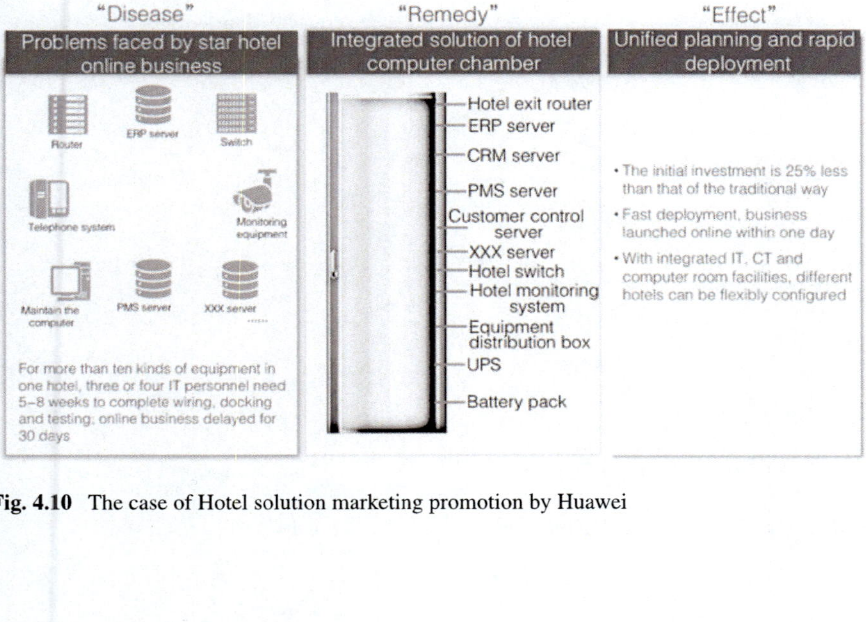

Fig. 4.10 The case of Hotel solution marketing promotion by Huawei

- The service can be opened anytime and anywhere, and has been highly praised by users for its safety and speed.

In the later stage, we should start from the commercial value of customers and turn the technical terms and "every potter praises his own pots" marketing into content marketing to solve customers' problems and create value for them.

In a word, high-quality marketing content oriented to customers is the foundation of marketing execution. The different combination marketing plans should be made according to the requirements of different customers "at the right time, to the right people, with the right content", so as to find opportunities and promote sales.

4.2.2.2 Digital Marketing as the Direction for the Development of Marketing

With the development of the Internet economy, the purchasing process and decision-making mode of B2C businesses and small and medium-sized enterprises (B2b) turn out to be quite different from the linear decision-making mode of large enterprises. The interactive purchase mode over the internet breaks the traditional flow buying behavior mode of "cognition—consideration—preference—purchase—loyalty". Online rankings, peer reviews, opinion leader reviews, friend recommendations, trends, etc. any one of these points may quickly promote purchasing behavior, as shown in Fig. 4.11.

In this mode, the most valuable users are not necessarily the ones who buy the most. Customers who always evaluate and comment on products are called product "contributors, whose characteristics are as follows.

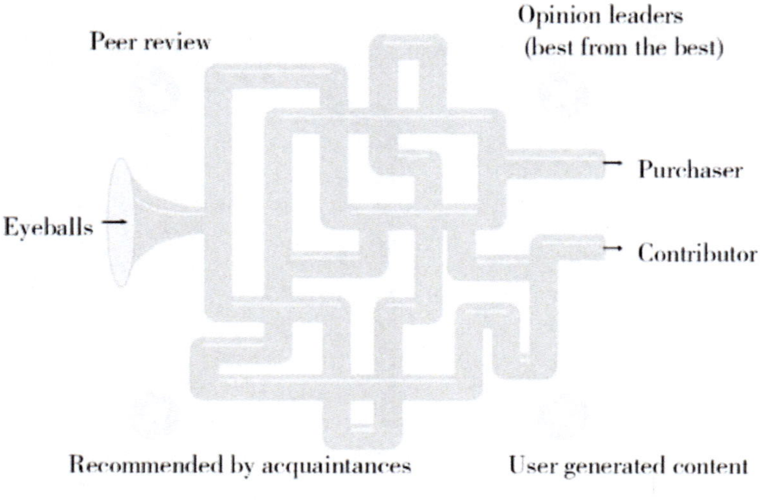

Fig. 4.11 The factors influencing users' purchasing behavior under the internet mode

- They play a greater role in the generation of effective product requirements and the improvement of products;
- They may affect the purchase behavior of 100 people around.
- Therefore, attracting customers' attention and transforming it into market leads with minimum cost, and transforming leads into sales opportunities through lead incubation activities are the key driving forces for the vigorous development of digital marketing.

The change of consumer habits promotes the development of digital marketing. With the development of Internet and IT technology, the original fragmented offline marketing activities and online marketing activities are coordinated efficiently, which greatly reduces the marketing cost of small and medium-sized enterprises. The essence of marketing management is to realize all-around management of various marketing activities, and realize closed-loop management through effective marketing assessment. The marketing panorama is shown in Table 4.1.

Outbound marketing is a relatively traditional marketing activity, while inbound marketing, is a new digital marketing activity. The marketing effect of the two is different for different industries and business models. Generally speaking, the average response rate of outbound marketing is 1~5%, while the average response rate of inbound marketing is 20~50%. The average cost of inbound marketing is less than half of that of outbound marketing. Some cases show that with the digitalization of marketing methods, the annual growth rate of the contact objects (customers) that can be located is more than 32%, the feedback on marketing activities is up to 105% every year, and the generated leads are up to 53% every year; The number of direct marketing decreased by 8% every year, and the number of marketing activities decreased by 35% every year, with the traditional marketing mode still important for the regions where online sales are not popular, as well as for large and medium-sized B2B business. Therefore, enterprises need to organically combine inbound marketing and outbound marketing to realize the integration of online and offline marketing. This kind of integrated marketing in the digital age is also called "digital marketing". In 2012, Huawei introduced MTL (marketing to leads) process and IT system, which can efficiently and automatically manage a large number of O2O marketing activities, potential customer information and marketing leads.

The process framework and main steps of MTL are shown in Fig. 4.12.

(1) **Flow aggregation**: Whether through offline marketing or online SEO (search engine ranking optimization) and other ways, the customers' attention will be centralized and attracted to the company's website or target landing page.
(2) **Capture leads**: Capture leads according to customers' requirements, problems and marketing content of the customers' concern.
(3) **Recognition of the quality of leads (modeling and scoring):** The leads captured can be divided into hot leads, warm leads and cold leads. Different industries need to summarize customer behavior, judge the quality of leads through the score after modeling and scoring customer behavior. At this time, the scoring of both content and behavior should be taken into consideration. Take content as an example, there is a big difference between customers

Table 4.1 The panorama of marketing

Strategic marketing	Outbound marketing	Inbound marketing	Marketing measurement
Market research • Basic market research • Related market research • Focus on customer base • Market Survey • Competitive analysis	**Advertisements** • Printed items • Radio and television • Online • Brand advertising	**Internet** • Web 2.0 • Search optimization SEO • Pay Per Click PPC • Micro website • Mobile applications • Live streaming online	**Traditional approach** • Directional telephone survey • Customer inquiry • Advertising survey • Database/CRM • Brief PR information • Market research • Leads generation/management
Plan • Strategic plan • Media program • Forecast, budget • Sales analysis • Incidence matrix • Instrument dial	**Promotion** • News release • News distribution • Articles • Media relations • News events	**Social media marketing** • Blog • LinkedIn • Facebook, YouTube • Twitter, Google+	**Internet** • Web analysis • PPC • SEO Tools • Number of registrations • ESP instrument panel • PR instrument dial • Google News
Strategy • Product • Market segmentation • Channels • Positioning	**Event marketing** • Three exhibitions • Demonstration • Training • Summit • Telemarketing • Mail	**Content marketing** • Manual • White paper • Product catalog • Research Report • Evaluation report	**Social media analysis or ranking** • LinkedIn • YouTube • Facebook • Twitter • Radian 6 • Google+

(continued)

Table 4.1 (continued)

Strategic marketing	Outbound marketing	Inbound marketing	Marketing measurement
Brand • Naming • Identification • Image and ID standards • Packaging • Price	**Sales enabling** • Sales tools • Leads management • Channel marketing • Sales and Promotion	**Direct marketing** • Directed email • Database and list management • CRM	

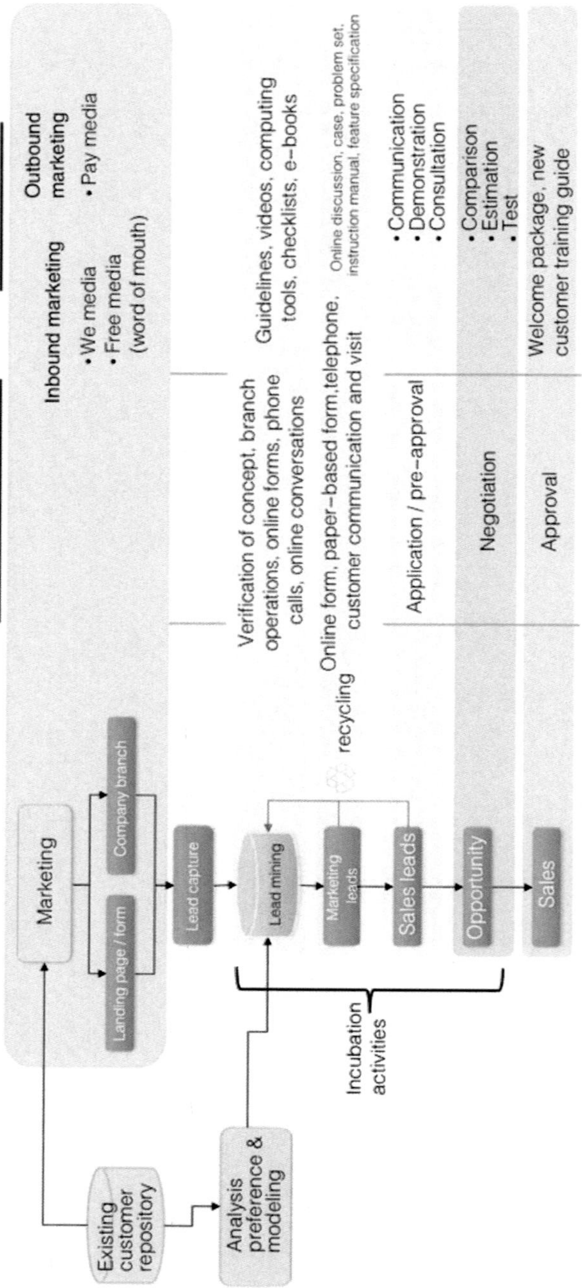

Fig. 4.12 The framework of the MTL process

opening e-mail to view marketing content and transferring related marketing content to friends. From the customer behavior perspective, if the customer visited the exhibition stand ten days ago, visited the pricing page five days ago, watched the product demonstration yesterday, and downloaded the RFP sample today, that means the customer is very active. If a customer registered and participated in an online seminar three months ago, watched four web pages and downloaded two white papers two months ago, registered for a new online seminar a month ago, checked the links in an email and watched three pages, and downloaded a white paper last week, it means that the customer is in a semi-dormant state, in that the above actions may be just for mastering dynamics or learning knowledge.

Lead scoring is to rank the purchase readiness and interest of potential customers or leads according to the pre-set model scoring method. When the score exceeds the preset threshold, the lead will be regarded as meeting the marketing standard, pre-sale and resale.

(4) Lead Incubation: When the score of lead does not exceed the preset threshold, we need to provide correct information at the right time through necessary activities to accelerate the transformation of the lead. It is necessary to manage the life cycle of resale leads, bring the customer information into the CRM system, and complete the sales process of new customer gift packages, cross-selling and customer retention. However, the low-quality leads that have not been transformed for a long time should be kept in the database and discarded after a certain period.

Lead incubation is a very important process to test the planning and execution ability of marketing activities, during which we need to match the customer's cognitive process and purchasing process to realize the linkage of combination marketing.

(5) Lead distribution: The enterprise needs to inform the sales staff of the quality and priority of the leads, and assist them to understand and contact customers through the database, with the follow-up activities of customer contact and leads left over to the sales staff.

(6) Closed-loop management of leads: The enterprise needs to turn leads into new sales, or discard invalid leads, and measure the efficiency of the whole marketing process.

Through the implementation of MTL marketing process and organizational change, Huawei has improved its O2O integrated marketing ability and built a complete set of the marketing automation system. Through the successful pilot in Europe and the global implementation, Huawei saw a qualitative leap in its marketing ability.

4.3 Management and Incentive Mechanism for Talents During Internationalization

The key to the formulation and implementation of an internationalization strategy is people. How to obtain and select the leading talents to adapt to the overseas market? How to establish an overseas talent pool and speed up the training? How to encourage overseas “soldiers” to fight for a long time? The lack of overseas talents is a common bottleneck for Chinese enterprises when “going global”. It’s even harder to get a leader who not only understands the company’s strategy and products, but also the overseas market. Therefore, the following three aspects must be done well in the construction of international human resources.

4.3.1 Breaking the Bottleneck of Overseas Talents Through Obtaining and Selecting “Generals”

The acquisition of overseas leading talents is the key to the success of enterprise internationalization, especially in the early stage. Some enterprises (represented by Huawei) adopt the talent strategy of internal selection, supplemented by “outsourcing”. Although it may take a long time in personnel training in this way, but the overseas leaders chosen this way, with a deeper understanding of the company’s strategy, will implement the strategies of the enterprise appropriately. However, many other Chinese enterprises have adopted the method of direct acquisition, that is, “directly introducing” for the eagerness of the development of the local market. At this time, the establishment of talent selection standards, cross-cultural management and incentive mechanism is particularly important. First of all, it is necessary to set clear overseas objectives and adopt a relatively flexible mode for management and control. For this, Sany Heavy Industry can serve as a good example in that it has given full play to the role of local leading talents in the local market in Germany. Secondly, we should formulate reasonable incentive mechanisms, such as commonly used equity, options, Huawei’s unique TUP, and the fund partner system of New Hope Group, which can greatly improve the sense of belonging and responsibility of overseas leading talents. Finally, we should establish an enterprise culture and an integrated talent management system to adapt to the development of globalization, so as to fundamentally solve the problem of obtaining overseas leading talents and enable them to play a sustainable role.

The identification and selection of overseas core talents based on the international leadership model refer to selecting the right people first before cultivating them, which will achieve twice the result with half the effort, for which strategic mindset, market insight, mobilization and implementation, and continuous motivation are the key elements for the identification and selection of overseas leading talents. In order to avoid the difficulties caused by the inadaptability of the business backbone staff in the overseas market, it is a compulsory course for Chinese enterprises to evaluate the quality of overseas backbone staff and formulate targeted training plans for reserve talents.

Practical ability, strategic mindset and strategic contribution are the key indicators for Huawei in identifying and selecting overseas leading talents. The necessary and sufficient conditions for a cadre to be promoted are to firstly to make his department profitable and secondly to make strategic contributions. The cadre who failed to make profits for the representative will be eliminated from the bottom, while the cadre who made a profit but not a strategic contribution can not be promoted. Both are necessary and sufficient conditions. "Now when we select cadres, we need to slowly adjust the structure, so as to make it more conducive to the direction of the advancement of the company."

4.3.2 "Concrete" Cadre Training Mechanism and "7-2-1" Overseas Talent "Double Speed" Plan

According to the theory of SPI, only about 20% of people are suitable for sales, of which less than 10% are "Eagle-like talents" for sales, who have strong sales and interpersonal skills, and can maintain the high performance for a long time. Huawei selects a large number of fresh university graduates to enrich the sales front line. Guided by the sales culture of "toasting together for victory, and resolution to help in face of failures", and the orientation with goals but not conditions or reasons, under the incentive of high-performance appraisal policy which balances individual contribution and team cooperation, Huawei's sales team turns more and more aggressive with high morale and desire to win through constant survival of the fittest by means of "helping and guiding the young members by the veteran members", with "loaded tasks" and "hotline promotion", Huawei established a rich pool of talent resources for the expansion of overseas markets.

"The enterprises will be crying out for talents only when they are in great need." In the initial stage, Huawei dispatched excellent domestic market representatives to overseas front lines according to the mandatory proportion requirements, which once affected domestic business and caused widespread complaints from domestic customer executives, which required extraordinary courage and courage. In addition to the establishment of a pool of talent resources in advance, the key is to quickly make the ability of these personnel meet the needs of overseas markets.

4.3.2.1 "Concrete" Training Mechanism for the Cadres

After solving the issues concerning the qualifications and ability of the sales personnel at the basic level, the management and training of the leading cadres of the sales department become very important. There is an unwritten rule in Huawei's sales department, that is, local people can not act as local sales directors. This is mainly to prevent the enterprise's customer relationship from becoming a private personal relationship, and thus the corruption caused by nepotism, as Huawei's foresight on this issue, which should be praised. Many enterprises contacted by the author in the consulting work are faced with the dilemma that there is no one to replace the sales "big frog" and they dare not replace it. Huawei once ed the leading group of the marketing department resign, which took a lot of courage and may have a direct impact on sales. To achieve this, an enterprise must have a big enough talent pool and a good cadre training mechanism. For example, the senior sales team of a leading coating enterprise, who has been working in the main "grain barns" for a long time, has gone away and taken away a large number of customers—because customers recognize people, not the brand or products of the enterprise.

Even if a non-local person acts as a local sales director, a long time at the position will lead to the formation of a circle of interests. Even if there is no corruption, when a person works in a very familiar working environment for a long time, he will be slack due to a lack of freshness and challenge. Therefore, Huawei will regularly rotate the regional directors and heads of representative offices to meet different challenges in different regions, which not only improves their sales skills and management ability, but also eliminates the possibilities of corruption. As the rotation has greatly improved the management level of the sales system and trained cadres, the cadre rotation system has gradually extended to the whole company, upon which personnel from R & D, supply chain, finance and other systems regularly flow to the sales system in proportion, and personnel from the sales system flow back to other systems. This "concrete" cadre training mechanism with one specialty and multiple abilities enables the employees of the platform department to fully understand the profound meaning of being "customer-centered" and the operation mode of the first-line market, so that the process formulated by the enterprise is closer to the business needs and the support for the first-line market is more in place. Accordingly, Huawei has built a set of unique "modes with front-line elite combat supported by a large platform" and a training mechanism for middle and high-level leaders.

4.3.2.2 "7-2-1" Overseas Talent "Double Speed" Plan

The practice has proved that Huawei's "7-2-1" overseas talent "double speed" training system[1] can greatly improve the speed and effect of personnel training.

In terms of training, Huawei attaches great importance to the summary of internal cases, experiences and lessons, and has developed corresponding training materials to make full use of them. At the same time, Huawei has carefully-designed plans to train internal gold medal lecturers, requiring relevant experts and leaders to invest in them and give corresponding rewards, among which, *Who Killed the Contract* and *Nine Moves for Successful Overseas Marketing* become classic courses for being very practical and comprehensive. Whether it is the training of grassroots employees

[1] Talent empowerment through 10% off-duty training, 20% tutorial system training plan and development feedback, 70% on-the-job action learning and job rotation.

to quickly adapt to the market environment, or the incentive for middle and senior managers to improve their overseas achievements as soon as possible, Huawei saw the obvious effect. Many enterprises have a large training budget every year, but the logic of their courses is not strong, and most of them invite external lecturers for training, but not using the internal resources. **The biggest waste of enterprises is often the waste of experience.** Making full use of and exploring the internal training resources of enterprises is an efficient and low-cost way of cadre training.

The key point of **"7-2-1" talent training system** is to strengthen the exchange of experience and ideas, as well as post-rotation empowerment "Upon the success in one area, a teaching team will be set up to train cadres on a large scale". By strengthening the construction of various strategic reserves such as a heavy brigade, major project department and project management resource pool, the enterprise can promote the circulation and flow of cadres, so as to make the whole team full of energy and improve the global vision and leading ability of cadres.

In the early stage, to encourage employees to work in less developed and difficult areas, Huawei not only provided subsidies, but also specified promotion opportunities. However, because the product requirements and business environment of underdeveloped areas are often lower than those of China, cadres who have not been promoted through the "7-2-1" system are often not suitable to be leaders in overseas areas. Ren Zhengfei once said: "The cadres stationed in Afghanistan have been there for many years and suffered a lot for us. They can only be heroes. They can't be generals even if the enterprise wants to promote them now, because they haven't been equipped with the skills they need through rotations. If people can be rotated for different positions, we will empower them. Why shouldn't they stand out? Therefore, we promote the rotation of the team to further enable all kinds of excellent personnel in the grass-roots combat team to "flow without corruption" in the rotating process, so that all levels of the whole company are moving towards the goal of victory and striving for progress."

4.3.3 Effective Incentives from Three Perspectives

The work overseas presents challenges from culture, environment, work and family. The establishment of a "striver-centered, open and inclusive" global cultural value, together with the establishment of a clear policy for cadre promotion and career development, and a reasonable short, medium and long-term incentive mechanism, are the key guarantee for the success of the internationalization of Chinese enterprises.

Huawei encourages its employees to take root overseas through career development (promotion opportunities), salary design and organizational atmosphere.

- By planning forward, the organizational ability of "the front line calling for support" was enhanced with further empowerment of the front line.

- The organizational system and atmosphere of leading charge were formed through the improvement of the cooperation mechanism between the front line and back end.
- The opportunities for career development (promotion) were increased with priority given to the promotion of cadres with successful overseas experience, especially those with working experience in overseas hard areas.
- The long-term incentive problem was solved through innovative TUP, upon adherence to the "striver-centered" corporate culture, in addition to the inclined salary and overseas subsidy system.
- An efficient overseas work and administrative platform was established to solve the worries of employees in their work and life.
- The long-term combat power of overseas teams was ensured in terms of culture and system.

Huawei's international strategy and implementation, after years of practice and summary, just echoed the performance of the dance named Avalokitesvara, the thousand-hand Bodhisattva, in which "those children who can't hear the sound at all, without any music coordination, conducted so neat and uniform actions, so exquisite performance, for which the hardships and efforts can be hard to imagine." In the process of globalization, Huawei constantly denies and surpasses itself. "Huawei is still far away from success. It has just climbed onto the beach in many overseas markets and will be driven back to the sea at any time. The industry and market are constantly changing, and some technologies and experiences just accumulated are once again facing self-denial. At this critical moment, we can't be distracted, we can't waver, we can't turn our back on our roots. No matter now or in the future, we have to work hard and harder."

The continuous enhancement of China's national strength has created ever-better conditions for Chinese enterprises to "go global". After more than thirty years of effort, China has more than 20,000 overseas enterprises, and can collaborate with each other and no longer fight alone against the competitors, when the Belt and Road Initiative has blown the trumpet for overseas Chinese enterprises to fight shoulder by shoulder with each other. If we can learn from Huawei's "spirit", follow Huawei's "form", and establish our own characteristics to formulate a clear international strategy and build a strong international executive force, then the success of the internationalization of the enterprises will be around the corner!s

Chapter 5
Transformation and Innovation of Business Model

The main reason why "business models" have been constantly thought highly of is that the development of Internet technology has subverted the original market pattern, and cross-border operation has brought about great changes in the boundary of enterprise management and business model. Unicorn enterprises have become famous overnight, such as BAT, LeTV, Xiaomi of the earlier generation, TMD (Toutiao, Meituan, Didi) of the new generation, bike-sharing, Pinduoduo, etc. According to statistics, in 2018 alone, 36 new unicorn enterprises emerged in China, accounting for about 1/3 of the global total.

Many entrepreneurs may dream of "soaring" through the innovations in their business model, or watch out in case their competitors will surpass themselves through the innovations in the business model. An ancient Chinese motto goes that "Gentlemen love money and get it through right ways", while Ren Zhengfei reminded people in this wave innovations of the business model caused by the Internet: tofu or tofu. What did he mean by saying so? What is the business model? What is the essence of it? In short, the business model is the source and way of making money for enterprises, but the essence of it is that whether the enterprises provide physical products or services (collectively referred to as offering), they must win the acception of the customers.

Huawei has undergone great changes in its business model in the three important transformations in its development, from seeing its income and profit through the transaction of hardware products in the initial stage to obtaining income through the sales of the combination of hardware and software products later, during which, Huawei found that the mode of selling software and hardware separately brought more profits to the enterprise, with the export tax rebate alone accounting for 17%.

In the later period, Huawei not only gained more revenue sources but also greatly improved the user viscosity through the sales of software and hardware products and services, as well as the sales of solutions including consulting, design, integration and project management, with the sales market expanding from domestic market to overseas market, while the customer group from telecommunication operators to government, power, finance, transportation and other industries with the scope of customer sources more and more extensive, and the trading mode developed from the

L. Tao, *Huawei Wisdom*,
https://doi.org/10.1007/978-981-19-1169-9_5

primary "cash-and-carry" to a variety of forms. More and more models that Huawei has never heard of, such as TurnKey, financial leasing and financial sales, Revenue sharing, RANsharing and integrated services, etc., are proposed by customers, especially after Huawei went into the overseas market, which had a big impact on the management, product forms, and even organizational system of Huawei.

5.1 Driving Force Behind the Change of the Business Model

The driving force of the great changes in the business model comes from the following four aspects.

1. **Macro trend of the development**
    - Social and cultural development: social and cultural development tend to be diversified, personalized and virtual.
    - Trend of the development of technology: With the formation of the national innovation strategy, technology upgrading is accelerated.
    - Changes in the laws and regulations: The regulatory policies turn to be more open, promoted by the market economy.
    - Social and economic development: the Internet has drawn a great impact on production and people's life.
2. **Economic driving force**
    - Economic globalization: Bigger market, more resources and stronger competition.
    - Capital market: The active capital market injects vitality into innovation.
    - Economic infrastructure: Belt and Road Initiative promoted its comprehensive development.
    - Commodities and other resources: The contradiction between the abundance of commodities and the shortage of scarce resources.
3. **Industrial driving force**
    - Value chain: The competition among enterprises evolves into the competition among value chains.
    - Shareholders: Shareholders shift from focusing on short-term interests to balancing short-term and long-term interests.
    - Competitors (including monopolists): "Big Mac" emerged in various industries.
    - New entrants (subverters): Cross-border operators broke the industry barriers.
    - Alternative products/services: The rapid development of information technology brought more alternatives to customers.

4. **Market driving force**

- Market issues: The major fluctuations of the economy presented tests of the adaptability of enterprises.
- Requirements and needs: Customers are increasingly desiring something higher than meeting the basic needs.
- Market segmentation: Personalized requirement became the mainstream.
- Switching costs: The low-profit model of "three-plus-one" trading-mix (custom manufacturing with materials, designs or samples supplied and compensation trade) has gradually become history.
- Income attraction: The embodiment of entrepreneur value.

In fact, the business model of all industries has undergone some changes. With the development of Internet technology, many industries closely related to people's daily life have been subverted, and people have to pay attention to the reconstruction of business model, for fear of becoming stragglers "not understanding, not learned and left behind". First of all, let's look at the industries that are most affected by the Internet. According to the research of American scholars, the industries that are deeply affected by the Internet in the United States are shown in Table 5.1.

Table 5.1 The industries deeply affected by the Internet in the United States

Industry	Substitution index (S)	The biggest online substitute
Music	0.73	iTunes
Books	0.73	Amazon
Household electrical appliances	0.6	CircuitCity
Footwear	0.47	Zappos
Groceries	0.4	Safeway
Automobile	0.4	eBay Cars
Legal service	0.4	LegalZoom
Clothing	0.33	Local Yelp
Renting	0.33	Local Craigslist
Hospital and doctor	0.27	WebMD
Catering	0.13	Local Yelp
Hotel	0.13	Priceline Expedia
Beauty leisure	0.13	Local Yelp
Domestic maintenance	0.13	Local Yelp
Dentist	0.13	Local Yelp
Exercise and fitness	0.07	Local Yelp

The situation in China is somewhat different from that in the United States, with daily necessities, clothing and fast food greatly affected by the Internet in China, but the overall trend is similar. The more the services/products call for personal experience, the less they are affected by the Internet. When an enterprise happens to be in an industry deeply affected by the Internet, in addition to carefully studying how to use the Internet for new business model innovation, it is more important for it to keep in mind the essence of the business model—to provide customers with better products/services, and to make achievement by satisfying its customers.

Take Qunar.com for example, before its acquisition by Ctrip, the author had once used the service of Qunar.com. When booking tickets online over Qunar.com, people can find the best bargain by comparing the prices. There would be no problem if the journey went as scheduled, but because of the typhoon, the flight we originally booked was canceled. My friend who bought his tickets through the Ctrip network changed his ticket within an hour, while it took more than three hours and more than 20 calls before we could change our tickets. When waiting for our tickets to be changed, I studied Qunar.com.

After being listed on NASDAQ, Qunar.com suffered an accumulated loss of US $5 billion, before it was reported that it would be acquired by Ctrip soon. The founder of Qunar.com said in his latest update of microblog then that what he was most proud of was that he had realized the financial freedom for his 1,500 employees, whatever Qunar's contribution to the market and customers would be... There is no problem in bringing financial freedom to his employees, but what should the measures and ways for that?

Many Internet enterprises start their financing with a good concept to obtain a number of online customers and traffic through financing quickly, and then obtain more financing through more customers, before they exit quickly after listing, after "collecting money" through the business of financial derivatives with the funds they raised. The key performance indicators of these enterprises are the number of customers and the amount of financing, with how to serve existing users well often put in the secondary consideration of work and evaluation. Such companies are neither to benefit customers nor investors, but to get rich quickly through the so-called "business model". With the development of the Internet economy and the gradual maturity of the investment environment, such companies will be quickly eliminated by the market.

After returning to the essence of business, and after creating values for the customers, the offering will bring different business results for enterprises through different business models. The standard to judge a business model is profit.

$$\textbf{Profit} = \textbf{revenue} - \textbf{cost}$$

The enterprises can business obtain revenue through the business model that meets the value needs of customers (Total Value Ownership, TVO). Just like UAV, which stimulates the potential needs of customers and meets the value orientation of customers, makes more profits though the cost for the products can be high. The business can also take the model that reduces the total cost of ownership (TCO mentioned above), which is easier for many follow-up enterprises to adopt.

5.2 Analysis and Summary of Typical Business Model Transformation

How can enterprises determine the most suitable business model for their own development from the many business models? Here we will analyze the design of the business model through several typical cases.

5.2.1 Retail industry: The transformation of the business model from Suning Appliance Co., Ltd.(short as "Suning Appliance" hereafter) to Suning Commerce Group Co., Ltd. (short as "Suning Commerce" hereafter)

5.2.1.1 The source of the crisis for Suning Appliance

The first is the traditional model of joint management: the traditional model of joint management makes retailers over-rely on the commercial real estate model, not understanding the products and the needs of consumers, thus the discourse and attention of consumers determine the fate of retailers.

The second is that brand enterprises take the initiative to connect the Internet: network channels enable them to regain their parts of the voice in front of traditional retailers, and at the same time enable them to access the needs of consumers quickly without opening physical stores in prime locations.

The third comes from the impact of online retailers: in 2011, Suning was still expanding vigorously, with 373 more chain stores compared to the number of 2010; In 2012, the situation took a sharp turn for the worse, with the net profit in the first quarter falling by 15%, and the annual decline at nearly 50%, in addition to the close of 178 stores at the annual net loss of 20, while in 2012, the revenue of JD.com reached RMB 60 billion, and that of Alibaba exceeded RMB 1 trillion yuan.

5.2.1.2 Suning's road for changes

To perish in waiting or to die for improper changes, anyway, Suning is sure to go off the stage if they don't change for even a chance.

The first stage, from 2010 to 2012: Suning showed uncertainty or reluctance in the exploration of its road over the Internet without substantial promotion on the path with vague directions despite a clear strategic direction.

- Early imitation of e-commerce: Suning experienced the separation and conflict between its online and offline operations;
- The common phenomenon in the early stage of the transformation of enterprises: there is neither real interests nor future value when the new business has yet to be developed and

The second stage, 2013: with the development of mobile Internet, O2O was proved to be a feasible path for the transformation from traditional stores to e-commerce.

- Determination on the business model with "one body and two wings": "e-commerce + physical stores + providers of retailing service".
- Combination of points and surfaces: With the overall layout on the surface and selected parts for specific pilots the hardware and software were ready for the transformation.
- In 2016, Suning formed strategic cooperation with Alibaba, and in 2018, its offline revenue surpassed that of its old rival Gome for the first time.

1. **Firm grasp of the essence of the transformation of the business model**

(1) **"Expenditure reduction"—overall cost reasonably reduced**

By analysis of Suning's own cost structure and careful comparison with that of JD.com, a model enterprise of pure e-commerce, Suning formulated key measures to reduce overall costs, as shown in Fig. 5.1.

Measure one is to optimize the relationship with the brand: the way to reduce the purchasing cost is to increase the sales volume and optimize the relationship with the brand. For example, in early 2013, Suning and Hisense signed a strategic target of RMB 30 billion in sales for three years from 2013 to 2015 to vigorously promote the cooperation of O2O integration through collaborative measures such as product strategy, channel expansion, supply chain optimization, organization docking and joint marketing between the two sides.

Measure two is to optimize the physical stores: the leasing of more than 1600 stores, as well as ancillary expenses and asset depreciation, is the biggest difference between the cost composition of traditional retailers and e-commerce, and also the orientation of cost reduction.

- Reasonable layout: for the first and second-tier markets, Suning mainly upgrades its flagship stores and closes unreasonable community stores that are not located

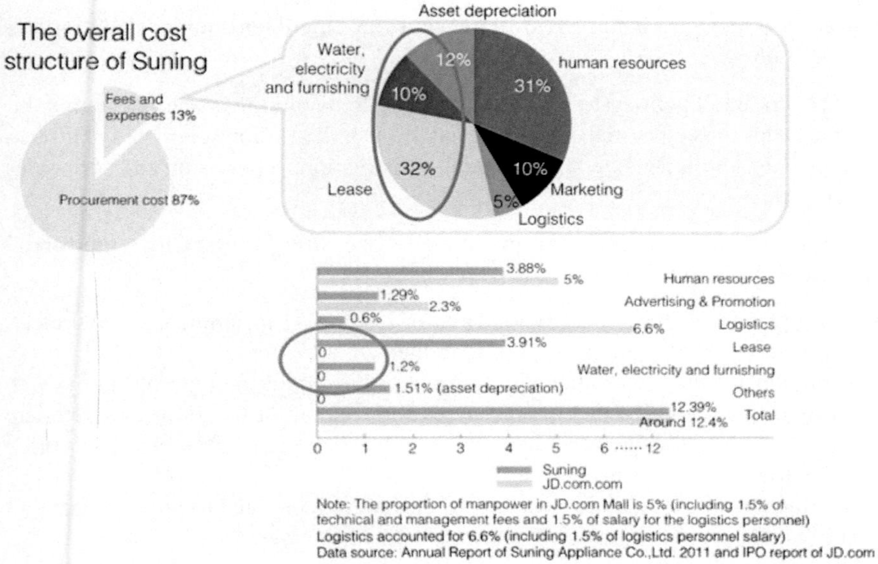

Fig. 5.1 Comparison of Suning's overall cost composition and JD.com's cost

in the regional center nor undertake the logistics functions; Suning focuses its development on the third tier markets. Suning is bound to continue to increase its efforts in open stores, as important nodes of logistics layout, in the third tier market and expand its O2O network; While in the fourth tier cities where the existing businesses in the circle are deeply rooted, Suning chooses to break through by e-commerce instead of spending energy on opening stores.

- Turning cost into a new source of income: Suning Appliance transformed the original huge cost into a new source of income through opening its offline resource platform to realize the marketization and socialization of resources with the establishment of a third-party logistics system.

(2) **"Open source" to increase the source of income**.

Suning Appliance was transformed into Suning Commerce with the value proposition of "all categories, all directions, all customers" "service as the only product of Suning".

The first measure is to increase business categories and break the price difference between online and offline operations.

- From home appliances and 3C products to department stores, daily necessities, books, food and virtual products, it broke the price difference between online and offline products and realized the same price for the same product nationwide, which greatly promoted the integration of O2O.

The second measure is to provide a 3C solution, intelligent home with "Suning privilege house service".

- It covers intelligent system solutions, air system solutions, water system solutions, audio-visual system solutions, and the overall solutions consisted of professional consulting, design, procurement, construction, supervision and after-sales services.

The third measure is to try a new profit model over the "Suning Cloud platform" opened in two ways.

- Through opening the "Suning Cloud Platform" (http:// sop.suning.com) to society, a third-party open logistics system is formed.
- High-end information value-added service: the mining of big data is open to partners, which will gather the resources and wisdom of brand makers, retailers and third-party service providers, and provide rich commodity selection, price comparison and personalized service experience.
- The business flow, logistics and capital flow were integrated to provide financial solutions to meet the needs of consumers and businesses.

2. **Reconstruction of Suning's core competence**

    - It possesses an efficient and low-cost logistics network system with hundreds of millions of customer resources, more than 1600 stores and access to more than 2800 districts and counties.
    - Omni-channel: The perfect integration of online display and convenience (such as price comparison) with offline experience and service-enriched retail operation experience and supply chain management experience, and better met the needs of users and supply chain.
    - Through "Suning Cloud Platform", Suning enjoyed the advantages of the Internet with its shortboard strengthened.
    - The new operation process supported with the advanced IT system and R & D capability (unified database of POS system and network system, real-time price system, real-time supply chain system, and development of Suning e-commerce mobile APP).

Suning spent a certain period of time learning the mode of online operation to develop its online business independently, while the Internet retailers such as Alibaba and JD.com have formed a comparative advantage in customer resources, with a strong impact on traditional retailers through the user viscosity to the platform, so comparatively, the number of active customers of Suning still presents as its big weakness. While due to the lack of offline resources, the logistics cost of Internet retailers remains high, so they urgently need to establish their own offline resources. Therefore, Suning and Alibaba, JD.com and Tencent quickly learn from each other and form a new competitive advantage by forming a strategic partnership.

5.2.2 *Manufacturing industry—from Foxconn to FIH Mobile Limited*

5.2.2.1 The source of Foxconn's crisis

The first is the sharp drop in customer orders: Too much dependence on several large customers such as Apple, Samsung and Nokia resulted in relatively stereotyped customers.

The second is the rising cost: The rising cost of raw materials and the serious shortage of workers lead to the rising of labor cost and other comprehensive costs; The promulgation of the new labor law, as well as the satisfaction of employees' requirements for a wage increase and welfare improvement, further diluted Foxconn's profits.

The third is the intensified competition and declined profits: Foxconn's profit margin has dropped from 6% a few years ago to 2%, while new competitor Pegatron adopted the mode of competition at an even lower profit margin (0.8%), which is "even lower than lower". Losses became normal to Foxconn, with its gross profit rate falling below 1%. In the first half of 2012, Foxconn saw its total revenue at US $2.5 billion, down 16.37%, with a loss of US $226 million; In 2011, the total revenue of Foxconn was US $6.3 billion with the net profit at US $73 million; The net loss of Foxconn in 2010 was US $228 million.

5.2.2.2 The path of the transformation of Foxconn's business model

1. **The essence of the business model transformation firmly grasped**

(1) **"Expenditure cut" by reducing operating costs**

Measure one: factories moved to intensive-labor areas in the mainland and overseas with a cheaper manpower.

Measure two: robots introduced to upgrade intelligent manufacturing.

With robots undertaking the heavy and repetitive work, the automation of production line and management was realized; One million of the robots developed through Foxbot project have been put into use in three years, for which the enterprise moved forward to industry 4.0 with future competence formed and the career development channel opened up for ordinary blue-collar workers to work in the science and technology industry, resulting in the reduced number of ordinary workers and labor costs greatly cut.

(2) **"Source opened"—the source of income added**

Foxconn's business group for channels was restructured with the introduction of five-channel businesses such as Wanmabenteng Project (Open ten million supermarkets of electrical appliance) and "Efeihu.com" for the accelerated transformation to new energy, new materials, cloud computing, etc.

Measure one, "Hon Hai Technology Group (short as Hon Hai) of manufacturing"—transformation from core manufacturing OEM to brand management.

- In 2013, Foxconn and local operators in Taiwan jointly released a cheap self-branded smartphone A5;
- TV set branded"RadioShack" tried the market of home appliances;
- The assembly business extends to the accessories business with higher profits, with self-made brand transmission cables, earphones, keyboards, etc.;
- Emerging industries: photovoltaic cells, lithium batteries, LED, etc.

Measure two, "Hon Hai of science and technology"—transforming from products to solutions.

- After buying 20% shares of LeTV with RMB 130 million, Hon Hai entered the field of mobile Internet and smart home with the help of the mode of LeTV and the integration of software and hardware.
- Hon Hai provided cloud services and IoT solutions upon the accumulation of technologies through the OEM server, storage, routing and switching equipment as well software and applications designed for the services.
- No longer sticking to manufacturing stubbornly, FIH Mobile Limited strode forward to both ends of the "smiling curve".

Measure three, "Hon Hai of Commerce and trade"—from independent operation to opening up the resource platform to the outside world. The following is the construction of its five major channels.

- **Offline:**
  - Its offline store, Cybermart, has accelerated its expansion
    - Media Markt, an electronic products store jointly developed with Metro AG;
    - Store in store through the alliance with other industries;
    - The Project themed Wanmabengteng with the focus on employees returning home to start their own businesses.
- **Online:**
  - Upon the combination of the advantages of traditional platform and Internet platform, e-commerce website "Efeihu.com" created a new open resource management platform and open up a new profit model.

(3) **Diversified choices on customers**

Measure one, customer resources expanded with less dependence on minor big customers.

By adding a number of emerging brand manufacturers such as Xiaomi, LeTV and Huawei, the production capacity can be lifted. But the OEM mode is still to give the control to others, for the diversified customers but reduced the degree of dependence.

Measure two, expands customers of the customers (end users), with an accurate grasp of the trend of customer requirement while increasing revenue sources.

- Electronic consumer groups expanded (mobile phones, TV);
- B2B enterprise customers expanded (government, enterprise and vertical industry customers faced by cloud services and Internet of Things).

2. **The core competence of FIH Mobile Limited Built upon the best use of its advantages to strengthen where it was weak**

    (1) **The world's shortest 3C supply chain, to achieve "982" (98% of the shipment completed in two days)**
    (2) **Core manufacturing and cost management (including 13 bases for automatic production and management)**
    (3) **R & D capabilities and patents, especially the world's leading mold design and manufacturing technology.**

        - The number of patents in the world ranks among the top three in China.
        - Hon Hai established a powerful mold development management system FRT, upon which Hon Hai can complete the designing and manufacturing of the molds within one to two days, which usually takes other manufacturers one week.

    (4) **Integration and reconstruction Value chain, with the core technologies mastered**

        - The enterprise merged Chi Mei, the second-largest LCD panel company in Taiwan, in exchange for shares.
        - The enterprise acquired 9.88% of Sharp's shares with US $836 million, becoming its largest shareholder, which enriched the LCD screen production line and, more importantly, enriched the core technology and intellectual property rights.

In 2017, Foxconn's revenue grew by more than 80%, which was the result of its strong expansion of Nokia function phones, smartphone manufacturing and auxiliary logistics and sales business in emerging markets, as well as the benefits from the drive of the mobile phone market in China and India, and the effect of joining Microsoft's supply chain.

5.2.3 Catering industry—Analysis of Haidilao business model

When dining in Haidilao, customers will be enjoying the real feeling of "consumers as the God", but at the same time wondering.

- Can the cost be controlled by using the service mode of high-end restaurants in mid-range catering?
- Will the continuous expansion be a flash in the pan? What is the core competence of Haidilao?

5.2.3.1 How Haidilao reduces its cost

For fewer expenditures in the TCO, the typical cost structure of the catering industry is shown as in Fig. 5.2.

Through the analysis of the general cost structure of the catering industry and Haidilao's case, we can find that the total cost of the catering industry is increasing year by year, with the part of expenditures on labor cost, store rent and the cost of storage, transportation and distribution increasing the fastest. With the development of the economy, the labor cost of all the industries is rising, while to improve the service level, we have to recruit quality personnel. Therefore, the most suitable part to save the cost is in the rent, storage and distribution.

Measure one, the cost of storage and transportation, distribution and period loss cut.

- Through the cooperation with HAVI group of the USA, the enterprise established distribution centers in Beijing, Shanghai, Xi'an and Zhengzhou, which were designated as distribution centers after being certified by Beijing Paralympic Games for its "health and safety" and "quality preservation".

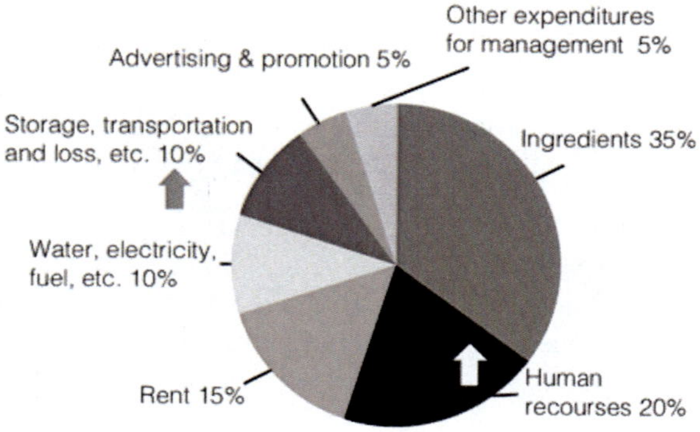

Fig. 5.2 The typical cost structure of the catering industry

- Each logistics center is equipped with a set of advanced cleaning, inspection, refrigeration equipment, in addition to a strictly standardized production chain;
- The planned consumption management of backstage distribution centers and front office restaurants is highly standardized.

Measure two, "No kitchens for the branch stores" as the ultimate goal of reducing the rent.

- Innovative preservation technology of semi-finished products;
- The application of automation technologies in its devices for adding soup to the hot pots, automatic dishwasher and touch screen for ordering the dishes.

Measure three, the "dehumanized" standard process.

- The "dehumanized" standard process in the background ensures the safety, high efficiency, low inventory and low store cost of the system of rear services.

These measures not only greatly reduced the operating costs, but also formed the core competence of the enterprise.

5.2.3.2 Open sources for Haidilao

Measure one, the catering industry relatively relies on a single source for its revenue, mostly diners.

- Customer loyalty became the main driving force of enterprise profitability and growth, as well as an important factor to the profits made by Haidilao.
- Customer satisfaction and loyalty are far more important than merely the addition or subtraction of the profit, but satisfied customers do not necessarily become loyal customers. Exploring customers who fit the restaurant concept upon the understanding of their needs turns out to be the "principle to find customers" of Haidilao.

Measure two, new sources of income continuously explored.

- Haidilao bottom material and dipping sauce are sold in supermarkets one after another, which are divided into three series with 17 varieties.
- Reference to the foreign fast-food business model (franchise fees, real estate, etc.).
- Haidilao opens its catering logistics platform.

To implement the service orientation of the store and improve customer satisfaction and loyalty, Haidilao has only two items considered in the assessment of its stores: customer satisfaction and employees' efforts, while financial indicators have never been the focus of the assessment system of Haidilao.

5.2.3.3 Haidilao built its core competence according to the needs of subdivided customer groups

The basic needs of the catering industry are cleanliness and good taste. However, the hot pots put relatively low requirements for cooking technology, especially for hot pots of Sichuan style, for which the cooking has little influence, for the guests will match seasonings by themselves, so the preparation of food materials is relatively simple. Therefore, the key point of competition lies in the quality of food materials and services. Haidilao is famous for its clean, fresh and suitable dishes.

1. **Market orientation and the selection of customers of Haidilao**

   - The market orientation of Haidilao is medium-grade catering.
   - Customer segmentation: The customers who focus on experience rather than efficiency and are not sensitive to time. For "customers who are too sensitive to time will not choose to eat hot pot, consequently, they will not choose Haidilao, a hot pot restaurant."

2. **The value proposition of Haidilao**
   The businesses of the catering industry are generally classified into places of convenience and low price, places of fashion, places for family and friends gathering, places for business negotiation and places for elegant and high-end experiences. Haidilao accurately positioned itself as "a place of quality service for gatherings of family or friends".

   - Haidilao offers an enjoyable experience for customers, who would take the initiative to promote it through new media for free, which makes it one of the top ten catering enterprises in terms of the number of fans over Sina Weibo, the average number of tweets, the average number of comments and loyalty of its fans.
   - The free service for the waiting area of the target customers turns the long waiting into a kind of public praise and the marketing cost into benefits.
   - Haidilao offers service for get-togethers to distant relatives, friends, or colleagues even "at the other end of the world" through its video conference system, which though resulted in controversial comments, yet fully embodied the value proposition of the enterprise.

3. **The construction of core competence of Haidilao**

   (1) **Humanized services at the front desk**

   - The service innovation of Haidilao, as the spokesman of differentiation, made the customer felt "overwhelmed" by the hospitality of the enterprise with "the long-expected feeling of being the God".
   - Service training, experience sharing.
   - Innovative "mentoring" mode and assessment system.

(2) **The "dehumanized" standard process and automation at the back**

- The safety, high efficiency, low inventory and low store cost of logistics system ensured.
- The physical labor of the staff at the front desk was reduced while better service for customers was provided.

(3) **Product and technology innovation**

- Haidilao planned to launch 1 or 2 impressive hot pot varieties every year.
- 5 to 10 new dishes will be launched every season.
- The self-created "Yuanyang (half spicy, half not) basic soup with no residues" and "basic soup with trotters, soybean and kidney bean" have become the supplement of traditional basic soup for Sichuan hotpot.
- Innovative initial processing and slicing technology to ensure the health and ease to use.

The business model of Haidilao is to transfer the cost to the back end of the supply chain as far as possible, so as to achieve large-scale management and efficiency, with the ultimate goal of no kitchens for the stores. To this end, it has implemented comprehensive improvement and digital management in the layout of the distribution centers, procurement management, equipment and processing flow of the distribution centers, logistics distribution and inventory management, so as to ensure that the fully processed dishes arrive at the table of each store in the freshest state, that is, the functions of the kitchens of its stores are constantly transferred to the distribution centers, with the separation between production and services to realize standardized and humanized management respectively. In terms of the incentive mechanism for the expansion of franchise stores, with the reference to the pyramid selling, or MLM mode, Haidilao developed the mode that franchise stores can draw profits from its upper authorities, so as to realize mutual profits as well as avoiding the traditional phenomenon of "master's death at the success of his apprentices". So, an enterprise can choose a mixture of multiple business models to maximize the benefits.

From the above cases, we can see that the essence of business model transformation is to rebuild the core competence of the enterprise from the basic starting point of creating value for customers and to "open source" for more profits by increasing the types of products and customers segmentation, or to "cut" for higher profit through the structural optimization of the cost.

5.3 The Framework for the Design of the Business Model

It can be seen from the above typical cases that the business model, which is relatively stable, determines the features and business model of the enterprise. Generally, the business model can be understood from the following aspects.

External showcase of the orientation of the enterprise.

- What market and customers to choose (customer segmentation)?
- What does an enterprise do and what not? What kind of money to make and what not (products and solutions, relatively focused or diversified)?
- How to build a value chain, how to determine their own position in the ecological chain (value chain positioning)?
- Sales mode: direct sales, ODM/OEM, self-owned brand, etc.

Reflection of the process model internally(Process Model).

- Planning and implementation of the business: the way, organization and process of the enterprise.
- What kind of key activities are to be adopted to build enterprise competence?
- Product innovation leading strategy.
- Merger and acquisition.
- Cost structure and profit model.
- The process model will change with the development of the market environment and technology, especially information technology and the Internet, which has a significant impact on the organization and process.

5.3.1 Introduction to the new business model

The growing impact of the Internet on business models also gives birth to more and more business models. Different industries can adopt different business model combinations, while many industries have relatively exclusive business models. The popular business models (in the narrow sense) of present days can be summarized as shown in Fig. 5.3.

Small and medium-sized products: The modes like distribution and online shopping are generally adopted for small and medium-sized products.

Relatively large equipment: Generally, direct sales mode will be adopted for relatively large equipment, for which financial sales or leasing mode usually will be chosen for large machinery to improve the utilization of equipment and ensure the light asset structure of the users. The modes of PAYG, revenue sharing and charge on "consumption ÷ time" are often used in emerging businesses (such as businesses of the cloud application) for the mode can reduce the initial investment, and share business risks between both suppliers and operators and develop customers together.

Engineering construction projects: TurnKey, EPCO, BOT are widely adopted for engineering construction projects, where the main drive is the expectation of owners to reduce management complexity, solve financing problems or reduce operational risks.

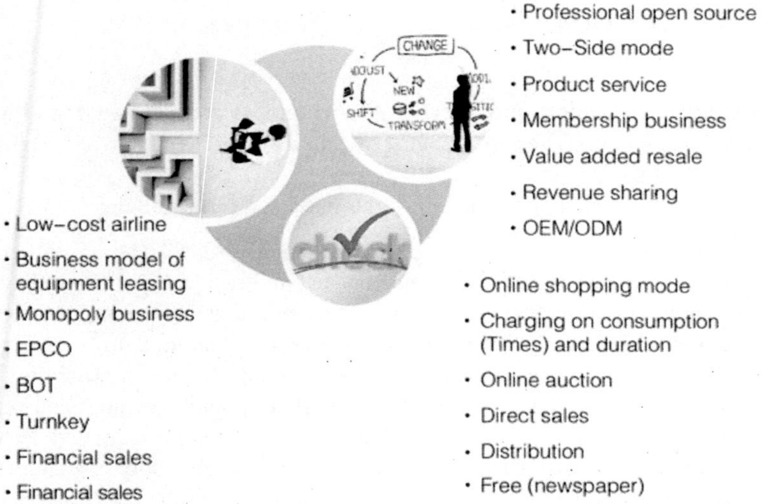

Fig. 5.3 The popular business models (in the narrow sense)

Value-added service and service platform: Many forms of business model, such as free mode, transaction frequency mode and double-sided mode can be applied to value-added services and service platforms. However, due to the commercial policies and regulations, the business models are constantly changing. Taobao has been very successful with its two-sided business model. On the one hand, Taobao charges for personalized design, advertising and ranking, transaction commission, credit management, etc. over its trading platform, while on the other hand, through the analysis of transaction big data, it provides accurate information on requirements of products to manufacturers, and collect value-added service fees through ranking and advertising. The ofo sharing mode, in fact, is the model to make profits for the two or even three parties by obtaining a large number of customers profit through the mode of leasing or even the free access in the initial period to lower the threshold. However, due to regulatory reasons, a large amount of deposit can not be used for the profit of financial derivatives. The analysis of the big data of the customers does not prove much commercial value, but serves as a source for Alipay to increase the registration of new users, but causes inconvenience for the users at the same time. If the expected business model fails to work, the enterprise will be in difficulties.

Through the above analysis, whether in the choice of customers or in the choice of products, whether it is for the marketing mode or the transaction mode, whether it is to save costs or increase revenue, a complete model is needed to help the entrepreneurs design the operation mode and business model for the enterprises.

5.3.2 *The framework for the design of business models*

The Business Model Canvas proposed by Alexander Osterwalder and Yves Pigneur in their *Business Model Generation* gives the framework for the design of the business model, as shown in Fig. 5.4.

The framework is mainly divided into four parts and nine modules.

1. The foundation for the operation for the enterprises: The key operational processes and activities, core resources and capabilities (competitiveness), value chain cooperation mode and strategic partnership together consist the foundation for the operation of the enterprises. For pan manufacturing enterprises like Huawei, the key processes and activities of enterprise internal operation mainly include product R & D process, marketing and contract management process, manufacturing and supply chain (including procurement and delivery) process and other main business processes, with human resource management process, financial management process and fixed assets management process, and the processes for the management of changes and IT system as the important support. The core resources and capabilities are the key elements that differ an enterprise from its competitors in the industry. Although external resources such as special customers and social relations, scarce capital or natural resources can also establish the competitive advantage of an enterprise, they are generally limited in time. Only by building internal core competence that can't be copied by others, such as Huawei's R & D capability and corporate governance structure, Alibaba's platform capability, DJI's innovation and product leading capability, can enterprises maintain an advantageous position in the competition.
2. The products, solutions and services(offerings): Through the products, solutions or services provided, the enterprises are meeting not only the basic needs of customers, but also the needs of higher value different from competitors, so as to realize the commitment and value proposition of enterprises to customers.

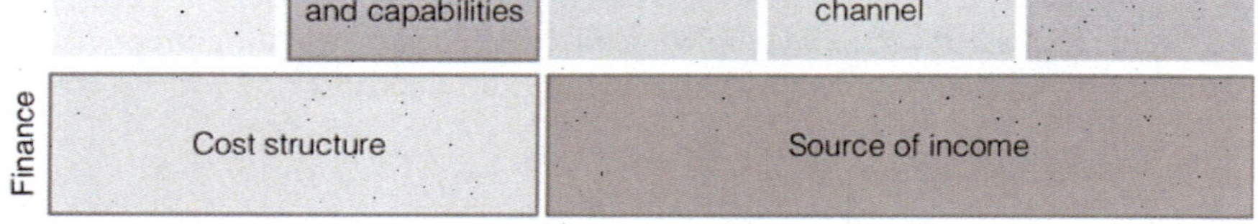

Fig. 5.4 The nine modules for the design of the business model

3. The customer interface: The customer interface includes three sub-modules: customer segmentation, sales channel and customer relationship. The enterprises establish relations with customers, and ultimately achieve sales upon the determination on the appropriate industry, and selection of the appropriate market segments and customer segments in the industry through a certain channel and sales model.
4. Finance: Finance includes cost structure and sources of income. By optimizing the cost structure, enterprises can optimize the overall profit model and improve the financial state by "cutting the costs" and "opening sources" through increasing revenue sources.

5.3.3 *Cases of the design of the business model*

According to the model, we can make a summary of the business model design of the previous three cases. Among them, the omnichannel business model from Suning Appliance to Suning Commerce is shown in Fig. 5.5.

The process of the reconstruction of the business model of Suning had its core on the reconstruction of the basis of enterprise operation and establishment of the O2O omnichannel platform internally though many modules were involved. In doing so, on the one hand, the number of products that could be sold and customers that could be served were greatly increased, thus the source of income increased; On the other hand, the layout and utilization of physical stores were optimized with the operating costs greatly reduced through keeping only a small number of flagship physical stores without reducing the contact area with customers. After the strategic

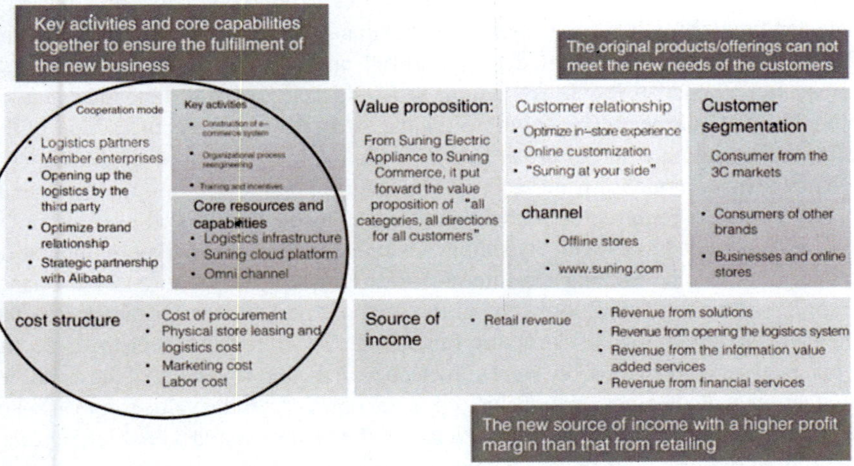

Fig. 5.5 The summary of the business model of Suning

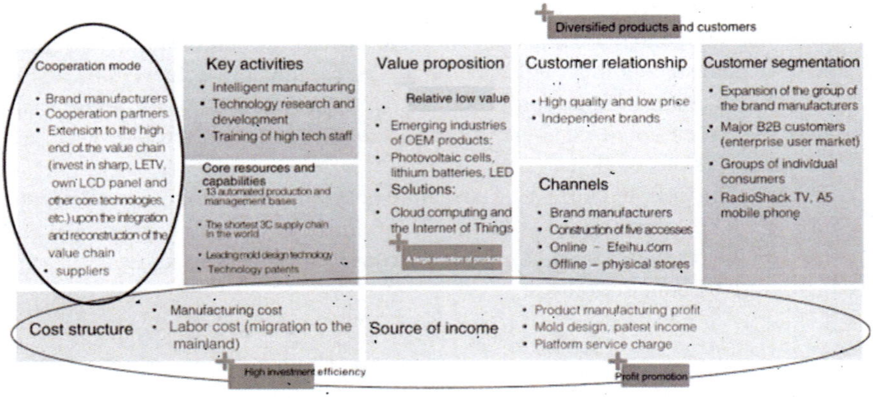

Fig. 5.6 The summary of the business model of Foxconn

partnership established with Taobao, Suning saw substantial improvement in its share and profitability.

The comparison of Foxconn's business model before and after the transformation can also be summarized as shown in Fig. 5.6.

Foxconn performed better in three aspects of its business model after continuous attempts though the transformation of its business model covers almost all aspects. First, in the financial aspect, especially in the aspect of optimizing the cost structure, Foxconn saw obvious effect; Second, in terms of expanding customer base, the cooperation with Huawei, OPPO/vivo, Xiaomi, and other customers has reduced its dependence on Apple, and the continuous growth of Chinese and Indian markets has improved the financial situation of FIH Mobile Limited; Third, FIH Mobile Limited returned to "its own core resources and capabilities". Based on maintaining the original world's shortest 3C supply chain and core manufacturing and cost management, FIH Mobile Limited accelerated the industrial upgrading of intelligent manufacturing, strengthened its R & D capabilities and mold design capabilities, and extended to the high end of the value chain through the integration and reconstruction of the value chain, aiming at the future industry 4.0 era to build its new core advantages.

The business model of Haidilao is shown in Fig. 5.7.

The customer requirements of the catering industry manifested even complex diversity. Haidilao has a relatively simple business model in the market segmentation of "hot pot". By optimizing the internal process of the back end and reasonably arranging all links of the supply chain, the goal of "no kitchens for the stores" has been achieved, with the cost structure fundamentally altered; At the same time, the humanized services of the front were enhanced with the improvement of the customer satisfaction and customer relationship, upon the practices of the value proposition of the enterprise. The continuous optimization of the business model enables Haidilao to maintain a certain advantage in the competition.

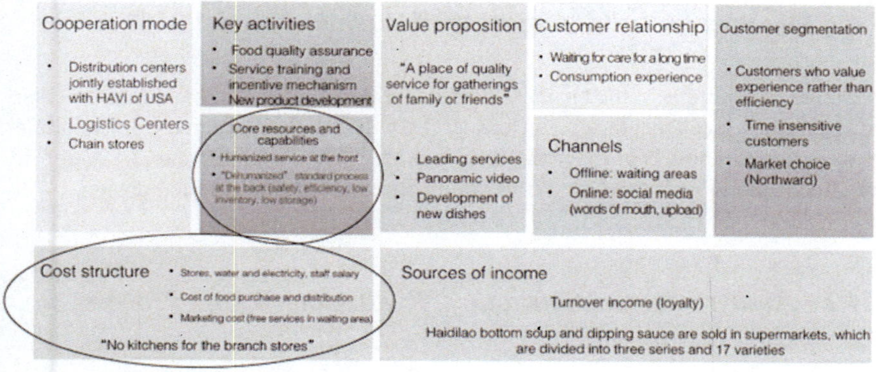

Fig. 5.7 The summary of the business model of Haidilao

After fully understanding the framework for the design of the business model, the seemingly complex business model of Huawei can be easily summarized, as shown in Fig. 5.8.

The business model of Huawei remains relatively stable despite it goes that "it will be strange for Huawei not to change for it will generally experience one big change every five years, one small change every three years." Due to Huawei's strategy with the "focus on the main channel", Huawei's business model mainly functions in the field of communication and information, with the expansion of its products and solutions from communication equipment to mobile terminals and cloud services, and the establishment of end-to-end solutions themed "cloud, channels, and terminals"; The businesses expand from domestic to global markets, with the customer base expanding from operators to industry customers and general consumers. In terms of revenue sources, Huawei is trying to move from cloud services to operation services, with a new profit model added and to be tested over time.

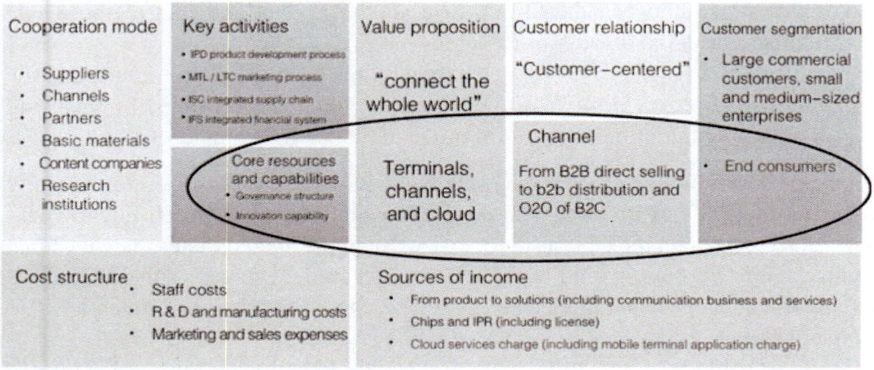

Fig. 5.8 The summary of the business model of Huawei

5.4 The way to Build a Successful Business Model

From the innovations of the business models for the above-mentioned famous enterprises, it can be seen that the changes generally will not take place in the nine modules of the business models at the same time, but start from modules 1 to 3. Therefore, we choose the most important four modules for analysis and detailed design.

5.4.1 Analyze the Cost Structure, Realize the Whole Process Cost Down

5.4.1.1 TCO Analysis

In the part of product strategy, we have analyzed the TCO of products. Here we will shift the focus onto the overall operating cost of enterprises. Both of the two can be calculated in a similar way, but with different meanings. The composition of TCO is as follows

$$\text{TCO} = \text{WACC}(\text{CAPEX} + \text{OPEX})$$

Note: WACC for Weighted Average Cost of Capital, CAPEX for Capital Expenditure and OPEX for Operating Expense.

- Capex belongs to one-time cost for equipment procurement in products, but from the perspective of the enterprise as a whole, it belongs to one-time investment fixed assets and infrastructure, both of which need to be depreciated and amortized annually.
- OPEX belongs to the annual routine expenditure on technical support, operation, guarantee, maintenance, training, labor cost, tax and so on.
- The difference between the OPEX of a single product and that of the whole enterprise lies in the breadth of its scope.
- Whether it is CAPEX or OPEX, all expenditures need to occupy funds, and the capital cost is reflected by WACC coefficient, which is determined by financing channels. Crowdfunding is a typical mode to reduce financing costs.

Fuyao Glass built its factory in the United States upon a choice made after carefully analyzing the TCO of its factory in the United States, during which Fuyao Glass found that that though the labor is more expensive in the United States than in China, the investment for buying land to build factories can be recovered through various government subsidies, and the energy price and comprehensive tax burden are also relatively low.

The reasonable reduction of tax costs is a common method to improve enterprise profitability. Generally, enterprises will choose areas with relatively low tax rates to register for reasonable tax avoidance. A typical example is Apple, which, through the establishment of a sales company in Ireland, reasonably avoids taxes by up to 38 billion US dollars every year. Another mode is to sell the hardware and software separately, which is typically represented by IBM, which takes advantage of its server software technology to control the profit of low-end servers at about 40%. By doing so, on the one hand, it has hit hardware equipment manufacturers like Huawei and Inspur in terms of sales, making them lose their price advantage or reduce their profitability; On the other hand, through the high profit from the sales of its software, the overall profit is maintained at a reasonable level. Since countries have different tax rates for the complete set of machines, hardware and software, the tax rate of the software is only about one-third of that of complete machine and hardware, which further improves the profit of software products. In terms of an export tax rebate, software products are also supported by more policies.

Therefore, enterprises need to design profit models and reasonably reduce various costs under the guidance of various national/international policies.

5.4.1.2 The trend of cost transfer

To reduce the cost effectively, we must consider the problem from the perspective of the whole process, but not from the part of it only. Huawei made detours in its early days, when in a cost reduction campaign, to reduce the cost of certain equipment, the R & D department cut out all the originally designed automatic detection circuit, remote monitoring and diagnosis function modules, and only retained the core business function modules, which greatly reduced the cost from the perspective of R & D, but brought a lot of trouble to the back-end technical support and operation and maintenance, and greatly increased the back-end service cost, in addition to the effects on customer satisfaction. Consequently, the cost was increased in general. In terms of structural cost reduction, the current days see several major trends.

1. **Enterprise level: enterprises of light assets**
    - Reduction of the investment in the production line through outsourcing of the production.
    - Reduction of CAPEX by leasing equipment and space.

For enterprises following this model, Xiaomi can be a typical example, whose production is almost completely outsourced, which is a very popular way in the early stage of the development of the enterprise. In this way, on the one hand, the initial capital investment can be reduced; on the other hand, resources can be concentrated in key areas. If the products launched are not welcomed by the market, the enterprise can make flexible adjustments. However, when the enterprise develops to a certain stage, a balance between self-production and outsourcing will generally come into being, so as to ensure the rapid verification of the products, rapid response to the market and increase the bargaining chips for business negotiation.

2. **Operation level: CAPEX transferred to OPEX**
   - To make up for the initial lack of funds.
   - Often to meet the needs of financial statements and business performance, such as to stabilize the stock price.
   - The result of the change of the mode of the decision-making on the investment, such as small amount purchase after centralized purchase of telecom operators.
3. **Product level: the transference of hardware assets to software assets (including design)**
   - The competitive advantages of enterprises were fully played. For example, IBM cracked down on low-cost hardware manufacturers such as Huawei, Inspur, and Lenovo by selling its servers at a gross profit of less than 40%, while achieving the goal of high profits through server software sales.
   - Adapted to the tax policy where tax is low for the software product, with a high export tax rebate.
   - Cost reduction in the whole process: The corresponding cost reduction measures were formulated upon the analysis of the cost structure and relationship of marketing, R & D, production, delivery, technical support and management. Through the research and development of chips and key modules, Huawei saw its profit of optical network products at more than 60% when there was generally only an average of 40% profit in the industry. The Kirin chip sets not only greatly reduced the cost of the mobile phones by Huawei, but also reduced the management cost of the supply chain and improved the supply security. Fuyao Glass has achieved a profit margin of 40% when the average profit margin of the industry is only 5% by improving the production process and optimizing the manufacturing process.

5.4.2 "Create Value for Customers" Upon Optimized Profit Model

Referring to Maslow's hierarchy of needs, the more the products can meet high-level needs, the greater the value of them to the customers. Especially for the mining and stimulation of customers' potential requirements, or the satisfaction to the requirements concerning the customers' life and death, the greater the customer value is, the stronger the premium capacity is, the simpler the profit model can be. For example, the cost of cocktail therapy (HAART) for AIDS is 300 thousand dollars a year, much higher than the sum of the price of individual drugs. This often requires sensitive market insights and huge R & D investments. Therefore, when designing a business model, the first core question to be answered is: what value does the product create for customers? How much is the customer willing to pay? On this basis, optimize the income mode, charging mode and pricing mechanism to achieve the optimization of business value.

5.4.2.1 Common ways for income

- Sales of valuables (physical goods or services);
- Leasing of valuables;
- Intellectual property license fee or software license fee;
- Operating revenue sharing;
- Membership fee/franchise fee;
- Royalty (such as the use of the brand, etc.);
- Auxiliary/subsidy funds (such as government subsidies, tax rebates, etc.).

When the type of income is determined, the mode of charging can take several combinations.

5.4.2.2 Common methods for charging

- One-time charge;
- Charge on time;
- Charge on quantity;
- Payment by installments;
- Payment after use;
- Multi-faceted charging mode (final consumers, manufacturers and channel merchants).

According to the market positioning and uniqueness of the product, we can also develop a more appropriate pricing mechanism to enhance the profitability of the product.

5.4.2.3 Common mechanisms for pricing

- Fixed pricing.

- Catalogue price
- Pricing on product characteristics
- Pricing on customer classification
- Pricing on quantity
- Pricing on binding sales.

- Dynamic pricing.
    - negotiation

- Benefits management and real-time market regulation
- Bidding
- Pay as you wish.

5.4.2.4 The evolution of the model for profits

Through the design of the mix of the mode for income, charging and pricing mechanism, the most reasonable profit mode would be determined, with different industries adopting specific profit models according to their own characteristics. The Internet has derived many new business models, which provide a typical example for the innovation of business models. There are four common models for Internet businesses.

1. **The long tail mode**

The typical representative of the long tail mode is Amazon online bookstore.

- High profits from the sales of niche products that are not originally covered;
- High-cost traditional stores are replaced by low-cost storage.

2. **The free mode**

The typical representative of the free mode is WeChat of Tencent.

- Free introduction of flow, with profit through other ways, such as advertising, value-added services based on big data mining.

3. **The platform mode**

The typical example of the platform mode is the iTunes of Apple.

- Businesses and individual developers both play dual roles as users and partners (content providers), in the Two-Side Model.

4. **Cross-border operation**

Cross-border operation is often conducted by an "outsider" who leads to the subversion and innovation of the business model by breaking the original rules after entering a certain field.

- Shi Yuzhu, a man from health care products to online game Zhengtu (Journey): Shi Yuzhu adopted the new mode of playing games for free but paying for props by subverting the traditional mode of paying on time. Besides, not only the game will be offered for free, but also the players will be paid, which was copied by most online games and mobile games.
- Qihoo 360 anti-virus V.S. Rising: Rising adopts the traditional software (also similar for hardware) sales mode, with payment and delivery (CD or license). Through the free anti-virus software, 360 has gathered popularity with the customers' desktops occupied and its revenue exceeding the sum of the previous

anti-virus industries by several times upon profits through 360 browser, search, navigation, etc.

- Taobao and eBay: The business model of eBay is "paid store + exclusive advertising over portal website". Considering the characteristics of the Chinese market, Taobao launched an innovative business model, namely "free store + grassroots website recommendation + credit guarantee", which lowered the threshold of entry for businesses and fully played the essence of digital marketing (increasing user base and attention, social media, SEO / natural ranking), with business miracles constantly created.

5.4.3 The construction of the core competence of the enterprises

To build a unique competitive advantage of an enterprise, we must first answer three questions: First, what materials, equipment, funds and resources does an enterprise need; Second, what needs to be built internally and what needs to be obtained externally; Third, what special competence does the enterprise have. Successful enterprises constantly evolve their own unique advantages through market competition.

- Customer base and customer viscosity/relationships, such as Taobao;
- Brand influence, such as Coca Cola;
- Intellectual resources, such as McKinsey;
- Technology patents, such as Qualcomm;
- Core technologies, such as Samsung's LCD and flash RAM, etc.;
- Core design capabilities and equipment, such as Foxconn mold technology, "Sky Whale" special equipment;
- Special resources, such as capital, land, government-business relationship;
- Corporate governance capabilities, such as process and IT for IBM, from application tools to competitiveness;
- Innovative model for profits.

It can be seen that the innovation of the profit models is only a part of the establishment of the competence of enterprises, and the business model cannot bring sustainable competitive advantage to enterprises for it is generally easy to copy. Returning to the essence of the business to create value for customers and build long-term internal core competitiveness is the best business model. Whether it is for innovation or for the establishment of the core competence, putting "customer at the center", breaking the conventions and thinking from the opposite are important mindsets.

The author re-summed the quaternion method for design upon reverse thinking proposed in *Blue Ocean Strategy* into RICE quaternion method, as shown in Fig. 5.9, which enterprises can follow, whose key point is the analysis of the key variables

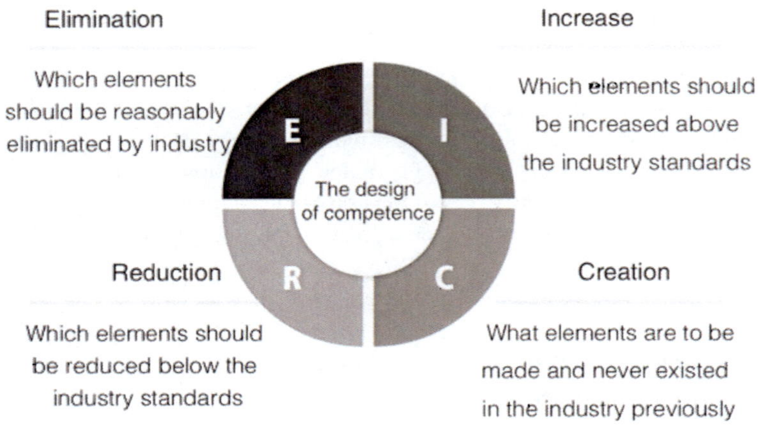

Fig. 5.9 The innovative quaternion analysis (RICE)

of the industry in which the enterprise is located, which can be multi-dimensional variables such as requirement points, solutions, competition points, investment points or value chain elements of subdivided customers, and can be illustrated through the following examples.

- Competition points: whether the industry focuses on superior customer value (function, performance, quality, etc.) or relatively low TCO.
- Market performance: whether the industry focuses on the customer base, number of active users, or customer satisfaction, loyalty, market share and profit.
- Resource advantages: whether the industry advantage is based on the reserve of physical resources, or superior skills and knowledge, superior intellectual resources and business processes.

Enterprises can use the method of quaternion analysis to design or reconstruct their core competence.

The first element of the quaternion analysis is the elimination, that is, which elements are recognized by the industry as elements that need to be eliminated. This is often an industry regulation established by industry associations to safeguard the interest chain.

The second element is reduction, that is, which elements are required to be reduced below the industry standards. This is sometimes even a special entry threshold set by leading enterprises on technical standards to prevent competition.

The third element is the increase, that is, which elements are required to be increased above the industry standards with its base to meet customer needs.

The fourth element is creation, that is, which elements never existed in the industry and are to be created to create value for customers and tap their potential needs.

We take the innovative design of Copycat Cellphones featured Dual SIM Dual Standby as an example to analyze the thinking process of RICE quaternion analysis method, as shown in Fig. 5.10.

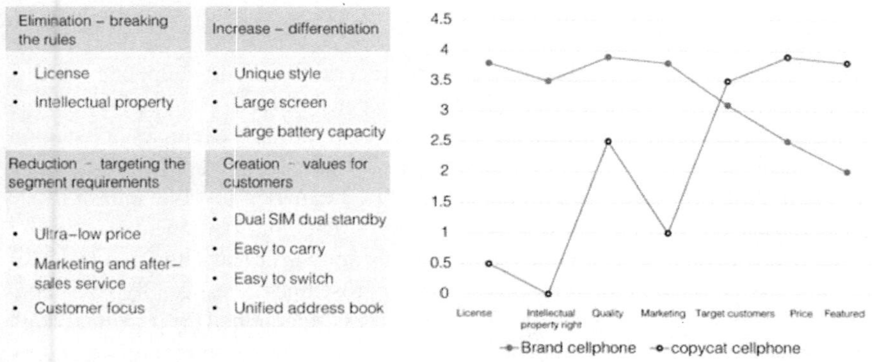

Fig. 5.10 The case of "dual SIM dual standby" RICE innovative design

1. Elimination—breaking the rules

In the early stage, the business of mobile phones belonged to the exclusive mode of operators and stood in a position of monopoly. In order to sell mobile phones, mobile phone manufacturers must obtain the mobile phone network access certificates of the operators, with their products generally sold through the channels of the operators. With the gradual opening of the market, especially in the 3G era when the lack of 3G mobile phones has seriously affected the development of the 3G business, more and more brand mobile phone manufacturers came to sell their products independently. In order to encourage the manufacturers for the engineering of more 3G mobile phones, the regulations over the operation have also been loosened, when the technology is gradually mastered by more manufacturers. Before the new laws and regulations, many characteristic manufacturers bypass the supervision through technical means, which promoted the prosperity of the mobile phone market.

Since most of the early domestic brand mobile phones were assembled with modules, there were few core intellectual property rights except the domestic standard TDM-SCDMA. Therefore, many copycat cellphones machines have successfully broken the inherent rules of the industry and won a large market share at that time. With the gradual standard regulation of the market and through the market selection process of "survival of the fittest", the surviving mobile phone manufacturers began to pay attention to R & D investment, patent application and intellectual property protection. If not, it is not easy for companies like Xiaomi to go abroad.

2. Reduction—targeting the needs of segment customers

For low-end users, the price of mobile phones can be greatly reduced by using low-cost chips and design schemes. When smartphones become the trend, mobile phones become "daily consumer goods". Upon ensuring the basic quality, the manufacturers basically give up the marketing and after-sales service, with the electronic market and maintenance stores shouldering the responsibilities responsible for the sales and services completely.

3. **Increase—differentiation**

Except for the differences in brands and appearances, the brand cellphones of that time presented nothing attractive, while the copycat cellphone equipped with large screens for game lovers, the mightier loudspeakers for morning exercises or listening to the radio, and bigger batteries for longer standby time won the popularity among users. Although most copycat cellphones stood in the market just like a flash in the pan, the practices that these weak manufacturers obtaining certain markets close to customers' needs by differentiated advantages are worth learning from by other enterprises. Meizu and Transsion are the typical representatives, especially Transsion, which, after the accumulation of "the first pot of gold", abandoned the previous rough development mode but maintained the differentiated competition mode oriented by customer requirements. In the African market, based on the consideration of the characteristics of African people's dark skin color and their passion in dancing, it enhanced its functions in photo taking and sound as a differentiated advantage, which won the acceptance of customers during its gorgeous transformation.

4. **Creation—Create values for customers**

In order to enjoy the favorite policies of different operators, or due to the needs of the circle of friends and business, many Chinese users keep mobile phones by different operators, which makes it troublesome to carry several phones at the same time. For example, when Huawei's sales personnel visit Unicom customers, they need to use Unicom mobile phones; When visiting customers of China Mobile, they need to keep mobile phones of China Mobile; Frequent entry and exit required constant changes of the SIM card, whose operation brought much inconvenienced, in addition to the constant synchronization and update of the address books of different mobile phones, which is time-consuming and laborious. Manufacturers of copycat manufacturers are the first to launch mobile phones featuring "dual SIM and dual standby", reflecting their extremely fast response and great innovation ability. The technology supporting dual SIM and dual standby were not only adopted by Huawei, Samsung and many other brand manufacturers, but also improves the switching control, unified address book, cloud synchronization and other functions on the basis of the original technology. In 2018, Apple had to lower its arrogant head to meet the requirements of dual SIM and dual standby in the Chinese market, with the release of the iPhone XR / XC mobile phones.

The essence of the design of the business model is to focus on customers and build core competence for both leading enterprises and backward manufacturers. At the product level, the extended $APPEALS model can be used to build the competence of products, while at the company level, under the guidance of the reverse thinking RICE quaternion analysis method, the specific direction of differentiated core competence can be found by determining the competitive elements of the industry (or the elements for the judgment of the enterprises by the customers). Different industries featured various factors for competence. In the TMT industry, the general factors for the competition include the function and performance of the products, brand, products type and solutions, products quality, customer relationship, sales channels, technical support, market coverage, innovation ability, financing level, supply

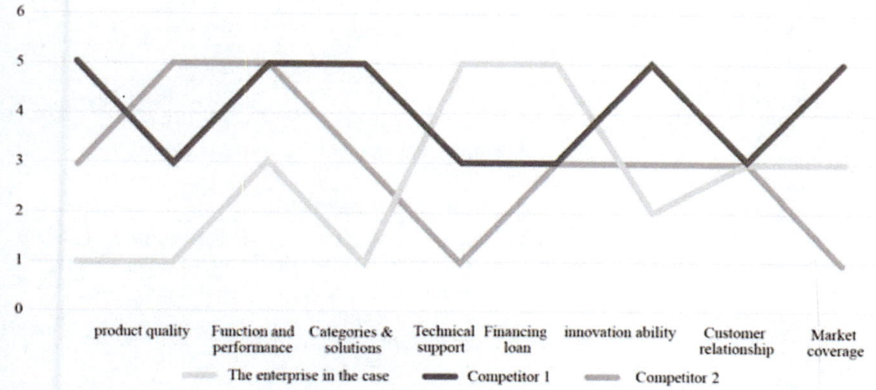

Fig. 5.11 The case of the construction of the differentiated competitive advantage for the enterprise

cycle, etc. From the side of the competitors, enterprises should distinguish the main learning benchmark, the main target, and the secondary competitors. In view of the main competitors, enterprises should find out the gap and build up the differentiated competitive advantage and core competence.

In the case shown in Fig. 5.11, the enterprise made a comparative analysis of two main competitors upon the determination of the main dimensions of the evaluation of customers when selecting suppliers. Being less-developed, the enterprise is certainly less known by the customers. So it is better not to include brand elements into the key elements for the competence of the less-developed enterprises, because it is often used as an excuse. Brand awareness, especially reputation, can be improved not by publicity, but by performance in the market. In addition, there is a significant gap between the enterprise and its competitors in terms of product quality, product types and solutions, and innovation capability. Through in-depth analysis and discussion, the enterprise was found having invested low in R & D for a long time, in addition to the low conversion rate of its R & D. Therefore, by increasing R & D investment, improving R & D management and assessment, the completeness of product types and solutions can be improved relatively quickly, and the gap in function and performance can be made up soon. To improve the quality of products, it takes a long time, as well as comprehensive improvement measures from design, R & D, trial production, production, technical services and other departments. In addition to increasing R & D investment, innovation ability needs continuous improvement and changes in innovative mindsets, key professionals, innovation mechanism and strategic strength, so as to truly build the core competitiveness of enterprises.

The principle for the construction of the core competence is also related to the industry and market positioning of the enterprise, which is similar to the choice of innovation strategy. See Table 5.2.

For an enterprise in the field of a single product and low cost needs to ensure the product quality, the engineering and manufacturing process of the cost advantage, reputation and customer relationship are the core competence. While for an enterprise

Table 5.2 The construction of the core competence matching with enterprise positioning

		Low cost	High cost
Scope of business	A wide product line or target market	Cost-leading • Integration and reconstruction of the value chain • Management system	Differentiation-leading • Core technologies • Brands
	A narrow product line or target market	Focus on costs • Customer relationship • Optimization of the and engineering and process of manufacturing	Focus on differentiation • Part-leading (to the extreme)

in an industry with a single product but high requirements for product differentiation, its core competence is the ultimate innovation and manufacturing capacity of its products, for which, the century-old small factories in Germany that provide permanent screws for high-speed rail can be very good examples. For an enterprise in the industry with a wide product line or a large variety of customers but low requirements on product differentiation, its core competence lies in its ability to control the external value chain and ecological chain, as well as its ability to manage different internal business sectors. Because involved in too wide a field, it is often necessary for the enterprise to go "from points to areas" to gradually strengthen its capacity in various sections. If it only wants to grow "bigger", the enterprise will easily fall into the quagmire of opportunism. For example, many family manufacturing enterprises in Zhejiang have gradually transformed from the original "doing whatever brings money" and pursuing the expansion of sales to the mode of "strengthening" themselves through diversified coordinated development. For an enterprise in the industry with a wide product line or a large variety of customers and high requirements for product differentiation, the enterprise must increase the investment in innovation and product R & D to ensure the leading advantage of multi-product differentiation, which is to build the core competitiveness, but it needs long-term capital investment and unswerving strategies. GE's strategy is the "top three" principle, for which it will resolutely shut down the business lines that can not be the top three in the industry.

5.4.4 Customer segmentation and customer selection

Huawei's "customer-centered" culture once confused some sales staff who had just arrived at the front line, for it seems they have to satisfy the customers for whatever they want. Ren Zhengfei explained that if "customers" want to take advantage of you all day, beat the price down at their will regardless of your life or death, or even want everything for free, then they are not customers, so why do you take them as the center? Therefore, it is the basis of the design of the business model to segment customers and meets the needs of the selected customers to achieve a win–win situation. The core issues of it are as follows.

- Who does the enterprise create values for?
- How to segment the market and customers to better meet customer needs?
- Which customers are to be served and which are to be ignored?

The methods of market segmentation in the industries are similar, and the common market segmentation elements are shown in Table 5.3.

The dimensions of B2B and B2C market segmentation are quite different. Generally, B2B market segmentation is more based on product, industry, country and the scale of customers. Comparatively, the B2C market segmentation can be much more complex, generally done by region, gender, age, occupation, income, education, etc. In the process of market segmentation, enterprises need to classify and sort different customers, find value customers, and implement different services to different customers, including the priority of requirements response.

Customer attraction and the competitive. position of enterprises in the eyes of customers can be used to segment and rank customers. Customer attraction includes

Table 5.3 The elements for market segmentation

Type of segmentation	Description	Examples(variables)
Geographic information	Market segmentation based on geographic location	Country, region, city, urban area, suburb, remote area
Demography	Market segmentation based on different demographic variables	Age, gender, income, education, social class, religion
Enterprise statistics	Market segmentation based on the specific variables of the enterprise	Number of employees, scale of the enterprise, large enterprises, SME
Behavior orientation	How customers buy and use products	Online shopping, price sensitive, old users, new users for the first time, non-users
Occasion (scenario)	Market segmentation according to requirements on product, way of purchase and usage of the product	Routine occasions, special occasions such as weddings, birthdays, celebrations, etc
Psychological orientation	Market segmentation based on lifestyle and personality	Shy, expressive, outdoor, single, athletic
Interest acquisition orientation	Market segmentation according to different requirements on the characteristics of the products	Convenience, economy, quality, image promotion, stimulation and taste
Industry characteristics	Market segmentation according to different industries	Government, finance, energy, education, retail

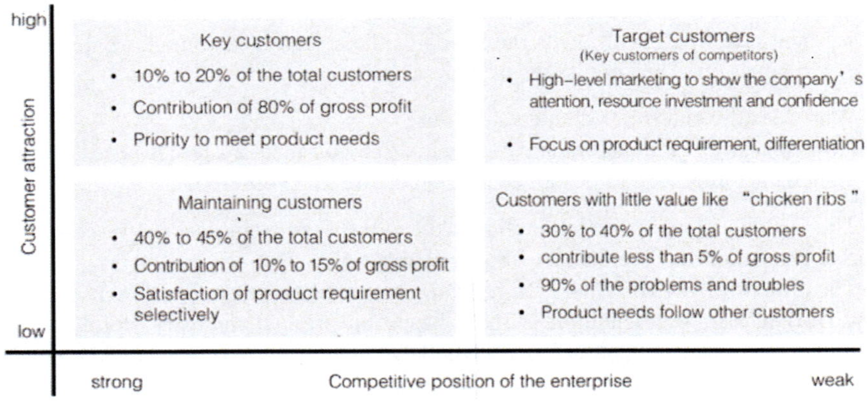

Fig. 5.12 The case for customer segmentation

market space (procurement volume), business growth rate, profitability, location, procurement method and process, customer financial status and reputation, etc. The competitive position of an enterprise includes product category, product performance, service quality, price, special services (such as technical consultation), brand image, experience, quality of sales personnel, quality of customer relationship, existing suppliers and competitive intensity. The enterprise in the case (as shown in Fig. 5.12) found its customers divided into the following four categories after long-term tracking.

Key customers: Key customers account for 10~20% of the total of customers, bringing 80% of the gross profit for the enterprise. The key people in the customer decision-making chain support the enterprise, especially the chairpersons and general managers. From the perspective of the plan of the investment, customers have maintained a medium and high-speed development in five years, with a strong intention to become a market leader. These customers belong to the value customers of the enterprise, so they need to give priority to meet the needs of these customers. In terms of the customer relationship, a strategic partnership should be built gradually through routine strategic communication and joint innovation between senior management of both sides.

Customers to be maintained: Accounting for 40% to 45% of the total customers, customers to be maintained contributed 10% to 15% of the gross profit to the enterprise. The sales ranking of such customers often changes, so it is necessary to find and cultivate potential value customers. By analyzing the industry changes and sharing the successful experience of value customers, we can selectively meet the needs of customers, so that customers can build differentiation ability in the competition. The enterprise needs to form a community of shared interests with potential customers for long-term cooperation and common growth. Some potential maintenance customers can be marketed through integrators, ISV and other channels to save the cost of customer management and sales.

Customers with little value just like the "chicken ribs": Accounting for 30% to 40% of the total customers, these customers contributed less than 5% of the gross profit, but created 90% problems and troubles related to contract management, technical support and complaints, as well as delivery and payment collection. This group of customers follows other customers in terms of the requirements, which calls for no special development. The causes of the problems should be investigated, and the problems related to the responsibility of the enterprise should be handled orderly. Indirect marketing mode is more used, which can be carried out through integrators, value-added distributors, distributors, and even networks.

Customers with potential value: They may be the value customers of the competitors or the large customers that the enterprise has not yet reached to. Customers in this group generally invest a lot and operate well, but the competition for them is also fierce. As enterprises are relatively weak, they need to invest more marketing efforts. Therefore, the enterprise needs to carefully screen these customers to be the "right ones". The enterprise should choose key customers for its investment, with priority given to them to meet the needs of the key customers, and build competence differentiated from that of the existing suppliers.

Customer segmentation is helpful for enterprises to concentrate superior resources, build competitive advantages in products and marketing for improved output and reduced costs, and better service and satisfaction of high-quality customers to ensure the effective operation of the business model.

The construction of enterprise cooperation mode and ecological chain is becoming more and more important in the development of modern enterprises, though cooperation mode is not elaborated on in this section. Establishing strategic partnerships with investors, value customers, key channels and core supply chain, or even allying with some competitors, can resist economic fluctuations, reduce business risks and hold a favorable position in the competition. The strategic partnership between Suning and Alibaba, JD.com and Tencent has basically determined the pattern of the retail industry. The strategic cooperation between Huawei and BOE in the 5G mobile phone project has put great pressure on Apple and Samsung. Xiaomi's ecosystem is even more complex, involving a large number of products and partners, which makes Xiaomi develop today, and also presents tests for its future direction. In a word, value chain cooperation is a very important module in the business model. Enterprises need to have the mindset of open cooperation to formulate clear cooperation strategies, so as to build a healthy enterprise ecological chain.

Business operation is a mixture of the nine ways shown in the business model of this chapter. The business model is a blueprint, which defines the overall operation mode and characteristics of the enterprises. At the same time, it should be noted that the successful design of the business model generally starts from two to three modules, rather than comprehensively. Some scholars described the development models of successful enterprises in China into five types: specialization model, diversification model, internationalization model, platform model and ecological model. No matter what the model is, it provides entrepreneurs with a thinking framework to formulate and optimize the business model.

The change of business model means the change of business philosophy. Therefore, the business model needs the enterprise strategy to point out the realization path, and to be implemented year by year through the business plan. The changes of the business model are often accompanied by reengineering of the original process system and IT system. In the 2C business of financial industry for general consumers, IT system is the key enabling tool to realize its new business model and the embodiment of its core competitiveness, while for the digitization, intelligent manufacturing upgrade of the enterprises, IT often determines the success or failure of the transformation. For example, Predix, the industrial Internet platform of GE, not only supports the internal digital transformation of GE, but also serves as a new source of revenue after its opening to the outside world. The changes of business model also need organization reengineering, and can make great changes to the target traction and evaluation incentive mechanism of enterprises.

Chapter 6
Huawei's System for the Planning of Strategies

6.1 Huawei's Strategy Management System and System Framework for Strategy Formulation

6.1.1 Why It is Often Difficult to Get the Strategies Implemented?

When the enterprise is small, "survival" is the biggest strategy. But many enterprises with a history of more than ten years of development, stable annual income and assets of over RMB 1 billion still have no proper corporate strategy. Some companies preparing to get listed will invite well-known foreign consulting companies to make business plans when they are going on the roadshow, but merely with the purpose to tell a good "story" to raise the stock price. Some listed companies even employ consulting companies or financial companies to help them formulate strategies, which are never really implemented to guide business development. One of the main reasons why the strategy is not implemented is that enterprises have never had one in its real sense, for many enterprises are used to using "tactical diligence to cover up their laziness in strategy". Even in some enterprises that have formulated strategies, entrepreneurs often complain that only they themselves are concerned about their development strategies, while most executives do not understand their ideas, so the strategies cannot be implemented. With the span of the management widened upon the continuous development of the enterprises, how to use strategy to guide the daily operation of enterprises and extricate themselves from complicated affairs has been on the minds of many entrepreneurs. According to statistics, 90% of strategies for China's enterprises failed to be implemented, upon the main reasons as follows.

- In the process of formulating the strategy, the leadership spent little time discussing the strategy and did not reach a strategic consensus with the top management. Consequently, the process of the formulation and implementation of the strategy often featured "three pats", that is, entrepreneurs patting their heads when setting

L. Tao, *Huawei Wisdom*,
https://doi.org/10.1007/978-981-19-1169-9_6

strategic goals, the senior managers patting their chest to show their determinations when assigned tasks, and in the end personnel at all levels patting their butts to show their innocence when the strategic goal cannot be achieved, with entrepreneurs being finally aware that the original goal was irrational and impractical, but to motivate everybody while others trying to find excuses to cover for themselves.

- The strategies were not formulated upon thorough consideration, with the key initiatives hard to be implemented or rated. The objectives and the implementation of the strategies should not overlap each other, with no effective action support and strategic decoding. Some enterprises prefer to set grand goals upon divergent strategies. Most enterprises made financial objectives the most exact strategies. However, if the enterprises paid too much attention to financial indicators, but failed to combine resource budget with objectives organically, it will lead to the phenomenon of "pushing the horses to run while not get them well-fed", failing to can't play the role of the strategies externally as "layout" and internally as "arrangements". Many enterprises often take their vision as the enterprise strategies, being not clear and focused, either too simple or too comprehensive. Generally speaking, nearly 70% of enterprises have relatively clear strategic vision, and more than 50% of enterprises have formulated relatively clear strategies to achieve the vision goals, but only about 18% of enterprises believe that their strategies have been implemented effectively.
- Lack of management system and organizational support for the strategies. The strategies were made in an irrational process of a short time and the chaotic logic order with the absence of the organizational responsibility. The quality and efficiency of the discussion over strategies will be affected for the lack of objective basis in strategy making and the daily accumulation of important external and internal information. Because the team is constructed in a haste, there will be no regular supervision, feedback, and correction in the process of strategy implementation. The strategies, based on the imitations of the so-called "classic model" upon strategic analysis lacking of the concise and practical tools for the methods, tools, templates, and other basic capabilities of strategic analysis have not yet been accumulated and optimized, are not practical and cannot be visualized.
- The objectives and the assessment of the strategies are out of line with each other. In addition to the apportionment of financial objectives, many enterprises still lack a logical strategic decoding process, especially the departments of the non-financial index. Only about 25% of managers connect corporate strategy with departmental goals, and departments of the enterprises never have the idea of joining with each other for the implementation of the corporate strategy. Only 5% of the grassroots employees at the level of strategy implementation understand the enterprise strategy and the relationship between individual assessment indicators and enterprise strategy and department goals.

6.1.2 *The Difficult Development of the Management System for the Strategies of Huawei*

Huawei, like many Chinese enterprises, has gone through many detours and experienced three stages in the development of its system for the formulation and implementation of its strategies.

The first stage with no strategies. A small number of senior executives of the company formulate strategies through meetings and discussions, with over fulfillment of the targets every year. Enjoying the "happy worries", they believe it is not important to formulate strategies for the enterprise, so the "office for the planning of the strategies for the product" by personnel appointed from outside of the enterprise turned out to be an "office of nonsense".

The second stage with strategies tangible but soulless. The ancients said that "people without long-term care must have immediate worries", while "people who have no immediate concerns must have long-term worries" just confirms the strategic crisis following "happy worries". After experiencing "internal and external troubles" such as PHS strategic decision-making, GSM and CDMA/TD-SCDMA strategic swing, and the leaving of the company's high-level managers, Huawei's three-year strategic "801 plan" made in a haste together with the strategic department established are merely an expedient measure for enterprise's $10 billion valuations and the introduction of strategic investment, but not really to service the business development, therefore, it is inevitable that the strategy and tactics are not matching each other well. To prove the significance of its existence, the strategy department applies for topics at various high-level meetings. The review of the company's three-year strategy report was also down with little participation and recognition of the top leaders.

The third stage with closed-loop management from strategy to implementation. To improve the capability of strategic planning, Huawei form closed-loop management between the strategies and the implementation of them upon the introduction of the methods, tools and templates from IBM, Accenture and Merce, and then extended the strategic organization system to regional organizations through the introduction of seed personnel and training, upon the consideration of the actual requirements of the product line and the requirements of actual regional goals, so as to realize the combination of strategy and campaign, the combination of objectives and resources, and the combination of objective and assessment. Great changes have taken place in the function of strategy, from trend intelligence analysis in the early stage to providing decision-making reference for headquarters in R&D investment, human resource planning and supply chain prediction in the medium term, and then to achieving collaborative strategic planning from headquarters to product line and front-line areas in the later stage. The strategic planning and business plan are effectively linked, and the strategic objectives and key measures are decomposed into the smallest combat units and individuals through strategic decoding, so that the whole staff can "march together" in the strategic direction of the enterprise. Strategy formulation has become a top project and a key means to enhance the leadership of leading cadres. The gradual

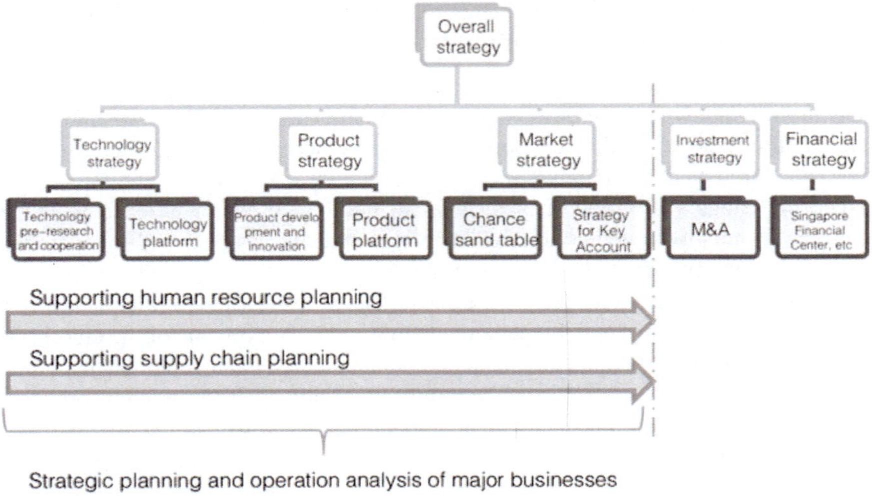

Fig. 6.1 The scope of the strategic planning of the main business

formation of the strategic behavior habits of the chief executives of the first level departments enables the whole enterprise to better balance the short, medium, and long-term interests, with the assessment of the strategic objectives clearer, which lays the organizational foundation for the strategic transformation of "the front line calling for support".

Huawei's three-year strategic plan mainly focuses on the planning and operation of its main business. The investment strategy and the main business strategy are coordinated, but relatively independent. The business scope of the enterprise's strategic planning is shown in Fig. 6.1.

The enterprise put the focuses on the main product strategy and market strategy, as well as supporting technology strategy, supply chain planning and human resource planning.

The first step of the formulation and implementation strategies is to formulate high-quality enterprise strategies. Therefore, the following three necessary conditions must be met.

6.1.2.1 Stable Teams

It is necessary to define a fixed role to undertake the organizational formulation, capacity building and routine management of the enterprise's strategy, including core members and peripheral members. When the enterprise is small, special strategic planning roles can be set up in the enterprise development department, business planning department, or president's office according to the organizational settings of different enterprises. When the enterprise reaches a certain scale, it should establish an independent strategy department, which serves as the secretary office of the enterprise's strategic planning committee, being responsible for the regular management of strategy. The strategic planning project team is composed of representatives from the strategic department, marketing management, product planning, human resources, operation management or finance departments, as well as fixed representatives from production, service, supply chain and other departments added as expansion members as needed.

6.1.2.2 Advanced Methods

As the old saying goes, "If you want to do a good job, you must first sharpen your tools". There are many methodologies, tools and templates for strategic planning. After integrating the methods of IBM, Accenture and Merce, and even learning from the templates of Microsoft, Huawei finally chose the business leadership model (BLM) of IBM, which has similar equipment manufacturing experience with Huawei, as the theoretical framework for strategic planning. However, BLM is a system model to help enterprises build strategic thinking, which cannot be directly used in the formulation of strategic reports. Some enterprises directly copy the BLM model, resulting in the strategic report as a hodgepodge of all aspects. On the basis of this model, Huawei summed up the key steps of strategy formulation of "five viewings (market, customer, trend, competition and self) and three decisions (strategy, target and core control point)", which makes the strategic planning closer to reality with highlights of the key points. In addition to formulating corporate strategy, Chinese enterprises especially need to closely integrate strategy with the business plan and target assessment. Therefore, in terms of strategy decoding, BSC and BEM are more popular, whose core ideas are similar, but the level of BSC is clearer and the structure of BEM is more systematic.

6.1.2.3 Rich and Accurate Sources of Information

After introduced the above advanced methodology, Huawei encountered a common problem for Chinese enterprises in the practical application of it, that is, the lack of necessary market data, competition data and other information, making the seemingly good visualization graphics and tools useless. To solve this problem, on the one hand, enterprises need to use third-party data, such as data from the authoritative market research company, investment bank analysis and consulting company analysis; On the other hand, enterprises need to establish an internal market intelligence system, which is a sustainable and most accurate data source; Thirdly, enterprises need to optimize the methods and tools of strategic planning in turn, and they can use qualitative and quantitative methods to adapt to the current situation of Chinese enterprises. This also needs a stable organizational system and IT as support to ensure long-term capacity and data accumulation.

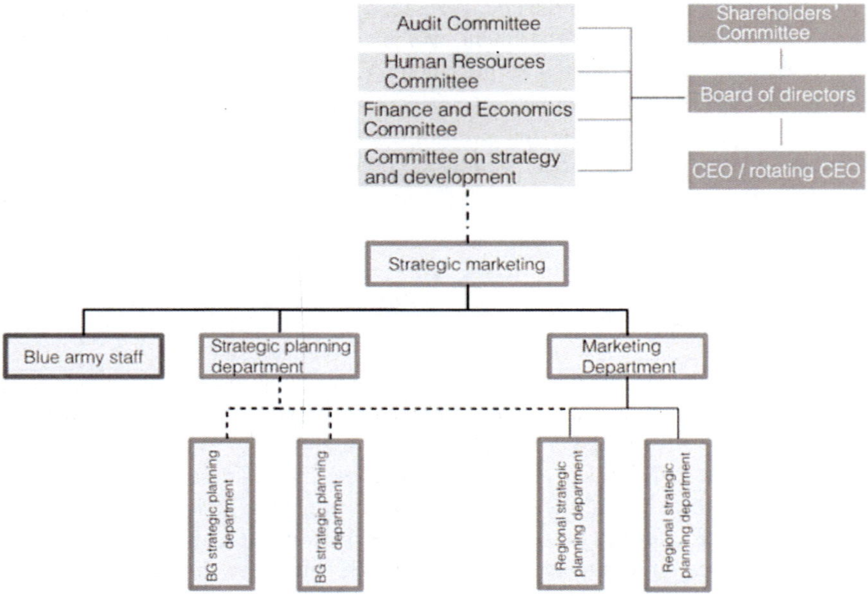

Fig. 6.2 Huawei's strategic organization system

After years of evolution, Huawei established a relatively complete strategic organization system, as shown in Fig. 6.2.

Huawei's strategic management system is divided into three levels, with the top decision-making level as the company's strategy and development committee, the second level strategic marketing department as the daily secretary office of the strategy and development committee, which is responsible for the organization and implementation of high-level theory-discussing meeting, strategic planning, strategy decoding and management in the process of strategy implementation. In this layer, the strategic planning department is the implementation subject of the daily management of strategic planning, while the blue army staff, as the role B of strategic planning, can find the problems and major risks existing in the strategy formulation and implementation of the enterprise from different perspectives, and escort the healthy development of the main business. The third level of the strategic organization goes deep into the three BGs and major market regions. The next level of product line and marketing department also have corresponding roles, which are subordinate to the product planning department and regional marketing department, and receive the guidance of strategic planning department in the business. Such a three-level organization realizes effective feedback of information from bottom to top and implementation of strategy from top to bottom.

6.1.3 System Framework of Strategy Making

Ren Zhengfei stressed that we should "cut off" the hands and feet of senior cadres, leaving only their heads to look up at the starry sky, to form insights into the market, to plan strategies, and to devise strategies. To establish a strategic mindset, first of all, six strategic questions should be raised:

(1) Have you foreseen the future trends and changes, and have profound and original insights?
(2) Have you defined the market segments/customers and given full play to your own advantages?
(3) Is the relationship between strategic decisions and scientific planning balanced?
(4) Are uncertainties considered and alternatives evaluated objectively?
(5) Is there a clear action plan and resource planning?
(6) Has a firm implementation system been established and a contingency correction mechanism been established?

To improve the ability of strategy formulation and implementation, Huawei introduces the business leading model BLM for strategy formulation, whose system architecture is shown in Fig. 6.3.

This model covers the main aspects of management, and can be used for work planning of almost any business unit, from culture (atmosphere) and values to key tasks. BLM defines eight interactive aspects of enterprise strategy formulation and implementation, which are strategic intention, market insight, innovation focus, business design, key tasks, formal organization, personnel, atmosphere and culture.

First, strategic intention serves as the starting point of strategic thinking, which generally includes medium and long-term strategic vision, strategic outline and specific strategic objectives. These strategic objectives should be adjusted appropriately according to the market results of last year's strategy implementation,

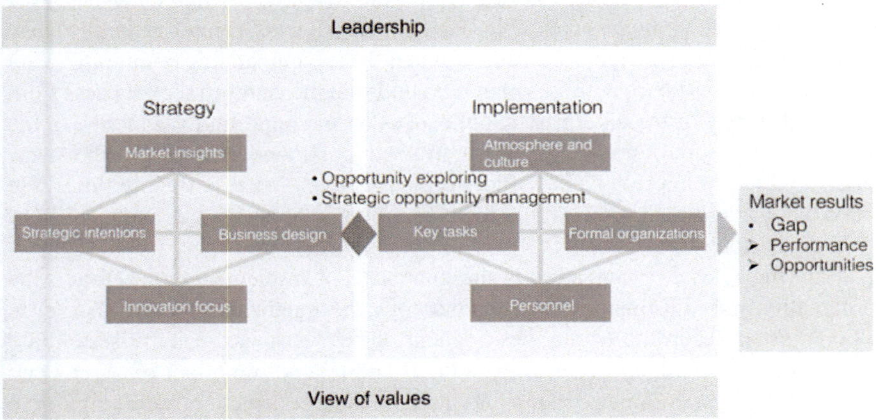

Fig. 6.3 Business Leading Model (BLM)

including the achievement of performance, the gap with objectives and competitors, and the change of major opportunities. Besides financial indicators, strategic objectives should also include market position, brand value and other indicators. Good strategic planning begins with the statement of good strategic intention and the expression of strategic objectives, which is the first step of strategic planning.

Second, market insight determines the depth of strategic thinking, which can be analyzed from the macro situation, technology and market trends, customer requirement changes, competition and other dimensions. This is for a clear understanding of the future opportunities and possible challenges and risks of the enterprise, perception and explanation of what is happening in the market and its impact on the future of the company.

Third, the focus of innovation is to determine whether the key point of innovation is product leading innovation, customer close innovation, excellent business innovation or category innovation according to the strategic positioning of the enterprise, whose purpose is to create value for customers and form the differentiated competitive advantage of cost enterprises in meeting customer needs. The "open" "customer-centered" innovation is the best innovation model for Chinese enterprises.

Fourth, business design is the key foothold of strategic thinking. On the basis of market insight and innovation focus, enterprises should choose the right customers, the right products/services and the right profit model. The good business design needs to answer two basic questions: can new business design be based on existing capabilities? If not, can enterprises get the new capabilities they need to develop their strengths and avoid their weaknesses?

Fifth, the key task is the key link between strategy and execution, which presents the key tasks and time nodes in strategy execution, including expansion opportunities of strategic opportunities, key activities at the customer level, specific requirements of internal operation efficiency and process transformation, key tasks of intellectual resource development, etc. The core of this part is the identification of strategic opportunities and the formulation of a strategic sand table. All measures and important tasks are carried out around strategic opportunities. Ren Zhengfei attaches great importance to the strategic sand table. He believes Huawei cannot generally view strategic commanding heights, but rather divides these commanding points into many positions, analyzes them, proposes plans and finds out measures to seek success from reality. All levels of the enterprise should focus on the opportunity window. In the future, Huawei should not only make a strategic commanding point on the sales, but also allow the representative office to plan its own strategic opportunities. He hoped that leaders at all levels would focus on strategic opportunities and take short, medium and long-term measures.

Sixth, the formal organization is the guarantee of implementation. Due to the optimization and adjustment of enterprise strategy, the organization system also needs to be adjusted according to the development of new business. Enterprises should not only ensure the input of human resources and related important resources, but also carefully design the leadership and human resource structure according to the characteristics of new business. At the same time, they should also establish the corresponding organizational structure, management system, management system and assessment standards, otherwise, the effects of the implementation will be greatly reduced.

Seventh, talents should have the corresponding skills to carry out the strategy, including the description of skills and the formulation of measures to acquire, cultivate, motivate and retain talents. Huawei has different requirements and definitions for key talents in the process of its three important strategic transformations. The first is the product strategy transformation (marked by IPD), which focuses on Solution Responsibilities, product planning experts and system engineers. The second is the globalization transformation, with the emphasis on the middle and high-level cadres with cross-cultural management skills. The third is the transformation of the business model. In BG, channel management experts, industry experts and solution experts are the key points; In consumer BG, industrial design, O2O marketing, channel and store management are the key points of talent supplement. Talent planning plays an increasingly important role in the implementation, but also should move forward, and should be involved in the early stage of strategic development.

Eighth, atmosphere and culture. Managers need to pay attention to every sector of the enterprise from the enterprise as a whole to single departments. The common management styles are compulsive, pioneering, coaching and authorized. In the era of a knowledge-intensive economy, most successful enterprises have formed an atmosphere and culture of openness, authorization and sharing. However, in the process of formulating the strategy, enterprises should not cover everything, but leave the relevant contents to be reflected in the key measures and the reform of assessment methods.

With the establishment and gradual improvement of the strategic organization system, Huawei's strategy making ability has been significantly improved through the guidance of consulting companies and the practical application of strategic tools and methods. The corresponding strategy making steps, processes and IT systems have been gradually improved, which makes the strategy making and implementation carried out orderly and safely. The steps and key points of strategic management are shown in Fig. 6.4.

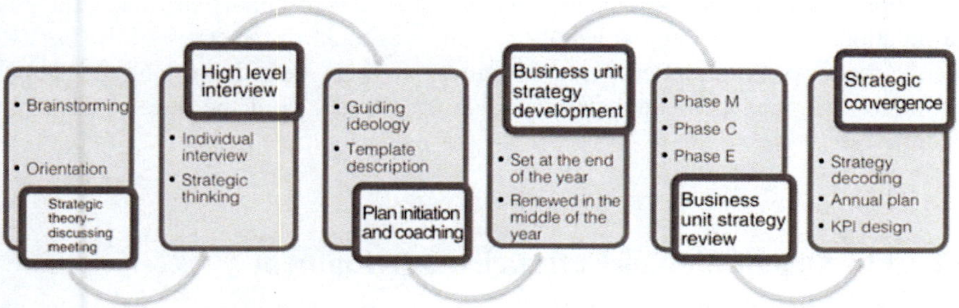

Fig. 6.4 Main steps of strategy formulation

Huawei starts the company's theory-discussing meetings at the end of each year, during which the strategic marketing department, investment cooperation department, future network research department and other main staff systems carry out necessary situation analysis and guidance to forming the guiding ideology of annual strategic planning and major research projects after the full discussion among the main business leaders at the meeting according to the information they each got. The company's Strategic Planning Department officially launched the annual strategic planning and issued the annual planning work calendar, providing annual strategic guidance and report template (including steps, tools and methods). The strategic part of each business unit starts and organizes the three-year strategic planning of the business department, and sets up strategic review points at the main nodes of external market analysis, competition analysis and internal core control point design. The head of the department presides over the review and determines the final key measures. After the review and revision, the annual strategic planning (SP) baseline is formed. On this basis, the company formulates the annual business plan (BP). After strategic decoding, the company undertakes the strategic objectives step by step and forms the annual assessment index. The company generally completes the signing of performance targets in the first quarter. Strategic reports will be greatly updated in the middle of the year, while the business plan will be continuously monitored at monthly meetings, and necessary upgrading and adjustment shall be made quarterly. The formulation and implementation management of strategic planning and business plan has become the routine work of each major leader. Through continuous re-selection, strategic and business plan formulation, process monitoring, result review and re-evaluation, the strategic formulation is no longer a time-consuming and arduous assault work, and various market data and competition data are no longer "patted" out randomly. The improvement of the accuracy of strategic planning can make the R&D layout, the search of investment target, talent planning and supply chain plan of the back end more purposeful and efficient, and the combination of strategy and tactics will be more closely linked.

In the process of its development, Huawei has experienced many strategic and tactical mistakes. However, under the guidance of the "customer-centered" business philosophy, Huawei has developed a set of corrective mechanisms from strategy formulation to strategy implementation, which ensures the success of Huawei's overall strategy. Entrepreneurs are not gods, so it is very important to establish a strategic management system suitable for the stages of the development of enterprises.

6.2 The Orientation of Enterprise Development Determined by Strategies

Many enterprises claim to have strategies, but after analysis, it is often found that there are many deficiencies. What is strategy? Strategy is that an enterprise should first understand its position in the market, what its future goal is, what path to take for its goal, and what is its difference from other competitors. Strategy is the way for an organization to achieve its vision and mission, including a series of goals and resource allocation. Michael Porter added the following to the strategy.

- Determination on the organization's unique value orientation (product leadership, operational excellence, or customer intimacy) and identification of a clear profit model.
- Clear choices for customers, products/services and regions.
- The strategy of competition and differentiation should be formulated upon the competitive position.

After the enterprise develops to a certain scale, strategy formulation focuses on "strategy", which needs to be specific and clear about what the enterprise should do and what not. Huawei's strategy is the "main channel" strategy, emphasizing the principle of phased focus and pressure.

How to make a good strategy? This problem has been perplexing many enterprises. Especially when enterprises are in the transition period or encounter development problems, they would rush to make strategies, so the perspective of strategy formulation is often how to make enterprises out of difficulties as soon as possible, which just violates the taboo of strategy formulation. The starting point of enterprise strategy formulation must be to create value for customers and develop themselves by satisfying customers. Creating value for customers is nothing more than two points, either reduce the overall operating costs of customers, or create new value for them. After defining the basic points of strategy formulation, choosing reasonable and effective strategy formulation methods and tools can help enterprises to systematically sort out and think about strategies, logically output key implementation measures and avoid strategic blind spots. After comparing and integrating the strategic planning methodologies of several consulting companies, Huawei integrated the BLM methodology as the main tool of strategic planning on the basis of the original MM process of market management. However, BLM is too large and comprehensive, so the formulation of strategy needs both systematic thinking and emphasis. By summing up the experience of Huawei and other Chinese enterprises in strategy formulation, the main work steps of enterprise strategy and business plan formulation can be summarized as shown in Fig. 6.5.

The whole process is divided into four parts: strategic analysis, strategic decision-making, arrangement (resource planning), strategy and business plan matching.

6.2.1 Strategic Analysis

When formulating its annual strategy, an enterprise should first clearly describe its strategic intention.

Fig. 6.5 The major steps of the formulation of enterprise strategy and business plan

6.2.1.1 Strategic Intention

Under the guidance of the enterprise vision, through the review and summary of the implementation of the strategy in the past years, combined with the annual strategic guiding ideology formed by the strategic retreat, a series of strategic objectives are initially set as an important input for strategy formulation.

Relying on its position as an innovation leader, Apple is not pursuing the largest market share, but maintaining its profit level, and seizing 80% of the smartphone market profit. Samsung, by its advantages in the chip, display screen, memory along the industrial chains, strives to occupy the first place in the global smartphone market share, ensuring the overall income and profitability of the enterprise.

1. General Description of Strategic Vision and Objectives

Compared with these international leading enterprises, many Chinese enterprises, based on their own development status, generally adopt the following ways to describe their strategic intention and business vision.

- The long-term development goal is to "maintain the healthy and sustainable development of the enterprise".
- The development goal of the next three years is to significantly improve the overall business, with the annual sales revenue reaching RMB 10 billion within three years, and the market share of the main business reaching more than 18%.
- In the future a certain year, the competitive strength of the products in strategic key markets reached the leading position, with the sales of its products in the industries of A and B topping in China as the first brand of domestic enterprises.

The strategic review is very important in this process, during which enterprises should examine the implementation of the strategies of the previous year, analyze the causes of the problems through root cause analysis, and formulate measures for the improvement in the new annual strategic plan and avoidance of the strategic risks.

2. Strategic Review: A Structural Root Cause Analysis

When summarizing and reviewing the past performance, enterprises often fall into the listing and comparison of financial indicators, but not analyzing the root causes of these financial indicators. For this reason, Balanced Score Card (BSC) will be introduced here. BSC is a management tool as well as a mindset to solve problems invented by Robert Kaplan and David Norton of Harvard Business School, with aims to find out the shortcomings and key points for the improvement of the enterprise's operation from the four dimensions of finance, customer, internal operation and learning and growth, so as to serve as an important input for key strategic initiatives for the continuous promotion of the implementation of the strategies and the healthy and orderly development of enterprises. Figure 6.6 shows the failure in analyzing the root cause of strategic objectives in the process of strategic review with BSC.

Judging from the dominant financial indicators of the enterprise in the case company, the enterprise has suffered serious profit decline. Through the BSC root cause analysis, the following problems can be found.

- Financial dimension: The enterprise found out the important financial indicators which play a key role in the operation and development of the company from the financial perspective. From the financial perspective, the decrease of the profit results from the fact that the sales growth of new products fails to meet the expectation and the slow sales outstanding due to the delay of product acceptance.
- Customer dimension: From the perspective of the customers, the enterprise found out the major factors for the failure to meet the important financial indicators of the enterprise. The product lack of competence with low customer satisfaction, resulted in the unwillingness of the customers for the large scale, as well as the

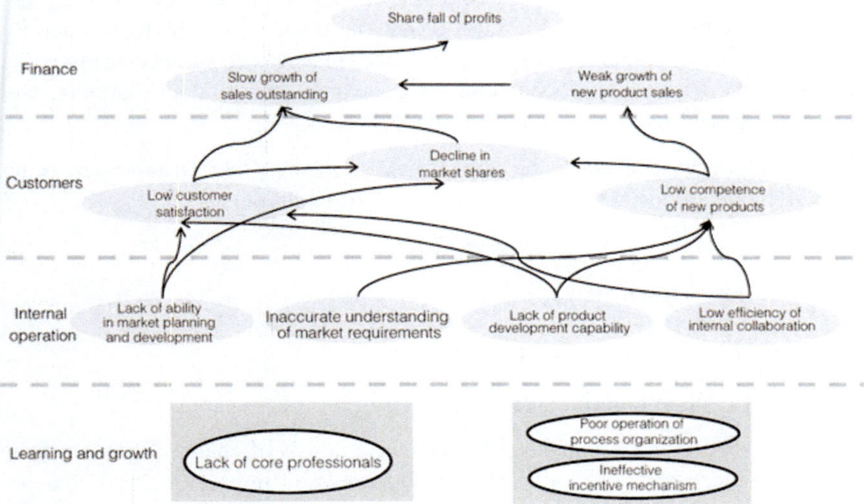

Fig. 6.6 The case of the root cause analysis in the strategic review

low share of the market. In addition, many quality problems appeared from new products with functions to be perfected, resulting in the delay of acceptance and payment collection.

- Internal operation dimension: From the perspective of internal operation, the enterprise found out the imperfect process that affected the financial goals and customer goals of the enterprise. Several factors will contribute to the low competence of the new products, of which in the front lies the lack of responsible departments in requirement collection, analysis and decision-making, and the lack of long-term attention and analysis of customer requirement, which leads to the inaccurate perception of the market requirement and the inability to form differentiated competitive advantages, while in the process of the development of the products, the lack of reliable forecast of sales volume, insufficient accumulation of key technologies, resulting in insufficient R&D investment, and no competitive advantage concerning the function and quality of the products, and in the back-end marketing, because of the lack of necessary marketing materials and new product sales incentives, the front-line sales staff is not to and will not sell new products.
- Learning and growth dimension: From the perspective of learning and growth, the enterprise found out the insufficiencies in ability and motivation to support the effective operation of the company, which affected the completion of customer goals and financial goals. Through the analysis of the above reasons, in the key measures of strategic planning, a three-level requirement management mechanism and IT system from front-line sales to R&D should be clearly defined, with the product planning organization of the marketing department as the first person responsible for requirement management and product planning. A two-way commitment between sales and R&D should be formed, that is, the front line's commitment to requirement acquisition and sales tasks, and the commitment of R&D over the function and quality of the products. At the same time, special incentive policies to the sales of new products should be formulated by the enterprise. In human resource planning, the plan should be necessarily made clear for the training and acquisition of the experts for product planning, key technology, and marketing for new products.

Through root cause analysis, the countermeasures can be formed and taken as the important inputs of business design and key task formulation.

6.2.1.2 Market Insights

1. Analysis of the Trend of the Market

It is generally done in four dimensions.

(1) Macro environment analysis: Through the analysis of changes in the macro-environment, mainly in PESTEL dimensions, the impact of these changes on the whole market would be identified. It should not be done by simply

listing macro data such as population and GDP, but called for specific analysis for different fields under the same macro environment. As shown in the example in Table 6.1, the macro environment of India's market will have completely different impacts on communication and high-speed rail equipment manufacturers.

(2) Value chain changes: By analyzing the changes that are taking place in the upstream and downstream links of the whole value chain, a judgment of their impact on the whole market can be made. Value chain analysis, as one of the core contents of market trend analysis, is especially significant for new markets, new industries and new products. The purpose of the analysis is to determine the market participants, advantages and disadvantages, positioning, value flow, and changes in the market, so as to predict the final possible results.

(3) Technology trend: Through the analysis and tracking of the trend of the future development of related technologies in the field, the possible impact and changes it will bring to the market in the future can be evaluated upon the understanding of its pace, so as to predict disruptive technologies. The analysis on subversive force still follows the classic Porter's Five Forces Model, but with new content given according to the new situation. The possible impact on customers and competition, as well as the changes of industry entry threshold, possible new products and new objects of competition and cooperation from the single or combined innovation of user experience, business model, technology and products, marketing and listing mode, organization, positioning, value chain and so on can be analyzed, so as to formulate countermeasures in advance.

(4) Market segmentation and analysis of market space: The methods for the market segmentation of B2B and B2C differ from each other, with that for B2B more based on products, industries, countries, customers (by size), while that for B2C more from the aspects of the age, gender, income, education, region, and religion. The existing known market segments should be sorted into a list, updated and maintained annually, with the existing marketing activities, current strategies or product line extension implemented, the stock market dynamics determined, and the results of the existing strategies and plans evaluated. Usually, a new market segmentation need to be done when the enterprises identify new requirements from existing customers among the greatly changed market, or when the enterprises enter a new market, formulate new strategies or plan new products. The purpose of market segmentation is to predict the scale and growth rate of the market segmentation accurately, so as to determine the future development potential of enterprises in the market and provide a key basis for decision-making.

The analysis of the market space can be done in two ways of "top-down" and "bottom-up" for the best outcome upon the verifications of each other. The top-down method to determine the market size means to obtain the statistical data of the market size that enterprises can participate directly after the continuous reduction from the global data over various filtering conditions upon a global market defined. The data

Table 6.1 A case of PEST analysis

Contests	Factors related to the enterprise in the case	Changes and trends	Impact (opportunity/threat)	Applicable countermeasures
Political	Foreign investment is encouraged, but being related to national security, communication system is greatly affected by politics; referring to the west for the communication standard of high requirements	The central government has gradually strengthened its control over the states	High standards, in addition to the frequent questioning over security issues by the Congress and the military institutions	The third-party laboratory of the UK opened to the relevant regulatory authorities in India
Economic/population	The economy has developed rapidly, with its GDP has increased by more than 7%, and the population ranks second in the world	Big population of the youth who pursue modern communication technology, but of low purchasing power	Serious competition at low price	Low-cost solutions landed in India
Sociocultural	An English speaking country with cultural diversity	Local culture and customs need to be considered	Diversified development of applications	Development of local applications upon the advantage offered by Institute of India Research to
Technological/natural	The local communication technology is backward and there is no strong local competitors	The government's obvious intention to support local communication manufacturers	Joint ventures may gain a better competitive position	Cooperation with Reliance

could be from professional consulting companies, market research reports and other financial research reports (such as Gartner, IDC, etc.), statistical data of industry associations, government journals, government procurement data, customs import and export data, etc. While the sales or production statistics accumulated during a long history of the enterprise and the organized regular market analysis from the front line of the market may present as more accurate market analysis. The bottom-up method to determine the market size means to get the overall market size upon the collection of the data of each market participant. However, if the market is highly fragmented, it will be very difficult and costly to estimate the overall market size by collecting data from each market participant, when it is more effective to collect the representative enterprise data in the market and adopt the method of weighted synthesis. The data sources include representative annual reports of friends and merchants, surveys of first-line bid answering projects, annual reports of major customer groups, customer investment plans, customer surveys, channel partner surveys, etc.

When analyzing the market space, people often make the mistake of exaggerating the market space in order to get the project established. Therefore, the overall market space and the market space that enterprises can participate in should be distinguished at least through the two dimensions of product and region, as shown in Fig. 6.7. Although the U.S. market accounts for nearly half of the global market of communication equipment, Huawei did not take the U.S. market space as the basis

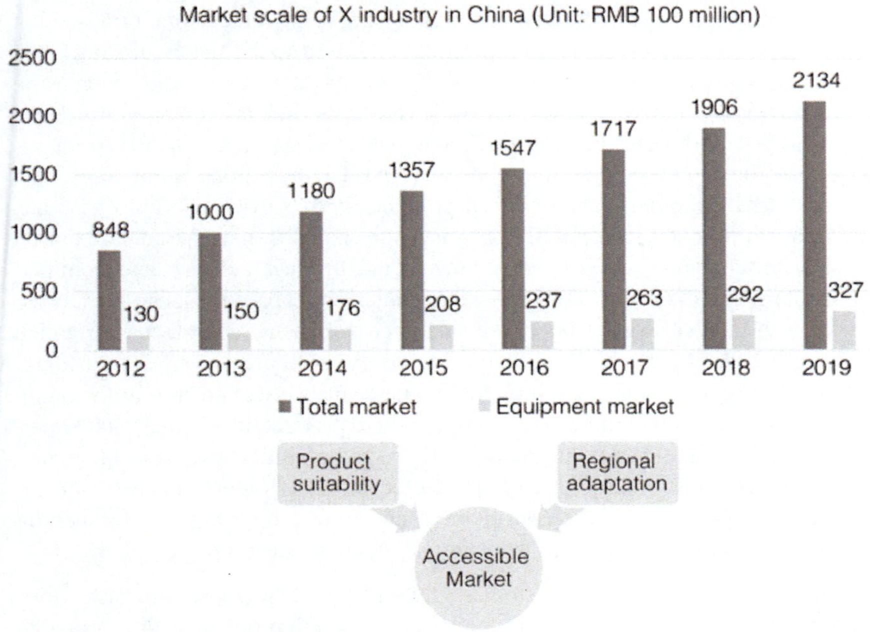

Fig. 6.7 The process of the convergence of the market space for participation

for market target prediction before 2008, for at that time, Huawei did not have the conditions to join the competition in terms of either customer relations or products.

2. Customer Analysis

By analyzing the changes of customers' requirements in business operation and solution, their impact on the future of the whole market can be identified.

(1) Customer segmentation: The customer groups are classified by a two-dimensional method based on opportunities (customer attraction) and the competence of the enterprise. Customer attraction can be measured from the perspectives of customer investment and investment planning, growth rate, profitability, industry influence (product traction, brand value, etc.), procurement methods and processes, existing sales, customer goodwill and even location, while the competence of the enterprise can be analyzed from the perspective of product range, product capability and experience, service quality, price, customer satisfaction, special service (such as consulting) ability, brand image, sales staff quality, customer relationship quality, and competitive position compared with other suppliers. Through the comprehensive evaluation of these two dimensions, development and marketing strategies for different customers can be formulated upon the identification of key customers through further customers segmentation.

(2) Customer behavior analysis: Customer behavior analysis includes the analysis of the changes in the customer purchasing behavior, customer transaction behavior and customer purchasing tendency. Based on the historical transaction records of customers, the weight of decisive factors in customer purchasing behavior is analyzed, and marketing strategies and investments are determined according to the customer's purchasing preference. The determinants of customer procurement are generally "hard" capabilities (such as product performance, quality and price) of products, and "soft" capabilities of enterprises or products, composed of key decision chains within customers, external key influencing factors (such as investors), product delivery and commissioning, life cycle costs and service management capabilities, can form 60 to 80% of the decisive factors of the customer purchasing equipment, for which the $APPEALS method can be used to verify the characteristics of customer purchasing behavior. Therefore, the product capability of an enterprise should be upgraded from simple price competition to product differentiation competitive advantage. The enterprise should have the ability to design integrated solutions to customer problems, and further help customers to carry out business planning and design consultation, and form a high degree of matching with customer strategy, thus achieving strategic partnership.

Analysis of the mode of the customers' transactions. The modes of transactions chosen by customers means the willingness of cooperation or the level of possible entry barriers. When customers choose income sharing, "Pay As You Go", "Pay on Requirement" or other modes of transactions with strong hedging nature, it shows that customers are just trying to deal with the enterprises for not trusting suppliers or not confident in their business development, an when customers choose BOT, turnkey, financial leasing and other transaction modes, it shows they are willing to cooperate, but lack of funds or cautious investment, and hope that suppliers can provide more options, while when customers choose transaction modes as operation outsourcing, joint innovation and intellectual property sharing, it generally means that the relationship between customers and suppliers grows into a partnership but not merely a business relationship. Therefore, a win–win profit model should be designed upon a full understanding of the requirements of customers.

In the analysis of the customer purchase tendency, the enterprises need to identify customers' purchase tendency, analyze the position of products in the market life cycle, select appropriate customers according to the market, and formulate reasonable product development strategies, and use different marketing strategies and means in different stages. The enterprises can recommend growth business to customers who pursue market-leading, mature business to customers who pursue stability, and mature business and extended recession business based on the reasonable design of profit model for the customers who are relatively backward and cost-sensitive.

(3) Customer pain point and value analysis: The market opportunities of enterprises can be predicted through decoding customer investment behavior, collecting internal and external analysis reports on customer development trends.

The enterprises can internally collect the analysis report of the customer strategic pain point, and summarize the trend of the evolution of the customers' business operation based on the report.

Externally, the enterprises can collect and listen to the analysis and judgment of the evolution of their business operation by industry analysts/friendly peers/customers.

The enterprises need to summarize the key evolution trends of customers from the perspectives of business operation and solutions, before the customer value analysis and corresponding business-related insights and suggestions can be given upon analyzing the changes brought by these trends to the market and the impacts and challenges brought to customers.

(4) Customer experience measurement: The measurement of the customer experience included supplier certification evaluation before becoming a supplier, and customer satisfaction (including satisfactions with customer relationship and transactions) survey after becoming a supplier. Key customers generally have a supplier certification process, such as BT, and NTT, who have carried out overall strategic supplier certification for Huawei, which plays a key role in Huawei's deep understanding of customers and improvement of internal management and external supply chain management. Customers will also conduct an annual regular satisfaction survey and ranking of present suppliers, which can also enable enterprises to have a deeper understanding of customer value orientation and their own problems, improve management and make strategic adjustments.
(5) Customer opinion analysis: Through social media analysis, the enterprises can understand customers' views on them and their products in a wider range, and

formulate preventive measures before the problems are completely exposed, so as to improve their reputations among the customers. In the present era of the Internet, it is more widely used in 2C business. For commercial users, they can enhance their interaction with customers and improve their ability to solve problems by establishing user community, participating in O2O user conference and building ITR (from issue to solution) system.

3. Competition Analysis

Only leading enterprises with strong innovation ability can worry less about competition, such as Apple in the era of Jobs. Therefore, competition analysis is a very important link in strategy making. In the competition analysis, enterprises need a comprehensive understanding of the intensity of the competition in the industry, whether a monopoly pattern has formed in the industry, what position the enterprise holds in the industry, what is the focus of competition, and how the main competitors are performing. However, due to the little experience accumulated, many Chinese enterprises are often unable to make reasonable judgments and formulate corresponding competitive strategies.

Take the two cases shown in Fig. 6.8 as examples. There are many third-party analysis reports for reference for the industry of video surveillance in China, which makes it easier to analyze the industry competition. As the secondary equipment market of the smart grid is relatively closed and highly regulated, most enterprises are unable to obtain comprehensive investment plans and complete information of their competitors. Due to the large amount of power equipment procurement, bidding is required according to the national regulations, with the main participants of the

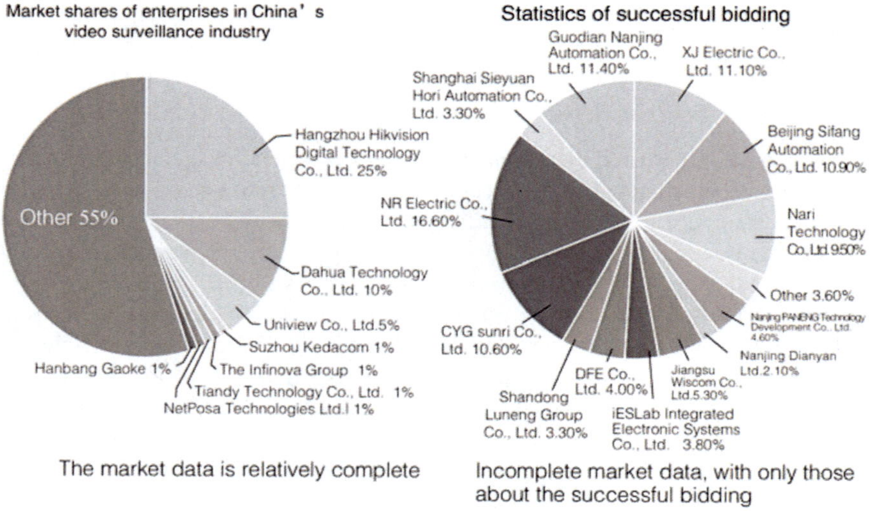

Fig. 6.8 A case of the analysis of the competition within the industry

industry participating in it. Therefore, the competition situation of the industry can be indirectly obtained through statistical analysis of the successful biddings.

The purpose of industry competition analysis is to come up with competitive strategies and provide input for the formulation of strategies. Therefore, in terms of the two industries in the above cases, the one has already seen leading enterprises in it, while the other still has its market "separated" by the close racers. Which industry should a newly-entered enterprise choose if the characteristics of the industry are not taken into consideration? Almost all theories of competition will support the choice of the second market for no monopoly has formed in it, which means that the threshold is low and suitable for the new entrants. Then, the right choice must be made according to the characteristics and advantages of the enterprises. Duan Yongping will choose the first kind of market, because his strategy is "dare to be the follower". The first type of market has seen leading enterprises, which indicates that the market is relatively mature. For the "Blue & Green corps" of OPPO/vivo, which has the advantage of late development, they can occupy reasonable market shares upon fully playing their advantages, rather than "washing saline alkali land". The second kind of market is divided, which means that the industry may be not mature or in a disorderly state of competition, such as smart homes, the green energy industry and so on. Therefore, the theories of competition should be taken upon the consideration of the realities of the enterprises.

The analysis of competitors should be carried out continuously in a long term, with the competitors divided into four categories: primary, secondary, optional and possible new entrants, and the regular monitoring of competitors carried out from nine dimensions.

- Enterprise strategies: including business strategy, marketing strategy, product/service strategy, etc.
- Finance: quarterly financial analysis and market share, revenue and profit sources, business model.
- Ecosystem: Alliance and ecological chain.
- Marketing strategy: Brand & image, market positioning, key information transmission.
- Product launch strategy: product launch dynamics and marketing plan, direct sales network coverage, regional and industry segmentation and coverage of major channel partners, customer.
- Organization: top management and decision chain, organizational structure, talent management mode.
- Customer information: customer list, customer positioning and share, key nodes of customer relationship.
- Strategic direction: company strategy, product strategy and investment strategy, etc., and possible response and actions to the strategies made by the enterprise.
- Weak links: to find out the key dependence through SWOT analysis, find out the way to benefit the enterprise, and identify the sales opportunities of the enterprise and its partners.

Around the selected market segments, regular monitoring of competitors should be carried out for special analysis of the competitors and alerts over the major actions of the competitors, so as to formulate corresponding competitive strategies.

Good tools can enhance the visualization of strategy, but upon the premise of enough market intelligence and data accumulation. The example in Fig. 6.9 shows the panorama of Japan's communication market in 2007 through the analysis with Mekko. The figure clearly shows the proportion of investment in various product areas of Japan's communication market at that time, as well as the market share and competition of major equipment manufacturers in different product areas. It also shows that Japan has an open market of huge growth potential as long as Huawei makes its products more in line with the requirement of the market. From the analysis of the Korean market with the same tool, it is found that the panorama of the Korean market is very "clean" with only about three manufacturers in the field of each product. Except for the products that Korean manufacturers can't provide, such as high-end routers and high-end optical networks that the public in Korea will choose those by European and American manufacturers, they almost choose "uniformly" Korean local manufacturers, for which Huawei only has a small share in low-cost optical transmission products.

In the decision-making process of market selection, even the former CFO, who knows little about technology, can easily make the decision of "no key investment in Korean market", which was later proved right by the facts. Huawei saw its revenue in the Japanese market later exceeding $2 billion, while the Korean market left managed by Huawei's Japanese representative office.

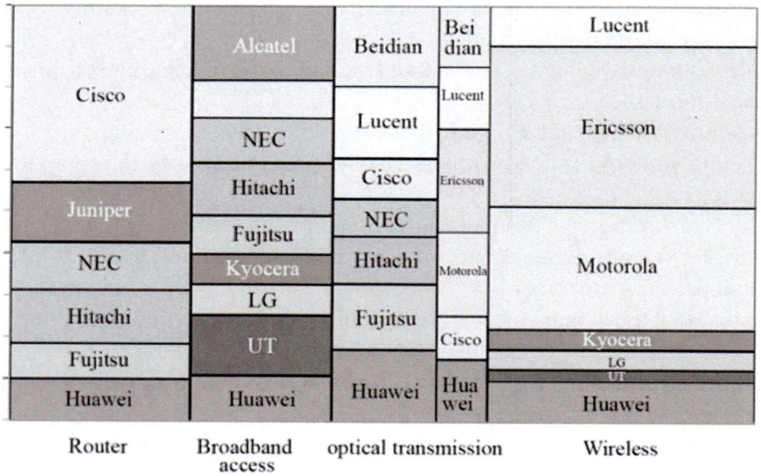

Fig. 6.9 An example of panoramic competition analysis with Mekko (Japanese telecom market)

6.2.1.3 Innovation Focus

First of all, enterprises should make clear their position in the market and strategic orientation of the enterprise in the industry. Leading enterprises in the industry generally adopt a relatively aggressive product leading mode before gradually build up a comprehensive competitive advantage. Generally, the followers will take a quick seize of the market share by building platform advantages and improving efficiency. The same enterprise can also adopt different innovation models for different business categories. The growth business generally adopts the product leading mode, that is, through technological innovation, it can quickly seize the market opportunity and lengthen the distance with competitors. Mature business generally has two kinds of innovation modes. One is customer intimate mode, which can meet more customer needs and improve customer satisfaction by expanding product types and upgrading product performance, and increase customer viscosity through marketing mode innovation such as consultant marketing, and experiential innovation such as fool-proof and intelligent operation. The other is the innovation of operation and management to achieve excellent operation, including E2E cost optimization, process innovation, management innovation, integrated mode innovation, and migration to the high end of the value chain. For the declining business, they can extend their life cycle, such as making profits and withdrawing from the underdeveloped market expanded.

It is very important to measure the innovation ability of enterprises effectively after defining the innovation focus. Generally, the proportion of R&D capital investment/R&D manpower and the proportion of new product income are used to measure the enterprise's innovation determination and innovation efficiency. The proportion of R&D investment can refer to the average level of the industry, which generally accounts for about 8% in the TMT industry and 3% in the traditional manufacturing industry. The R&D investment also reflects the strategic positioning and trend of enterprises. Huawei and Lenovo are both TMT industries. Huawei's R&D investment is between 10 and 15%, while that of Lenovo is about 3%, which naturally leads to the difference we see today.

When establishing the innovation mode, enterprises also use the classical VRIO analysis model (see Table 6.2) to find out the advantages or disadvantages of products or enterprises by answering the questions about value, rarity, imitability and organization of the company's resources and capabilities.

Through this tool, the enterprise can objectively evaluate the resources and capabilities that the organization has now, and carry out business design according to the characteristics of the enterprise itself upon the strategic review.

6.2.2 Strategy Decision

On the basis of strategic analysis, enterprises can establish strategic controls through business design; It can further form a variety of business portfolio schemes through product market portfolio analysis; achieve strategic decisions and form key measures

Table 6.2 VRIO analysis model

A resource or capability…						
Valuable	Rare	High cost for imitation	Adopt by the organization or not	Advantage or disadvantage	Competitive significance	Economic performance
N	–	–	N	Disadvantage	Competitive disadvantage	Below normal
Y	N	–	↕	Advantage	Competitive parity	Normal
Y	Y	N	Y	Advantage	Temporary competitive advantage	Temporarily higher than normal
Y	Y	Y		Advantage	Sustainable competitive advantage	Above normal

to ensure the realization of strategic objectives with the help of the analysis tools like SWOT, SPAN and FAN.

6.2.2.1 Business Design

Value-driven business design (VDBD) is a key thinking tool for business design, whose core idea is to choose customers, products and profit models properly to create value for customers through keen insight into the value transfer trend of the industry. The six elements of business design are as follows.

- Choice of customers: What kind of customer groups are the main products for? What kind of customer group is not in the scope of services? How to coordinate the existing market groups and emerging market groups?
- Value orientation: What high-value customer opportunities should be the target? What unique customer value orientation does the enterprise have? How can enterprises win competitive differences?
- Profit model: How the enterprise is to make money? Is it traditional product sales, service agreements, licenses, royalties, or intellectual property sales? What are the main ways to make a profit in the field of your business? What are the main competitors? What role does the enterprise play? Have you designed other profit models for the enterprise?
- Strategic controls: How can enterprises better ensure the provision of long-term and sustainable value-added services to customers? Are enterprises well positioned to lead the implementation of open standards? Is the orientation of value capture effective? How can companies benefit from disruptive or pre-emptive business actions to enhance their competitive advantage?
- Scope of business: How much added value have you achieved? How much do you depend on the partners who make profits together, such as channel partners

and suppliers? What other profit models have you designed? How interested are partners in them? How satisfied are they? How much do you consider about risk?
- Risk management: How to ensure the identification, understanding and management of uncertain factors? Is the underlying reason behind them understood? Is the risk of management independent or systematic? How can we increase the possibility of success and reduce the possibility of failure through better risk management? How can we use other business units or functional departments of the company to better manage risks?

It can be found that VDBD is very similar to the thinking mode of business model design with nine modules in chapter five, except that the business model design in chapter five is more systematic. In fact, the ways of strategic thinking are interlinked and need to be integrated in practical application. The key point of business design is to find and create strategic controls for the sustainable development of enterprises. Huawei has chosen the key customer strategy in the operator market. Through deep insight into customers, long-term and continuous R&D investment and management reform, Huawei has constructed the product innovation ability and management ability that are difficult to copy, and formed a unique strategic control point.

6.2.2.2 Develop Growth Strategy and Find Market Opportunities

Welch, a master of management, once said that the company's biggest strategy is to achieve effective "sustained profit growth". Through the ANSOFF combinatorial analysis matrix in Fig. 6.10, enterprises can find new growth opportunities for four typical situations, and form different modes for growth and strategies for the implementations.

Fig. 6.10 The ANSOFF combinatorial analysis matrix

For section C: The products have gained a certain share in the market, and a certain foundation of the relationship between the brand and customer. Therefore, enterprises need to expand market share continuously to increase revenue. However, in order to reduce the risk of suppliers, customers usually adopt a multi-supplier strategy when selecting suppliers, and will not let one supplier dominate. Therefore, there is a ceiling for the growth of market share. New opportunities generally include the following.

- Stock operation: Through the analysis of the life cycle of the equipment, the enterprise should find out whether there are any requirements for relocation and reconstruction or possible sales opportunities? Is there a need for upgrading and intelligent transformation? Are there any parts for sale? Are there any service sales beyond the maintenance period?
- Portfolio sales: For the promotion of enhanced new products, in addition to the current products, do customers need integrated solutions and professional services such as EPC, agent maintenance, operation and maintenance or consulting?
- Competitors' equipment relocation: Enterprises can analyze competitors' equipment life cycle, guide customers to replace and relocate as soon as possible.
- Excellent operation: Enterprises can improve profit margin by reducing comprehensive costs.

For section D: Enterprises can use existing brands and customer relationships to expand new products in the current market. It often takes time for customers to accept new products, and new products often have quality problems. Therefore, in order to seize the market opportunity and promote the rapid improvement of new product quality, especially for strategic new products, special incentive policies are often needed. In sales strategy, the focus should be put on the market growth rate and the breakthrough of the target market and target customers, while in terms of product strategy, enterprises should emphasize the improvement of product quality and build differentiated competitive advantage.

For section A: This section stands for the expansion of existing products to new customers in new regions and new industries. At this time, there is no support from brand and customer relationships. Moreover, the products should be adjusted according to the needs of customers. Especially in overseas markets and markets of different industries, large adjustments are often needed in terms of the standards for product access, qualifications and industry characteristics, with matching strategies for the development of products. In terms of sales strategy, focuses should also be put on the market growth rate, as well as the breakthrough of the target market and target customers. Especially for strategic customers, it often needs a long expansion cycle. During this period, there is no sales performance, but enterprises need to send a strong force to attack, which tests the enterprise's strategic determination, and needs the necessary strategic investment policy and incentive policy upon assessment. When Huawei saw "no harvest" in the first three years when it began to break through BT, the first bridgehead of the developed market, in 2002. After becoming a strategic supplier of BT, Huawei has been steadily increasing its sales in BT until now, especially in 5G procurement, BT has given Huawei great support.

For section B: Here lies the most difficult growth path. The new products need to be tested by the market due to the lack of support from brand and customer relationship, coupled with the unfamiliar industry rules too do with the new products, so it is difficult for new products to achieve growth in a new market. In the aspects of organization management, R&D investment, market strategy and assessment and incentive, enterprises need to carry out a careful design. Enterprises need to tolerate certain failures and put the key work of the region on finding out the market rules, selecting the market segments or friendly customers, achieving a market breakthrough, and forming market model points. In order to realize the industrial transformation, many traditional enterprises often cut into the "tuyere" industry through independent innovation and acquisition and merger.

At this time, it is necessary to adopt a relatively independent management and operation mode for the new industry, but in terms of quality management, large-scale production and marketing platform, the formation of collaborative effect is the best choice. For example, in the process of industrial transformation and upgrading, Hangzhou Boiler Group (HBG), a subsidiary of Zhejiang Xizi UHC, established an independent business unit for new products/new industries, which opened up all links of market, R&D, production, delivery and service. The business unit can make decisions quickly according to market requirement and organize forces to seize market opportunities. At the same time, in terms of product quality and marketing platform, it can cooperate with the large-scale system. In the initial stage, the group adopted a certain strategic subsidy policy for the new business unit, which enabled the new business unit to overcome the difficulties in the second venture period. After a short period of three years, the income of the new business unit has accounted for nearly 50% of the group. Some enterprises, however, either adopt the old method to manage new business and "die as soon as they manage it"; Or completely laissez faire, because the new business can not take advantage of the strength of the big platform, so it turned out that the new business unit of dozens of employees was fighting against the whole enterprises of the competitors.

Therefore, through the analysis of directions for the growth, market segmentation and market space, enterprises need to explore market opportunities, sort the opportunities, and adopt different strategies for investment and expansion for different opportunities.

6.2.2.3 Select and Identify Key Strategies

In the process of strategic analysis, enterprises have clearly defined the market opportunities and risks, their own advantages and disadvantages. Therefore, the classic SWOT analysis method can be used to formulate and refine the key measures.

SWOT analysis is a classic analysis method, but in the practical application in many enterprises, there are often some basic errors. The typical mistake is that there is no logical relationship between the analysis of opportunities and risks, advantages and disadvantages earlier with the following measures later. Often measures have been taken long ago, but the market analysis is just done as a mere formality. The other is that too many strategies are formed through SWOT analysis, which makes convergence difficult. Therefore, it is necessary to return to the goal of the formulation of the strategy, and make strategy combination and convergence in the two directions of seizing opportunities and preventing risks. In SWOT analysis, the strategies of SO and ST are easy to deduce, while generally, the strategies of WO and WT need to be discussed carefully. Figure 6.11 shows the formation of WT strategy by taking Huawei's strategy formed when facing quality and information security challenges in overseas developed markets as an example.

In the process of the breakthrough in overseas developed markets, BT, the UK's largest telecom operator, presents as the first bridgehead for Huawei. As one of the typical high-end customers, it is not sensitive to price, but is highly sensitive in the requirements for product innovation and sustainable development, product quality and service, and product safety. At that time, Huawei's brand awareness was very low, with its customer relationship just beginning to be established, let alone the relationship between government and business. At the same time, influenced by political factors and the development of China's manufacturing industry at that time, the British government, the military and security departments were skeptical about the introduction of Huawei. While giving full play to its advantages, Huawei formulated a risk management and control (WT) strategy to make up for its shortcomings quickly. First of all, Huawei hired opinion leaders from local industries, such as John Suffolk, Huawei's global network security and privacy officer. He had once served as the Chief Information Officer (CIO) of the British government. When Huawei broke through

Internal capabilities	
Advantages	Disadvantages
S1: R & D capability, customized, fast fulfillment	W1: Brand awareness
S2: various products, low comprehensive costs	W2: Weak relationship between government and commerce
S3: Market coverage	W3: Fulfillment capacity

W2: Weak relationship between government and Commerce
W3: Fulfillment capacity
T1: Product quality standards
T2: Information Security

External environment		
	Opportunities	O1: Developed countries need to introduce low-cost manufacturers due to economic recession
		O2: New technology upgrading (broadband, 3G)
		O3: Local enterprises in developed countries lack of competitiveness
	Risks	T1: Information security
		T2: Product quality standards

Fig. 6.11 An analysis of Huawei's WT strategy in developed markets

the British telecom market, he, as the CIO of the British government, had carried out a certification process strictly upon Huawei. After that, he accepted Huawei's invitation in 2011 and became Huawei's first global network security director. Secondly, Huawei conducted active cooperation with standards organizations and third-party independent testing organizations to open the source code. Anyone who has doubts about Huawei can verify it through formal channels, and the partners can help clarify it; At the same time, Huawei has also established an administrative center, financial center, and local R&D and delivery team covering Europe in the UK, which has greatly improved the understanding of customer requirements and quality standards and fulfillment capability. This laid the foundation for most European countries to adopt different policies from that of the United States towards Huawei.

When formulating the key strategy implementation measures, it is necessary to ensure that the main business units such as R&D, products, sales and services, supply chain, etc. of the enterprise form a combination strategy of products and solutions when facing the market segments, and form an interlocking assessment target, rather than each unit fighting alone.

The following is an example of an enterprise's overseas market expansion to illustrate the importance of product and solution portfolio strategy. The product line of the enterprise is very strong, but the regional sales organization is relatively weak. Before the strategic optimization, the product line is working independently. It often happens that the same customer is visited by different product lines of the enterprise; Or the product line pushes its own products without considering the interests of the company when the customer clearly needs the products of other product lines of the enterprise. At that time, they failed to consider the interests of the enterprise, establish a platform for customer relationships, or form a clear product mix strategy. In the later stage, when the enterprise formulated the strategy implementation measures, the main business units formed the product portfolio strategy as shown in Fig. 6.12 after full discussion. In section one, they focused on expanding the first-class products by building local factories; In section two, according to the local climate conditions and engineering requirements, they focused on customized product development to meet the needs of local customers; In section three, through the acquisition of local brands, they entered the developed market quickly for the future sales opportunities of portfolio products. In the design of the evaluation index, the regional sales manager's evaluation index is based on the regional sales index, plus other medium and long-term performance requirements and organization construction evaluation requirements, so as to ensure the consistency of strategy and tactics.

6.2.2.4 Application and Cases of Strategic Decision Tools

After the previous internal and external analysis, core control point construction and the formulation of the combination strategy of market segmentation, the management needs to select and make decisions on key strategic measures such as product strategy and market development strategy. Many enterprises regard strategic reporting as

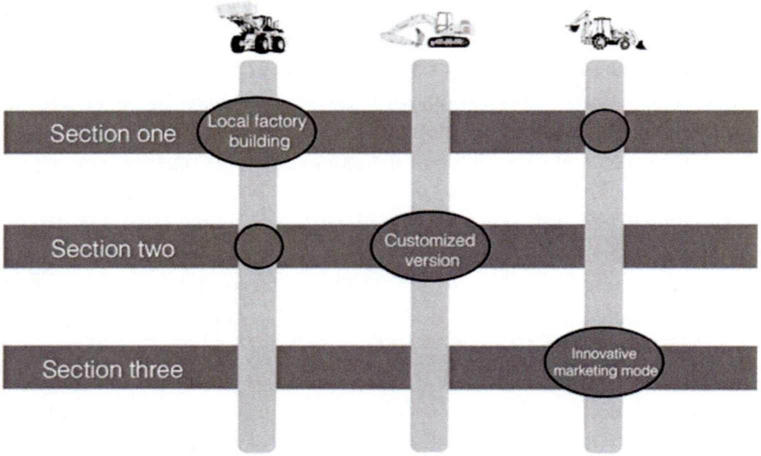

Fig. 6.12 A case of the strategy mix for products and solutions

situation notification meetings, thinking reports of the lower management or brainstorming. This is wrong, for the strategic report must get decision-making involved in. To make correct decisions, besides the entrepreneur's sensitive intuition, there are also some tools to assist entrepreneurs in scientific decision-making. Here are several tools commonly used.

1. BCG Matrix for Business Portfolio Strategy Decision

BCG matrix can help enterprises determine which businesses are suitable for investment, which businesses are easy to make profits under management, and which products should be eliminated from the business portfolio, so as to achieve the best business portfolio. The principles are as follows.

- Collecting the data of the enterprise's annual sales, annual market growth rate and the annual sales of its competitors.
- Calculating the relative market share, that is, the income of an enterprise's business divided by the income of its biggest competitor.
- Establishing the market growth share matrix (draw a circle with the coordinate point of the business on the two-dimensional coordinate as the center of the circle, the size of the circle represents the sales volume of each business, and sometimes it can also be used to represent the profit, as shown in Fig. 6.13) by marking each business on the matrix according to the relative market share and market growth rate.
- According to the change of the position of the important reference year in BCG matrix, the enterprise's business portfolio is evaluated. For products located in stars section, enterprises need to focus on investment for product leadership and market leadership. The products located in the cash cow section should ensure the maximization of financial indicators, and at the same time, make a reasonable

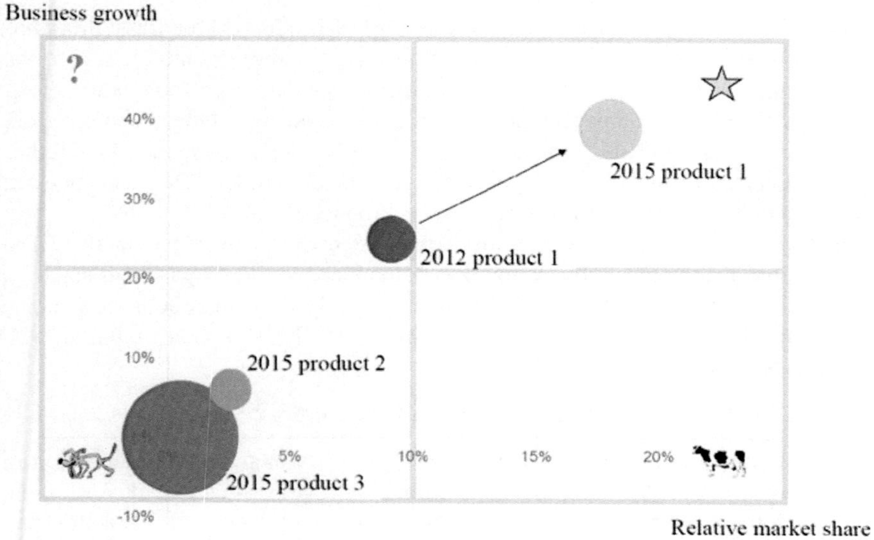

Fig. 6.13 A case of BCG matrix analysis

investment to achieve business growth through the upgrading of the versions or products, or opening up new markets. The products located in the question marks section should be focused on, in that although the business growth is fast, the relative market share is not high. The most likely situation is that the overall industry develops fast or has a large space, while the competence of the enterprise's own products is insufficient. The enterprise needs to accelerate the establishment of product differentiation advantages, narrow the gap with the biggest competitors, and strive to develop products into star products. For the products in the dogs area, enterprises should consider closing down, stopping, merging or transferring the business to improve the current development of the product.

After analyzing the performance of three types of its products, the enterprise in the case finds that Product One has maintained rapid growth after years of efforts, and the gap with its biggest competitors is getting smaller and smaller, so it belongs to the star product. Products Two and Three belong to dog products. Product Three has the largest market space, and the enterprise has invested in R&D for a long time, but only to find itself "being late in the market though get early in the morning". Over the past few years, the market position of products has not improved, but gradually deteriorated. In the final analysis, the enterprise found that the reason was that the company was not determined to invest, but taking it as a try, with no clear strategies for product or market. Through the analysis, the enterprise can make a decision like this: maintaining investment in Product Three, with the focus put on the advantageous market of Product One, and expanding Product Three with the combinatory solutions for Product One and Product Three; Unifying the marketing platform for the enterprise's joint efforts, to achieve market success and customer recognition quickly, and accelerate the maturity of Product Three through market inspection, so as to make product 3 develop independently gradually after it has been recognized by the market in terms of function, performance and quality upon a unique differentiated competitive advantage; Because the overall development space of the industry is small and there is disorderly competition in its market for Product Two, the enterprise decided to give up the market for Product Two and focus its resources on the industry of Product One and Product Three.

In the actual operation, the enterprises often fail to obtain the actual market share of competitors and other information due to the lack of sales department capacity, lack of market data. But generally, they can get the information about the winning rate of the bidding project, so they can also use the analysis method similar to BCG matrix to assist decision-making.

2. SPAN Analysis Tool for the Decision on Combinatory Strategy

The SPAN analysis method is shown in Fig. 6.14. By analyzing the attraction of different markets and the competitive position of enterprises in the market, different combination strategies can be formed. For the market with high attraction and competitive advantage, investment needs to be improved in both product R&D and market expansion to obtain the maximum benefits; For the market with high attraction but no obvious competitive advantage, enterprises need to find out the aspects to form differentiated competitive advantage as soon as possible to achieve the breakthrough of market scale; For the market with high competitive position but insufficient attraction, enterprises need to further segment the market to find valuable customers and realize the effective growth of the enterprise; For the market with low competitive position and insufficient attraction, enterprises should consider withdrawing to focus resources on high-value market.

Market attractiveness can be determined by the "weighted sum" of the following factors.

Fig. 6.14 SPAN analysis method

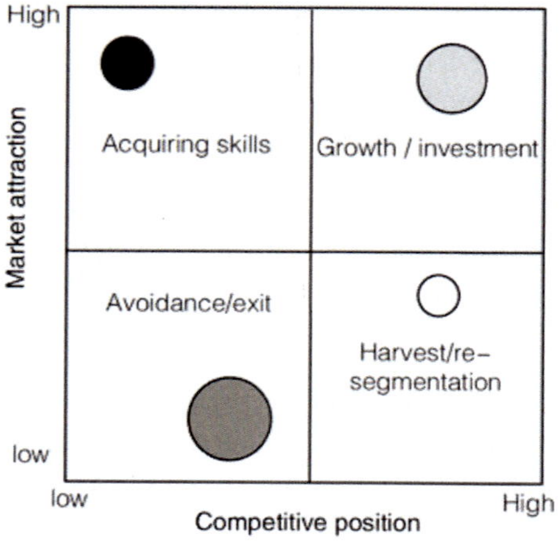

- Space for market segmentation;
- Market segment growth rate;
- Profit potential: direct/indirect competition intensity, entry threshold, customer/supplier pressure, customer reputation, etc.;
- Strategic value: the strategic value of entering the market segment for the enterprise;
- Methods and process, even locations, etc. of purchase

The competitive position is mainly based on the "weighted sum" of the key factors selected by the company and the best competitor in the industry on $APPEALS, which generally includes the following contents.

- Category, functional performance and quality of the products;
- Service ability and professional services (such as technical consultation);
- Price, life cycle costs;
- Brand image and experience;
- Qualifications of the sales staff, quality of the customer relationship, etc.

For products in different quadrants, action plans can be further refined, especially in marketing activity planning, sales and channel management, market pricing strategy formulation, cost control, etc., and can also be used to optimize investment, manufacturing, operation, R&D and product strategy. The example given in Fig. 6.15 has a great value for reference.

	Investment for growth	Maintaining market position and making profits	Selective input	Get cash	Looking for entry opportunities
Distribution	Expansion of the distribution channels	Maintaining current channels	Market segmentation	Reducing channels	Limited coverage
Cost control	Control – seeking economies of scale	Capacity reduction cost – variable cost	Strict control	Strictly control of the costs	Control – appropriate risk taking
Production	Expanding investment	Capacity utilization maximization	Increase productivity	Releasing capacity	Investment
R & D	Expanding investment	Focus on some projects	Selective investment	No	Investment
Market share	Maintaining the advantages	Maintaining or reducing slightly in order to earn	Selectively maintaining, Maket segmentation	Giving up the share and earning profit	Investing selectively and gaining share
Products	Differentiation, product line expansion	Streamlining and forming differential advantages in major market segments	Emphasizing product quality – differentiation	Great reduction	Expanding differentiated product lines
Price	Leading – aggressive pricing for share	Price stabilization/price increase	Maintaining or raising prices	Price increase	Getting share with aggressive price
Promotion	Vigorous promotion of the sales	Limited promotion	Selectively maintaining	minimization	Getting share with aggressive price
Personnel	Improvement of the quality of personnel in the core areas	Maintaining and reward efficiency and strict control of the organization	Exploring the full potential of the staff	Cutting organizations	Investment
Investment	Increase of the investment	Limit fixed investment	Selective investment	Opportunistic investment minimization or non– investment	Increasing investment
Working capital	Reducing process credit	Strictly controlling the credit – reducing accounts receivable – improving inventory turnover	Reduction	Great reduction	Investment

Fig. 6.15 An example for the reference of the market portfolio action plan

3. The Ranking and Decision of Strategic Opportunities in the Case of Limited Resources

Under the condition of limited resources, in order to focus on resources and ensure the capture of strategic opportunities, enterprises need to sort the market opportunities reasonably to avoid the situation that "only the crying children will be fed" and seize the strategic development opportunities.

The priority ranking method of opportunities is shown in Fig. 6.16. The specific method is to analyze the market attraction and competitive position of the opportunities through SPAN, before making financial analysis (FAN) on the R&D investment cost, possible sales revenue and profit that these opportunities need, and then calculate the weighted sum of the two data, and sort them according to the final score. The weights are determined by the quadrant of ANSOFF matrix. For old products and old market areas, the financial weight will be high; For new products and new market areas, the future growth and strategic value of opportunity have high weight; For the old products and new market areas, enterprises need to balance the relationship between the two, with the focus more on the competitive position; For new products and old markets, enterprises also need to balance the relationship between the two, but with the focus more on income growth.

Enterprises need to focus on investment to the top 20% of the opportunities to ensure the acquisition of strategic opportunities; For the next 30% of the opportunities, enterprises should keep the investment for the maximum profit; For the next 30% chance of ranking again, investment should be limited, together with close observation of the operation for possible adjustment in time; Attention should be paid to the last 20% of the opportunities, for timely adjustment when there are free resources or in remote (phone, mail, etc.) ways.

6.2.3 Arrangement

This includes planning and layout of tangible and intangible assets/resources such as processes, organizations, talents, knowledge, funds, special equipment and capacity.

- Organizational capacity planning: the organizational capacity required by the implementation of the strategy to mobilize and maintain the change process, including the consistency of understanding of the organizational strategy, the organizational system and control mode with cultural identity and efficient cooperation, the core business process (marketing and customer management process, innovation management process, integrated product development process, integrated fulfillment process, excellent operation process), and the core business process, incentive system to guide the members of the organization to be active and dedicated.
- Human resource planning: including the quantity and quality of professionals with the skills and talents required to implement key strategic activities, as well

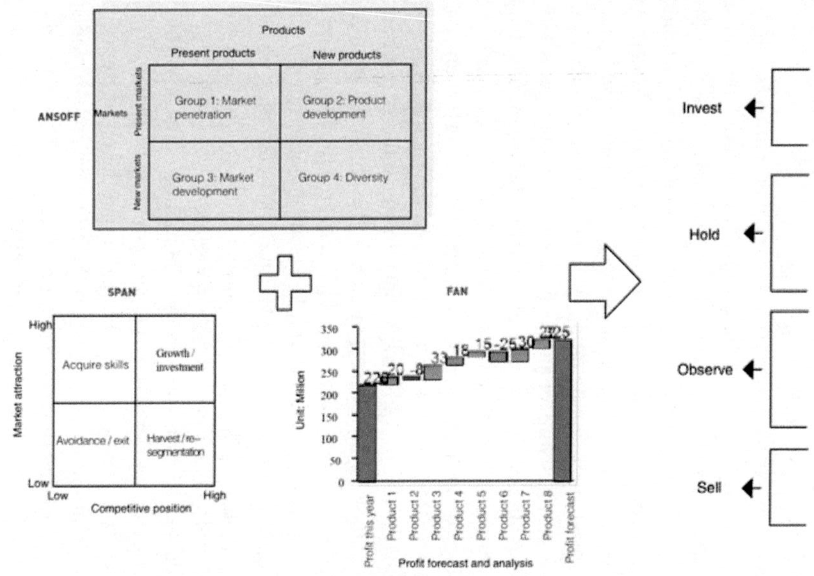

Ranking of opportunities

Grouping	Points	Projects
1	85.33	Item 22
3	83.22	Item 31
2	80.25	Item 12
2	73.33	Item 18
4	72.8	Item 3
1	67.43	Item 1
3	66.55	Item 15
4	64.35	Item 8
2	60.22	Item 82
3	58.33	Item 20
1	52.06	Item 17
2	51.22	Item 7
1	48.08	Item 10
3	43.44	Item 13
4	42.11	Item 16

Fig. 6.16 Method for priority ranking of opportunities

as the ability to rapidly introduce, transfer and cultivate high-quality professional resources in the whole organization.

- Information capital planning: supporting information system (ERP, CRM, IFS, MTL/LTC, etc.), knowledge sharing and application (knowledge base, case, etc.) and infrastructure capability (IT network, application system, database, etc.) required by the strategies.
- Strategic capital planning: the planning and layout of core intangible and tangible assets required by the strategy. It includes the layout of core intellectual property and patent, strategic capital preparation for quick access to key resources through investment or merger, research and development of key special equipment or precision machinery, and layout of core capacity.

Ren Zhengfei believes that per capita efficiency is the core competence of an organization. When enterprises are making the arrangement, certain constraints should be there for both human resource requirement and resource planning, especially the concept of unit capital and per capita benefit should be emphasized to ensure that the growth rate of performance is greater than that of cost. The core purpose of strategy is to realize the effective growth of enterprises.

So far, the process of making enterprise strategy is over. This set of strategy making method and strategic thinking modes based on BLM model but not completely copying BLM model can also be used for subsidiaries, business lines, product lines and sub-product lines of enterprises, but with different degrees of attention.

The overall strategy for the whole enterprise is similar to the strategy for business lines in methodology, but with different focuses. At the enterprise level, the market position of the enterprise in the whole industry should be determined; It is necessary to carry out the overall policy impact analysis, the overall analysis of key customers and major competitors, the analysis of the consistency between industry investment distribution and enterprise income source, the analysis of key customers' income and contract structure (determination of "grain area"), the performance comparison and trade-off decision of different product lines, and the management of enterprise level strategic opportunities; It is also necessary to study the coordination strategy of different business lines in the market, including the company platform planning (R&D, market, supply chain planning), new business area planning, overall financial forecast and resource planning (manpower, key equipment, strategic capital preparation for M&A, etc.), as well as the completion of business plan convergence and the first level department KPI strategic indicators. In short, the focus should be on enterprise level and cross business strategy development.

The business line focuses on the strategic planning of its own business area, which includes decomposing the above relevant contents of the enterprise into the corresponding parts of the business lines. For example, the competence comparison between product lines should be changed into the comparison between sub-product lines in the field, so as to determine the choice of sub-products. The business line must include the construction of product competitiveness and key strategic control. Compared with the formulation method of product innovation strategy in Chapter

Two, it can be found that product strategy focuses more on technology trends, key differences of technological innovation, etc., while product competence is analyzed in more detail based on $APPEALS tool, and output strategy rather than using blue sea strategy tool in company strategy for general analysis. In addition, it should also include matters of special concern in the field, such as talent requirement different from other business lines, introduction and development of special equipment, etc.

Chapter 7
Huawei's Strategy Implementation System

7.1 A Clear and Feasible Annual Business Plan as the Key to the Implementation of the Strategy

After the formulation of the strategic planning (SP) of the enterprise, one of the core measures for the implementation of the strategic planning is to formulate the annual business plan (BP) based on the strategy. The logical relationship between SP and BP is shown in Fig. 7.1.

SP focuses on determining the enterprise's strategic direction and strategic points of opportunity through strategic insight to realize the innovative business design, clarifying and grasping strategic control points, and forming a key milestone of the enterprise's strategic development.

BP, on the other hand, emphasizes clear opportunity, annual sales targets and predetermined market targets (major projects with difficulties, key customers, etc.). The annual action plan and strategy to achieve these goals must follow the principle of SMART, with the work allocated to the specific person in charge, the required resources and budget, as well as the key annual indicators, organizational KPI and personal business commitment (PBC) clearly defined. Finally, the incentive policies should be implemented upon the assessment through the KPI and PBC performance evaluation, so as to achieve closed-loop management.

7.1.1 Strong Logic Between Annual Business Plan and Strategic Planning

The strategic planning and business plan of many enterprises are separated from each other, for the management actually pays more attention to the annual business plan and annual budget, for it is directly related to the recent operation and assessment of enterprises. Some enterprises had once passed the enterprise's three-year strategic plan quickly, but debating hot and could not decide the annual business plan. Because

L. Tao, *Huawei Wisdom*,
https://doi.org/10.1007/978-981-19-1169-9_7

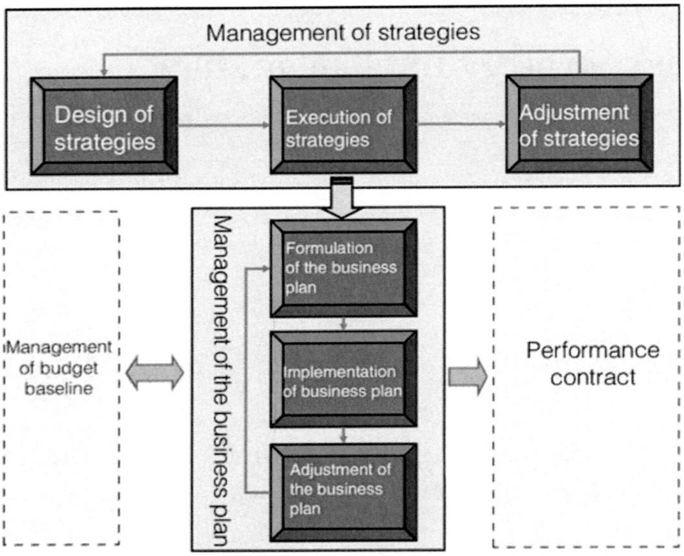

Fig. 7.1 The relationship between the strategic planning (SP) and the business plan (BP)

people habitually believe strategy as something "virtual" with no direct relationship with the business plan. Therefore, in practice, the three-year strategic plan is better operated following the pattern of "1 + 2" year strategic plan, that is, in the first year, clear objectives and key tasks should be determined, and in the second and third years, the direction should be clearly seen and updated. An enterprise can directly input the objectives of the first year in the strategic plan into the annual business plan, which, together with other annual key work and the corresponding financial budget, can be used as the "performance contract" between the top leaders of the enterprise and the leaders of various business departments. The contract can also be used as the basis for the leadership responsibility and authority of the business departments. The leaders of the enterprise guide the operation of each business department through strict questioning and assessment of the operation/budget plan of each business department, so as to realize the strong logic between strategic planning and business plan.

The principles for formulating the annual business plan are as follows.

- The objectives of the annual business plan come from the objectives of the first year of the strategic plan, and the financial budget starts from the objectives of the business plan;
- The enterprise's headquarters formulate indicators for the expected performance, and the president and senior leaders ensure the realization of performance expectation indicators by strictly questioning and assessing the business plans of each enterprise and business unit;

- The annual business plan provides clear business and financial performance objectives as the basis for the evaluation of the performance of the business unit leaders;
- The quarterly performance assessment includes questioning the person in charge of the business unit, with solving problems as the fundamental starting point, rather than explaining problems.

7.1.2 Six Components of the Annual Business Plan

7.1.2.1 Overview of the enterprise's Strategic Planning and the Objectives of the First Year

- Corporate vision and strategic intention;
- The objectives of the first year in strategic planning.

7.1.2.2 Major Indicators of Operating Performance and Plans

It is necessary, for items such as annual and quarterly sales plans, to reflect the detailed requirements and objectives of the enterprise in terms of income, profit, payment, cash flow, costs, expenditures, efficiency and quality.

7.1.2.3 Specific Measures

In order to achieve the strategic objectives of the first year and the main operation measures, schedule and key milestones, responsible persons and resource requirements, the annual business plan should follow the SMART principle, namely, the objectives should be clear, concrete, measurable, attainable, responsible and clearly planned by time.

The key measures in the enterprise strategy for the next three to five years are often highly generalized and not clearly defined, so the most important point in the business plan is to refine the action plan in the strategic plan. Figure 7.2 illustrates the key actions in strategic planning, i.e. how to refine the annual key measures in the annual business plan.

7.1.2.4 Reviewing the Differences Between the Progress of the Plan and the Enterprise's Objectives and Requirements and Corresponding Measures

Enterprises generally review the annual BP quarterly and monthly. When there is a big gap between the planned progress and the enterprise's original goal, root cause

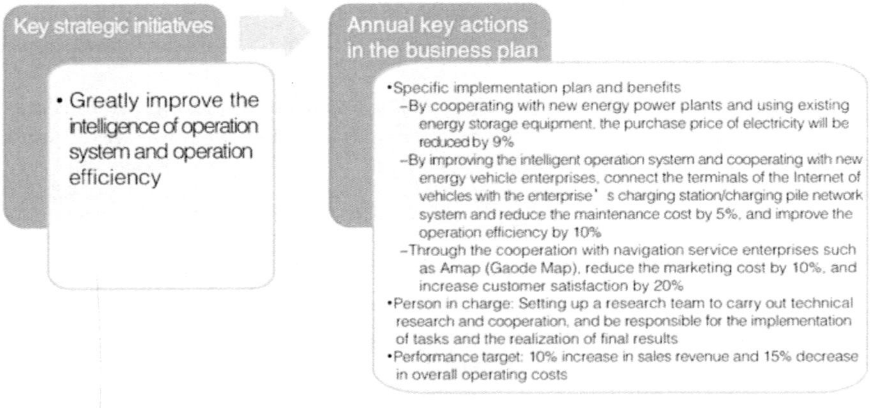

Fig. 7.2 An example of differences between key strategic initiatives and annual key initiatives

analysis should be carried out to find out corresponding measures. For example, when the product sales significantly exceed the original target, enterprises need to make adjustments in the aspects like the target, bonus, capacity planning, and tasks for sales.

7.1.2.5 Major Opportunities and Risk Management

The possibility and impact of major opportunities or major risks affecting the completion of business plan objectives should be predicted for the formulation of the corresponding measures. For example, the early warning should be given before the state issues major favorable policies, or the enterprise has a major crisis public relations events or quality accidents, etc., with timely response measures put forward in BP.

7.1.2.6 Detailed Financial and Resource Budget Plan

- Major financial budget (income statement, balance sheet, expense budget, etc.);
- Annual budget of human resources;
- Annual requirement for strategic funds;
- Annual budget of production capacity and fixed assets, etc.

7.1.3 Strengthening the Management of Annual Business Plan

Generally, enterprises pay more attention to the management of the annual business plan, but most of them will put the focus on the completion of financial indicators and sales tasks, and some enterprises even put the financial department responsible for the daily management of business plans, often ignoring the process management of key measures and key tasks highly related to business. Therefore, in the process of business plan management, it is necessary to clarify the relevant responsibilities and management processes of the main departments.

7.1.3.1 Main Activities and Responsibilities of the Enterprise Headquarters

- Reviewing the business unit strategy and revise it as necessary;
- Prioritizing resource allocation;
- Ensuring that there is enough flexibility for the plan;
- Authorizing the business unit manager to implement the plan and clarifying the responsibility for the effects of the implementation.

7.1.3.2 Main Activities and Responsibilities of Business Units

- Modifying business unit strategy as needed;
- Identifying key actions and initiatives for the year;
- Determining the performance contract of the current year;
- Ensuring adequate financial and human resources to achieve the objectives;
- Empowering individual managers to clarify responsibility for implementation effectiveness.

7.1.3.3 Main Departments for the Management of the Business Plan

It generally includes the business plan management department, strategic management department, finance department, human resources department and other relevant functional departments, whose main activities and responsibilities are as follows.

- Formulating relevant strategies, formulating and carrying out business plans;
- Providing relevant templates and guide relevant business units to complete relevant contents;
- Conducting daily management of the implementation effect of business plan and provide relevant data;
- Ensuring the availability of relevant resources and support the implementation of the business plan;
- Early warning and tracking of major issues and risks.

Enterprises should formulate a clear and efficient annual business plan management process and management calendar according to their own actual situation, so as to make each department have clear roles and a clear division of labor.

To win the enterprise's resources and realize the enterprise's growth expectations, some enterprises have estimated the market and goals too optimistically in their strategic planning, resulting in unreasonable planning or waste of human, material and other back-end resources. Only when the business plan is to formulate and confirm the annual target, will the feasibility of the early strategic planning be seriously analyzed and questioned, which greatly reduces the seriousness and preciseness of the strategic planning. Therefore, the business plan should directly undertake the strategic objectives of the first year, and first of all, achieve a "strong correlation" on the annual objectives. Secondly, it is necessary to decompose the strategic measures and action plans step by step through strategic decoding, so as to make them specific, clear, measurable and traceable, so as to ensure the strong logic between the strategic plan and the annual business plan and their implementation.

7.2 Strategy Decoding as the Foothold of Strategy

Strategy decoding is the process of vertical decomposition of tasks from top to bottom according to the organizational structure of enterprises, and horizontal decomposition of tasks from left to right according to business process structure, and the implementation of the enterprise's strategic intent and strategic objectives to each organizational unit or even individual. Strategy decoding is the key to ensure the consistency of the understanding of the enterprise strategy, especially the behavior consistency.

If a strategy cannot be clearly described, it cannot be measured, if it cannot be effectively measured, it cannot be effectively managed, and then the strategy will turn out to be nothing, said Robert Kaplan, the master of management. How to effectively decode the strategy? There are two main methods: one is the classic method for the decoding of strategy based on Balanced Score Card (BSC), the other is the decoding method based on Business Strategy Execution Model (BEM). The main characteristics of the two methods are compared and analyzed as followed.

7.2.1 Brief Introduction of BEM for Strategic Decoding

The BEM decoding mode adopts the structural model corresponding to the BLM strategy making mode, and the overall architecture is shown in Fig. 7.3.

Critical success factors (CSF) are the key elements that need to be seriously managed by the organization to achieve the vision and strategic objectives of the enterprise, so as to ensure the differentiation of competitive advantage. These CSF are all refined from the four dimensions of finance, customer, internal operation and learning and growth according to the BSC. The refined CSF is decomposed into annual key work Y by years with clear indicators for assessment and measurement. The concept of Critical-to-Quality (CTQ) is introduced here to make the goals

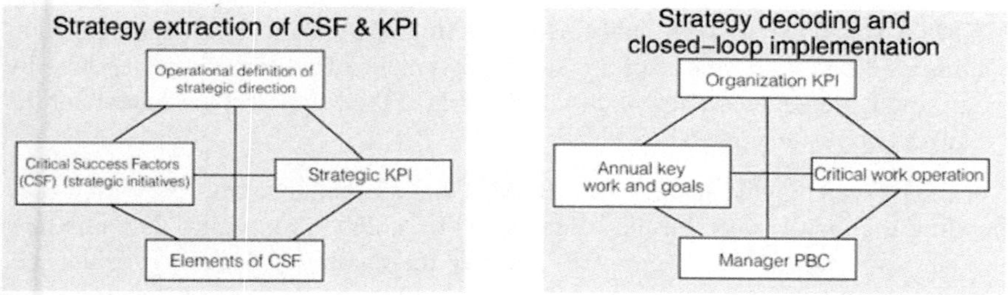

Fig. 7.3 BEM structure

following the SMART principle. The decoding process includes the following six steps.

Step one, define the strategic direction and its operation.
Step two, export CSF and make the strategic map.
Step three, export strategic KPI.
Step four, export CTQ-Y (export annual critical quality control points).
Step five, decompose CTQ-Y (decompose annual critical quality control points).
Step six, export the key work.

The first step repeats the process of the formulation of SP and BP to further understand and clarify the strategic direction and objectives; In the second and third steps, the CSF, strategic map and strategic KPI are all derived upon BSC. What is more innovative here is that IPOOC, a screening method of KPI, is proposed. IPOOC decomposes CSF in detail from four dimensions: Input (generally including resources), Process (critical activities, and processes that affect the achievement of CSF from a strategic perspective), Output (direct output based on process perspectives, such as the non-financial output of products, systems, customers and target markets) and Outcome (revenue from the perspective of internal and external customers), Based on the four evaluation criteria of strategic relevance, measurability, controllability and excitability, KPI indicators are to be selected by scoring, though the scoring criteria are subjective.

The main purpose of the fourth, fifth and sixth steps is to output annual key work following the SMART principle. For this reason, the methods of affinity, induction, task tree and other auxiliary tools such as TPM/BPM/CPM are introduced.

- TPM (Total Productivity Management) comprehensively deconstructs the comprehensive objectives through total analysis to ensure that the decomposed objectives can support the total objectives. The quantity outline of the upper and lower decomposition indicators should be consistent, generally aiming at financial and economic issues, such as income, cost, etc.
- BPM (Business Process Management) is to decompose and export objectives and measures following the business process and with the customer at the center, usually aiming at efficiency and cycle matters.

- CPM (Critical Parameter Management) aims to find the critical influencing parameters in the system, and support the improvement of system characteristics by improving the key parameters, usually aiming at the R&D product matters or the causes and results.

It can be seen that the advantage of BEM is that it is better structured, with its key decoding logic still based on the balanced score method, but with only some new auxiliary tools added to appropriately improve the quality of decoding results (i.e. key work and assessment indicators). Therefore, this book focuses on the method of BSC for strategy decoding.

7.2.2 *Method for Strategy Decoding Based on BSC*

In the front-end part of strategy making, this book has initially introduced the root cause analysis of adopting the balanced score method to carry out the recovery. In fact, The Balanced Scorecard is an important method to decode strategy, optimize the annual business plan (BP) and derive key KPIs. The decoding architecture is shown in Fig. 7.4.

7.2.2.1 Strategic Clarification

Strategy clarification is done upon the enterprise's strategy plan (SP) and annual business plan (BP). In many enterprises, only a few senior executives participate in the formulation of strategy, while other senior executives, especially the executive backbone, have no overall view or inconsistent understanding of the overall

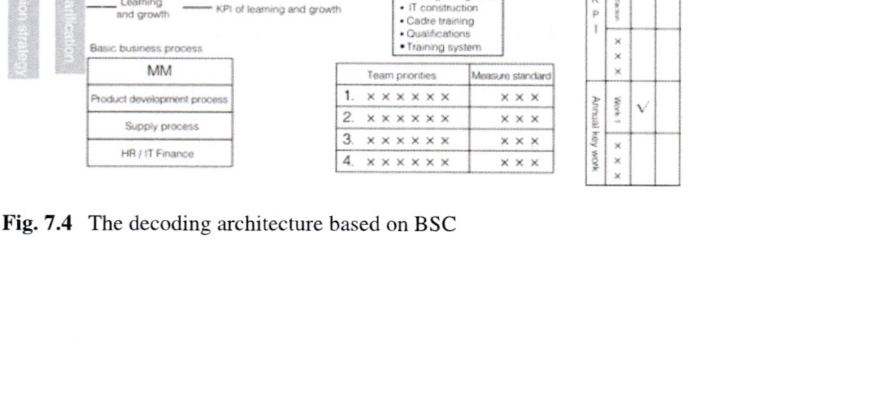

Fig. 7.4 The decoding architecture based on BSC

strategy, resulting in poor implementation. The reason is that corporate strategy is only the entrepreneur's strategic intention, no better than a strategic outline, but not the complete business strategy. Therefore, it is necessary to clarify and reach an agreement on the strategic direction, strategic objectives, opportunity identification, realization path and resource requirement. On this basis, the key measures in BP can be further optimized based on the BSC, and the key KPI indicators can be derived.

7.2.2.2 Detailed Explanation of Strategy Decoding Method Based on BSC

The BSC strategy decoding is a top-down vertical decomposition of strategy based on organizational structure from four aspects of finance, customer, internal process and learning and growth under the guidance of strategic objectives. It is necessary to ensure that the responsibilities were carried layer by layer from the enterprise to the department, and then to the post, to implement the Department's undertaking and responsibility to the goals by the upper levels, to provide the basis for the determination of individual performance commitment, so as to ensure the consistency of vertical undertaking; At the same time, based on the enterprise's "end-to-end" process, the joint liability and cooperation between departments are established, and the horizontal direction of the upstream and downstream of the process is decomposed to ensure the horizontal consistency. The selection of indicators should be done in a balanced manner and reflect the characteristics of the responsibility of different departments. The selection of indicators should be combined with the four dimensions of the BSC and the strategic orientation of the current development stage of the enterprise, so as to realize the balanced consideration of department responsibility. The detailed four-layer decoding structure of BSC is shown in Fig. 7.5.

The first is the financial level. This level describes the financial objectives to be achieved by the enterprise strategy, and the outcome indicators are to achieve shareholder value and improve the return on investment. The corresponding driving strategies and indicators include two directions: one is to improve the cost structure and asset utilization to achieve the strategy of improving productivity; The second is to realize the growth strategy of enterprises by realizing customer value and increasing revenue. Financial performance improvement is the goal of all strategic pursuits. Enterprises should choose one of the most important financial goals. Generally, the optional indicators are Return on Investment (ROI) and Return on Capital Employed (ROCE). For different types of business such as mature, growing and new business, the design and weight of financial indicators should also be different. For example, mature businesses pay more attention to the improvement of market position, the expansion of market share and the improvement of profit margin; The growth business needs to focus on revenue, profit, growth rate and contract quality; For new business, we need to relax the financial indicators appropriately, focus on the growth rate and the realization of market goals, and do not overemphasize the absolute value of financial indicators.

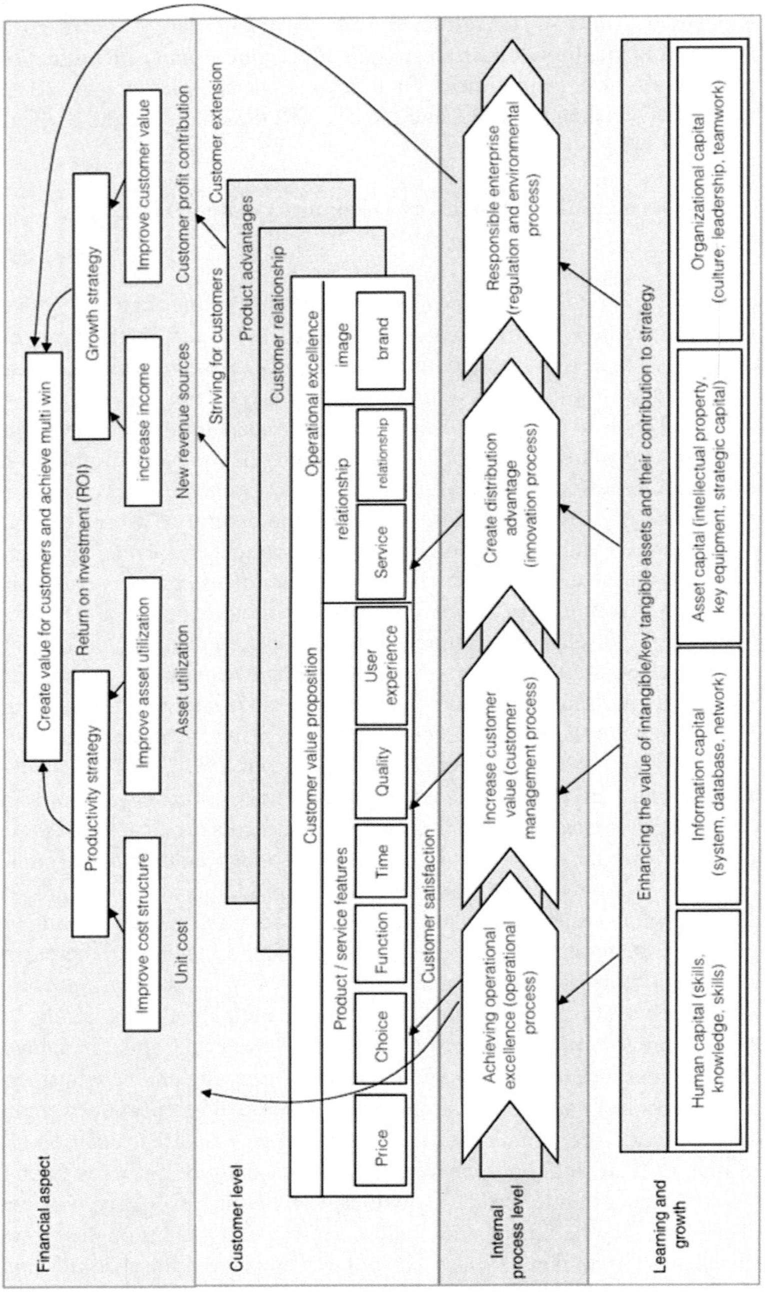

Fig. 7.5 Detailed four-layer decoding structure of BSC

The growth strategy focuses more on the profitability of long-term finance, with the goal of obtaining new revenue sources from new markets, products and customers, and improving customer value (increasing the profitability of existing customers and project renewal). The efficiency strategy focuses on the realization of short-term financial results, aiming at reducing operating costs (end-to-end cost reduction, increasing per capita output) and improving asset utilization efficiency (reducing inventory, increasing turnover, etc.).

The second is the customer level. To achieve financial objectives, the enterprises must "take customers as the center", providing competitive products, services, or solutions by establishing enterprise brand, as well as customer relationships. The products and services provided by enterprises should either create value for customers or reduce costs for customers, whose requirements for price, quality, function, marketing mode and time of fulfillment may vary from each other, therefore, it is necessary to focus on meeting the customer's needs for different customer value propositions, as shown in Fig. 7.6, which is marked as the part of different factors.

- **For customers focus on the costs (cost priority type)**: The most competitive price should be put forward on the basis of quality assurance. For leading enterprises, they often need to examine the long-term development potential of such customers, help the customers out of the misunderstanding of focusing only on transaction cost, and make customers truly "smart" customers, through product mix and solutions, upon the concept of life cycle cost.
- **For customers who prefer innovation and risks (product priority type)**: It is necessary to provide the most advanced products with unique functions that are not available or rarely seen in the market so that customers can take the lead in the market or show their uniqueness, such as Huawei's 5G mobile phone with a foldable screen.
- **For mature and stable customers (customer intimate type)**: Enterprises need to focus on customer needs closely, and provide personalized products and solutions for customers by establishing long-term organizational customer relationships and allowing customers to participate in the design or joint innovation. Therefore, at this level, enterprises can further optimize the key action plan and determine the financial and non-financial indicators for different customers by combining the market segmentation and customer segmentation analysis in SP and BP.

For the support departments that do not directly face external customers, they should regard internal customers as their own customers according to the relationship in the stream or organization setting principle of the process. It is necessary to sort out the upstream or downstream relationship within the process, especially the fulfillment relationship among the process with a clear definition of the deliverable between the above links, and take it as an important basis for the formulation of key measures and mutual assessment.

The third is the internal process level. The internal operation is mainly supported by the process, and the process is the steps formed by summarizing the best business practice, which is the soul of enterprise internal operation. The internal operation describes how to link customer value proposition, how to support long-term financial

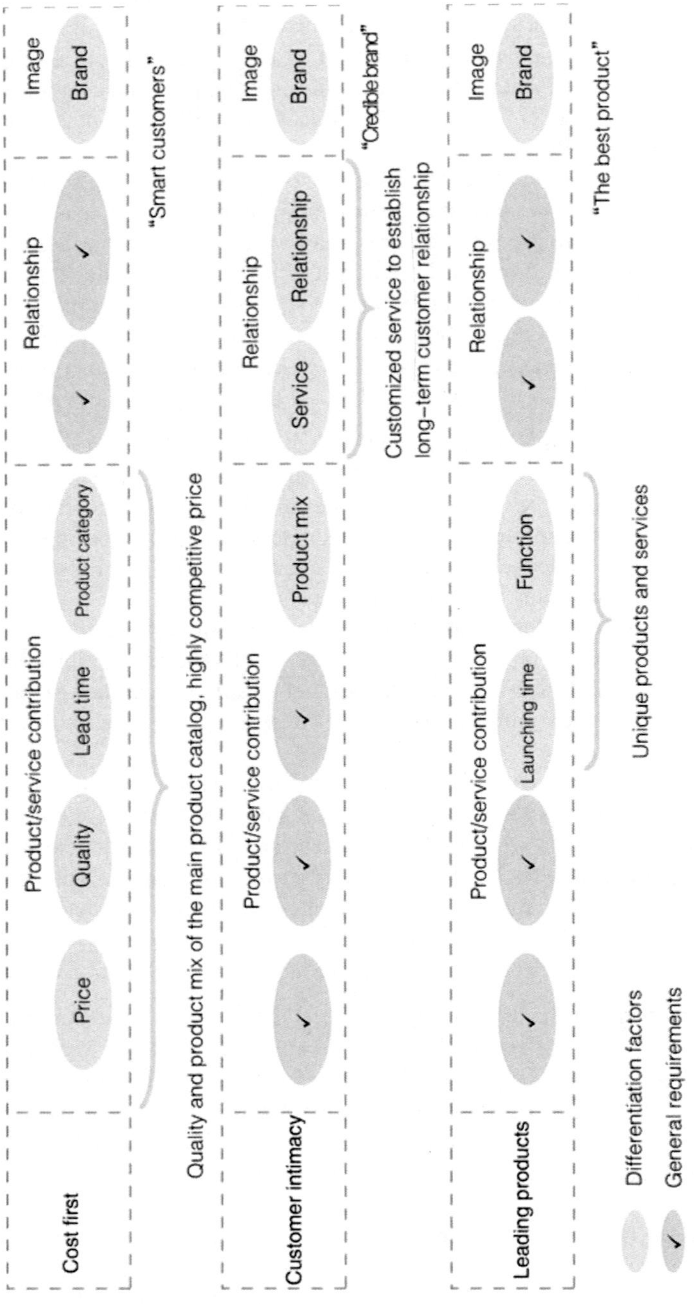

Fig. 7.6 Value proposition and focus of different types of customers

ability and short-term financial achievements, how to build a professional operation system, how to integrate professional service resources, and how to quickly breed, cultivate and develop the core competence of enterprises. The internal operation is the core driving force of the implementation of the whole organization strategy, connecting the preceding and the following so that the organization and talents can truly create value, which is the most personalized key level of the enterprise. Different enterprises have different processes, and when choosing these processes, enterprises must consider what stage they are in and what processes they need to establish and optimize, in addition to the consideration about which processes can create value for shareholders and customers in the short term and which processes can create value for shareholders and customers in the long term. This is the strategic choice of internal process, as well as the core idea of this level.

In the process of value creation from understanding customer needs to meeting customer needs, the key processes that have the most important impact on the strategy are as follows.

- Marketing management process: including management of brand, channel, business opportunity, and contract, etc., whose purpose is to achieve financial objectives through product/service sales. In Huawei, it is mainly supported by MTL/LTC process.
- Customer management process: including the selection, acquisition, maintenance, growth and retention of customers, whose purpose is to establish and utilize customer relationships for the sales of the product/service. In Huawei, it is mainly composed of CRM/PRM (Prospect Relationship Management) system, which is completed in cooperation with MTL/LTC process.
- Innovation management process: to develop new products, services, business models, processes and relationships based on market and technology trends, to seize market opportunities or improve competitive position. The difference between it and the development management process lies in the assessment mechanism, in that the innovation management process emphasizes agile development, as well as rapid market validation and iteration.
- Development management process: it involves requirements management, integrated development management, release and listing, engineering design, support and improvement, etc., whose purpose is to meet customers' needs with "customers as the center". In Huawei, the most typical development management process is the IPD integrated product development process. According to the characteristics of different products, Huawei integrates CMM (Capability Maturity Model for Software) and UCD (User-Centered Design) in the development management process.
- Operation management process: to ensure continuous and efficient service to customers, including the management of the fulfillment (procurement, manufacturing, logistics), finance, cost, data, risk, and problem, etc. In Huawei, it includes processes like ISC (Integrated Supply Chain), IFS (Integrated Finance System) and ITR (Issue to Resolution).

The fourth level is the level of learning and growth. It describes how to build the core competence around the internal operation that competitors can't copy. It closely cooperates with the internal process level of the enterprise to make intangible assets and key tangible assets provide the maximum value for the enterprise and customers, which is also the most critical factor to measure strategic readiness. It includes the following four aspects.

- **Human capital**: it refers to the skills, talents, technical know-how and other abilities required for the implementation of strategic activities, and the organization service mode enabling the rapid transfer of high-quality professional resources in the whole organization (such as the use and deployment of Huawei "Heavy Brigade"), which belongs to the strategic ability of the enterprise.
- **Information capital**: it refers to the information system, knowledge application and infrastructure capacity required to support the strategy. In addition to IT basic network, general application system (such as the database of ERP, MRPII, CRM, and OA), it is more important to carry the key business process and corresponding knowledge, data, case and other strategic information, which reflects the information conversion degree, information solution efficiency and information technology completion rate required by the strategy of enterprise internal operation. Huawei always adheres to the policy of "IT planning and construction ahead of business change planning", with the Internet as the core tool to improve enterprise operation efficiency. The scale of Huawei's internal network (including data center) connecting the world is second to none in the national and even global enterprise intranet, which supports the efficient operation of Huawei's more than 800 billion global businesses, covering all aspects of marketing, R&D, procurement, manufacturing, fulfillment and service, as well as human resource management and administration. Information assets have become one of Huawei's core assets, and Huawei has also become the practitioner and leader of enterprise digital and information construction.
- **Organizational capital**: The organizational ability to mobilize and maintain the change process required by the implementation strategy includes the establishment and recognition of advanced corporate culture, the consistency of understanding of organizational strategy, the efficient control and authorization system of the organization, the efficient coordination system of the organization, and the incentive system to make the members of the organization maintain a high degree of initiative, generate a willingness to pay and dedication. It belongs to the internal strategic environment to ensure the effective implementation of the strategy.
- **Strategic capital**: It is the core intangible and key tangible assets required to support the strategy, including core intellectual property, strategic capital and special equipment. Especially for the manufacturing industry, special equipment or precision machinery are strategic capital, even the embodiment of core competence, such as the "Sky Whale" to construct or extend islands. Strategic capital can be used for the early development of strategic products or markets, and also for investment or mergers to obtain key resources quickly. With the core intellectual property becoming more and more important in the global competition. Huawei

is relying on excellent core intellectual property and strong strategic capital to develop and grow in the world.

The core idea of BSC strategy decoding is to establish the logical relationship of decoding at all strategic levels. The process of strategy decoding is illustrated in detail in Fig. 7.7, with the key account strategy as an example. Key account strategy is an important part of enterprise growth strategy. The more high-value customers an enterprise has, the more sustainable and stable its business income and growth will be. In order to achieve this financial goal, enterprises must pay attention to the needs of key customers by providing innovative products and solutions. In order to fully understand the customer needs and long-term development strategy, so as to better serve the key customers, enterprises must establish the key customer relationship management process and IT system, and establish a solid organizational customer relationship with the key customers. Therefore, qualified key account managers, as well as the "first-line iron triangle" marketing organization suitable for key account expansion and a platform supporting organization system that can quickly respond to the first-line needs are needed in enterprises. These four levels are closely linked with each other upon a strong logic.

In this sense, any strategy consists of a set of development paths with strict causal hypothesis and strong logic. The management system must clearly explain the relationship (hypothesis) between indicators (or objectives) at all levels, so that it can be managed and verified. Balanced Score Card not only requires a good internal logic

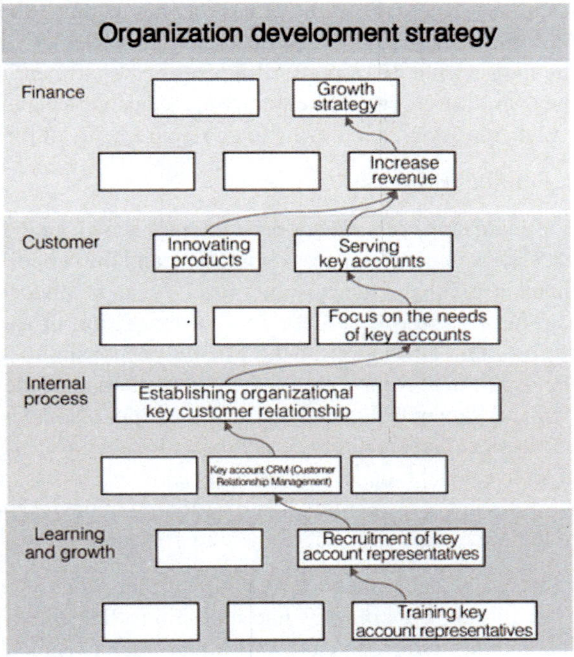

Fig. 7.7 Key account strategy decoding process

between the strategic objectives and strategic initiatives of all levels, so as to optimize the key tasks in BP, but also requires a good internal logic between the indicators (result indicators and internal driving indicators), so as to guide the KPI indicators.

7.2.2.3 Key Output of Strategy Decoding

In order to better decode the strategy, so that the enterprise's objectives can be decomposed layer by layer and form corresponding key measures, necessary input and reasonable guidance process are needed.

1. Important Input of Strategy Decoding

- The overall strategy of the enterprise;
- Strategic and annual business planning of upper departments;
- Annual key work of upper departments;
- Organizational structure and responsibilities of the department;
- Requirements of the enterprise and upper departments for the department (fields);
- Requirements of customers (including internal customers) for the department;
- The weakness in the construction of the department;
- Others.

The premise of strategy decoding is that the enterprise has formulated a clear overall strategy, which includes strategic objectives, enterprise level key business and management measures, and resource planning. Subordinate departments need to have the clear results of the decoding following the decoding process according to the long-term core responsibilities of the department designed by the organization, the overall strategy of the enterprise, the business planning of the upper departments, and the upstream and downstream requirements of the process.

2. Guiding Process

The main steps of strategy decoding are shown in Fig. 7.8, where are some differences between the business department and the support department, especially at the financial level and the customer level. It can be divided into the following six steps.

The first step is to determine the position of the department responsibility center. The attribution of the relative responsibilities is determined according to the department responsibilities, the contribution of the departments to the organization and the control or influence of the input resources. Different positioning of the department responsibility center directly affects the organization's acceptance of the objectives of the upper departments and the process, and then affects the design of the assessment elements. Clear positioning of the responsibility center is the premise of the organization to carry out strategy decoding.

- Business department: a department that directly contributes to the enterprise's profits by creating revenue and controlling the corresponding costs, which is generally referred to as profit center, such as regional sales, product line, etc.

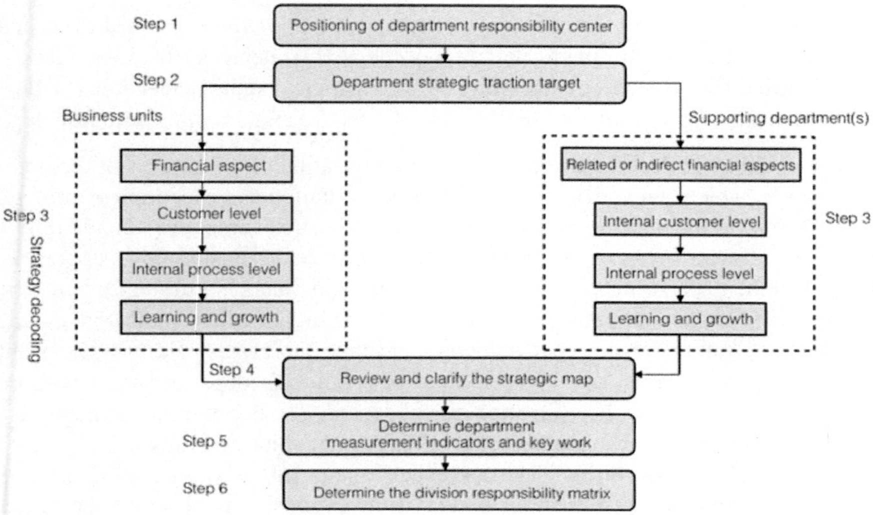

Fig. 7.8 Major steps of strategy decoding

- Support department: a department that provides the best services or products at the best cost to support and serve the main business department, which is generally referred to as a cost center or expense center, such as the human resources department, finance department, etc.

There is no grade difference in the positioning of various responsibility centers, but different responsibilities and division of labor. Upon the clear definition of the main responsibility types of the department, the financial evaluation indexes can be designed more accurately for better evaluation and motivation. Based on the change of business management mode, the position of the responsibility center may also change. Huawei's early technology support department, for example, was a cost center, and later turned into a profit center. The positioning of the specific sub-department responsibility center within each responsibility center may not be the same as that of the upper department, and it is related to the responsibility. For example, Huawei has both an expense center and profit center in its financial system. The Ministry of market finance and economics is a typical profit center, so the financing sales volume has become one of the important assessment indicators of the department, with the design of financing and sales solutions as the key work of the department.

The second step is to determine the strategic traction objectives of the department. According to the positioning of the department's responsibility center, the core objectives of the Department's business implementation, including the enterprise's annual objectives, superior/process objectives and key work will be determined, whose focus should reflect the unique value of the department, so as to support the effective achievement of the enterprise's strategy and upper/process objectives, and point out the direction for the formulation of the next strategic clarification chart.

The third step is strategy decoding. A highly logical strategic decoding will be done from four aspects: finance, customer, internal process, learning and growth.

- **Financial level decoding**: it is the final manifestation of the success of the organization, which can verify whether the implementation and execution of strategy contribute to the improvement of the revenues. Financial objectives should reflect the department's responsibility and responsibility center positioning, support the achievement of strategic traction objectives, and financial strategies must be conducive to the sustainable development of the organization. Indicators can be efficiency improvement, cost reduction, revenue increase, scale growth, profit margin requirements, risk control, etc. For supporting departments, it is more important to evaluate the utilization rate of expenses (it is better not to simply use indicators such as "absolute cost saving") and per capita performance.
- **Customer level decoding**: The target customers of the organization will be defined, upon the identification of the value proposition/appeal of the target customers, so as to make sure of the target objects for the next step to determine the core process to realize the customer value proposition. The realization of customer value proposition needs to support the finance, and should be able to create differentiated and sustainable value for target customers. For departments, customers include not only external ones, but also internal ones. For internal customers, the description of value growth should reflect the results of service, and the process requirements should be put on the internal level. For the supporting department, if defined by the upstream and downstream of the business process, internal customers are also customers, as shown in Fig. 7.9. The R&D does not directly face external customers, for the sales department is the internal customer of R&D, and R&D is the internal customer of the supply chain. Similarly, the enterprise's business department is the internal customer of human resources and other

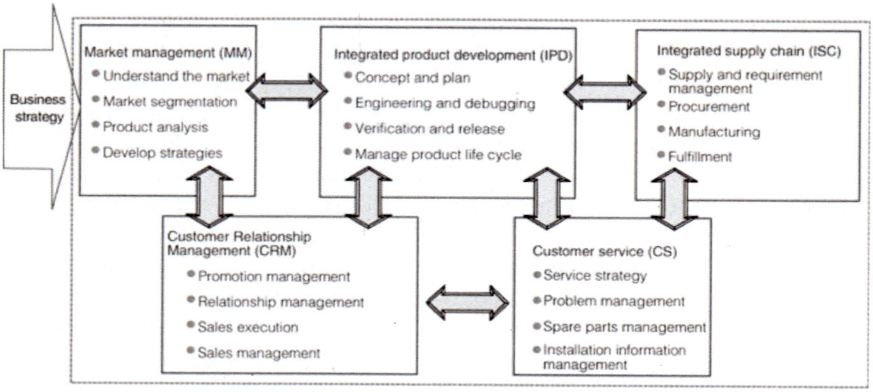

Fig. 7.9 The interface relationship between processes

service departments. Through the analysis of the relationship between the main processes within the enterprise, the assessment indicators and key collaborative measures can be formed to serve internal customers.

One of the problems remaining a headache for many enterprises is the problem of departmental barriers. Some even say that "they can do well the customers, but can't do well with the interior problems". Therefore, the internal customer satisfaction indicators can be formed between the main upstream and downstream business units by clearly defining the deliverable between the processes, so as to determine the assessment content between each other and realize the interlocking of the assessment indicators, so as to achieve efficient collaboration and jointly create value for customers. If defined from the upstream and downstream of the process, marketing is the internal customer of R&D, then through the design of reasonable indicators to realize the mutual lock of both sides' assessment, it can promote the sales of new products and the cooperation of both sides. For example, the market system can assess the response speed of customer requirement, the completeness of marketing materials, the quality of new product development, etc. of the R&D system, and vice versa.

- **Internal process level decoding**. There are two key elements to realize enterprise strategy, one is to create value for customers, the other is to achieve financial goals at reduced costs. The internal process level is the premise of identifying strategic human resources/information/assets/organizational capital in the next step. The focus is to determine the core management process that needs to be established and optimized most to achieve the strategic objectives, rather than a simple process summary. It determines the key tasks of process change, as well as the internal operation efficiency and process maturity.
- **Decoding at learning and growth level**. To drive the improvement of internal business operation performance through intangible and tangible assets will make it play the biggest leverage role in delivering value to customers, shareholders and communities. Enterprises should pay attention to the special talents, abilities and characteristics (human resources, organization, information capital, intellectual capital and key equipment) needed to support the operation of key processes determined at the internal level, which can be measured by the arrival rate of key resources, per capita efficiency and other indicators. Make sure the key strategies to effectively support the core process operation in terms of team and staff capability improvement; Make sure the key strategies in IT infrastructure and information system construction to effectively support the core process operation; To ensure the effective implementation of the strategy, the key strategies in intellectual property rights, key equipment, strategic funds, etc. should be determined, in addition to the key strategies in culture, leadership, coordination and teamwork to ensure the effective implementation of the strategy.

The fourth step is to examine and clarify the strategic map. Examine the logic of the four levels of finance, customers, internal processes, learning and growth, and see whether they are consistent with the strategic traction objectives, business planning, organization's shortboard construction, and superior/process requirements. The four dimensions of the strategic map should not only support all levels, but also support the realization of strategic traction goals; Each element of the strategic map should include the core content of business planning, and reflect the undertaking of upper and process objectives.

Figure 7.10 is a strategic map of the transformation of an OEM manufacturer. It can be seen from the figure that in order to realize the strategic transformation of enterprises from OEM manufacturers to brand manufacturers, the key indicators in the financial level are the sales revenue of brand products and the proportion in the total revenue, and then the profitability and break-even point of brand products need to be assessed. In order to achieve this financial goal, the enterprise must implement three key measures at the customer level: first, make clear brand strategy, formulate clear brand marketing plans and activities that can improve brand awareness and reputation, and formulate assessment indicators to measure whether brand awareness has improved or not; The second is to make clear the strategy of brand products, including the distinction between brand products and OEM products, especially the design of brand products should be based on the needs of customers, in addition to a differentiated competitive advantage compared with the products of competitors; The third is to formulate service strategies for direct customers. OEM manufacturers did not directly contact customers. Therefore, it is necessary to formulate customer expansion plans and service level strategies for different customers, and formulate assessment indicators such as customer satisfaction. In order to support the three strategies at the customer level, the enterprise must establish and optimize the four core process systems at the internal process level. The system includes the formulation of efficient offering requirements (OR) management process, the integrated product development (IPD) process based on customer requirement, the direct marketing mode for large customers and channel mode for small and medium customers, and the issue to resolutions (ITR) process to speed up customer response. In order to implement these four core processes accurately and efficiently, there must be qualified key talents, especially those who can adapt to the stage strategy of product innovation and brand product marketing; Organizational capabilities should also match the needs of strategic transformation and core processes. Therefore, it is necessary to formulate a clear intellectual property application and protection strategy, establish an efficient knowledge and information sharing mechanism to realize the organizational optimization of R&D organization and regional marketing platform system, upon an assessment and incentive mechanism for brand products. At the same time, the enterprise needs to improve the arrival rate and organizational ability of these key resources and develop clear and quantifiable assessment indicators, such as the arrival rate of resources, the maturity of organization and process, etc.

It can be seen from the case that there is a strong logic between the process of strategy decoding and the strategic map formed, which can closely link the objectives, key success factors to achieve the objectives and key tasks, as well as the results and assessment indicators, so as to better carry out closed-loop management and supervision.

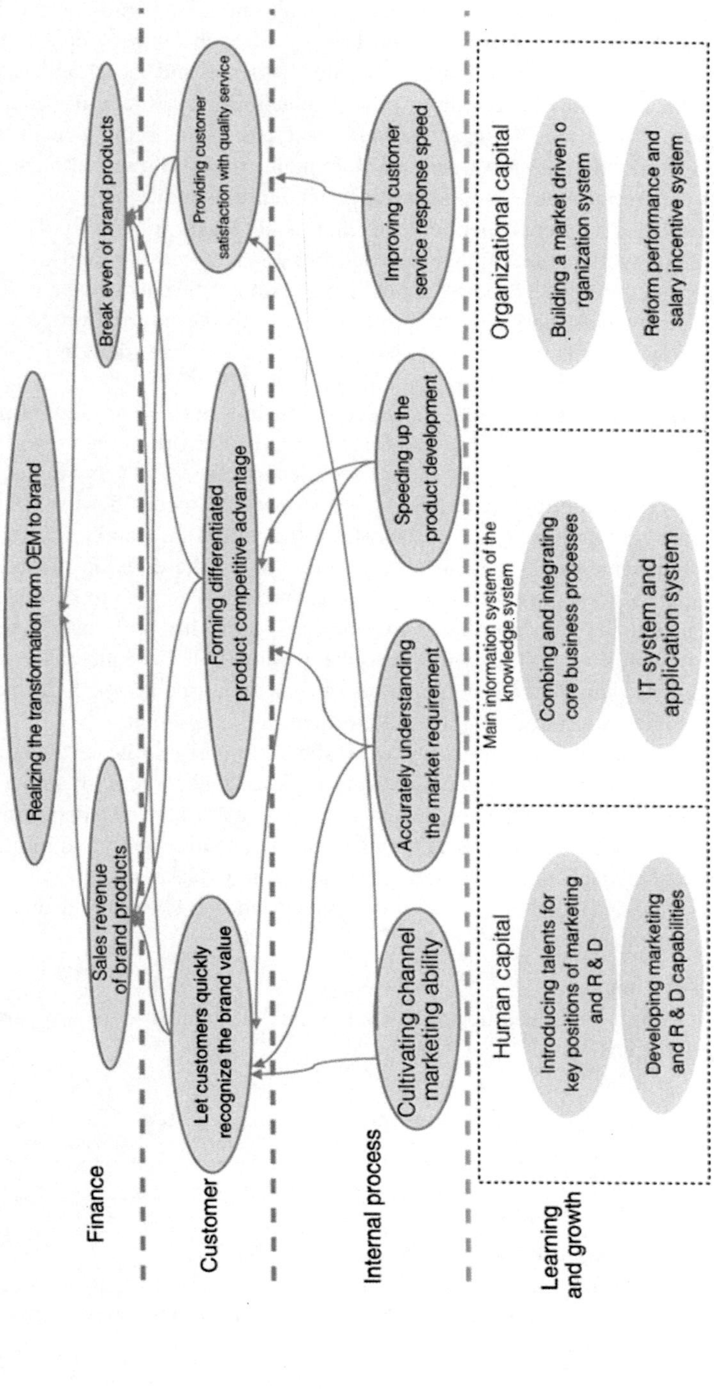

Fig. 7.10 Sample strategic map of the transformation of an OEM manufacturer

The fifth step is to determine the assessment indicators and key work for the department. The elements of the strategic map should be transformed into measurable assessment indicators, with the priority of each element determined. Indicators should reflect the responsibilities of departments, and the granularity of indicators can be determined according to the responsibilities of departments. The financial level, customer level, internal process level and learning and growth level are prioritized to identify the most important elements and put them into the key work. Priority determines the evaluation weight of each indicator.

In order to achieve the department objectives, it is necessary to identify the most critical and priority work of the team, so as to optimize the key measures and key work in BP. Key work and measures at the financial and customer levels can be classified as key business measures, and key work and measures at the internal process and learning and growth levels can be classified as key management measures. These important measures should follow the principle of SMART.

The sixth step is to determine the decomposition matrix of department responsibility. In order to ensure that the objectives and key work of the upper level can be implemented at all levels in the subordinate departments, and some indicators may be undertaken by multiple departments, it is necessary to consider the responsibility allocation among horizontal departments. Individual indicators sometimes even go cross departments, so it is necessary to determine the division of responsibilities and matrix according to the process relationship. The weight of relevant assessment is also different according to different responsibility undertaking situations. The responsibility matrix decomposition shown in Table 7.1 reflects the relevant responsibility weight in the KPI indicators of each department, which promotes the further implementation of relevant work by means of assessment.

One of the purposes of Huawei's "cutting off the bottom of middle-level cadres" is to break the departmentalism, and equip every middle-level cadre with an overall view but not to work only from the perspective of the interests of his own department. To achieve this, it depends not only on the individual's education level and mindset, but also on the enterprise's process system and the baton of "assessment".

So far, the strategic decoding has been completed, and its core output includes the following contents.

- Output strategy map;
- The key work and task decomposition of the annual business plan are further optimized to form BP+;

Table 7.1 Responsibility matrix decomposition

KPI	Sector 1	Sector 2	Sector N
KPI1	○	×	*
KPI2	*	×	○
KPIn	×	×	○

Note ○ indicates complete acceptance, × indicates direct partial undertaking, * indicates indirect partial undertaking

- Establish the KPI database of the organization, form the evaluation indexes of each department, and allocate the evaluation weight according to the responsibility.

Among them, the strategic map may output multiple strategic maps according to different directions and departments, so as to facilitate the publicity and implementation of the strategy. The above content does not need to be dogmatically output as a formal deliverable, but it is a strong structural and logical way of thinking, which is very important for optimizing work focus and refining key assessment indicators.

The enterprise generally selects no more than 7 indicators for the assessment. Specific subjects need to be selected according to the annual business plan and key points. The selection process emphasizes the presentation of unique value, and the weight of each indicator is designed according to the work priority and responsibility. In principle, the senior leaders pay more attention to the achievement of long-term goals and the improvement of organizational ability; while more grass-roots staff pay more attention to realistic and specific goal achievement and their own skills. The target value can be set as "bottom line", "standard" and "challenge", or only "standard" and "challenge". Table 7.2 shows the general template of performance target

Table 7.2 A general template of performance target setting

Enterprise performance target (annual)							
Department							
KPI category	Index library	KPI item	Weight	Bottom line 80	Standard 100	Challenge 120	Score
Finance	Income						
	Profit						
	Cash flow						
	…						
Customer	Customer satisfaction						
	Market target						
	Customer requirement						
	…						
Internal process	Time						
	Quality						
	Cost						
Learning and growth	Human capital						
	Organizational capital						
	Information capital						

setting, on which the annual evaluation indicators suitable for different enterprises can be designed.

After adding the strategic map and annual evaluation indicators upon strategy decoding to BP as the last part for the optimization of the key work in BP, the formulation of the whole annual business plan and the decoding of strategy are completed. It can be seen that in the formulation of enterprise strategy and annual business plan, the enterprise needs to further optimize the BP through strategy decoding, and form the assessment indicators with strong logical relationship, to ensure the implementation of the strategy under the regular closed-loop management of enterprise strategy and business management organization system.

In the process from survival to development, most enterprises will adopt market-oriented "opportunism" for a long time. As a result, enterprises begin to diversify passively or actively due to the pursuit of market hot spots and the direction of industry supported by the government. Few companies have determined the strategic boundaries of enterprises through the basic law in the early stage like what Huawei did.

There are many successful cases of enterprises adopting diversification strategy, but in China, enterprises are more worried about adopting diversification strategy. Especially after repeatedly comparing the growth paths of Lenovo and Huawei, it will be found that diversification seems to be one of the original sins. In fact, if an enterprise adopts the diversification strategy, as long as it establishes a reasonable management and control mode, formulates clear development strategies and objectives for different business units (like GE, all business units must be top three in the industry), and solves the contradiction between platform sharing and independent operation efficiency of the business unit, then the enterprise can still achieve healthy development. The strategy formulation methods of each business unit are similar, and this book will not repeat them.

In a word, creating value for customers is the starting point of strategy formulation, so enterprises should determine the product investment plan and development plan based on customer requirement, so as to ensure that customer requirement can drive the implementation of the enterprise's strategy. Only in this way can the strategic direction of the enterprise be roughly correct. The formulation and implementation of the strategy emphasize "planning before moving". Once the strategic opportunity comes, it is necessary to firmly implement it and build a continuous leading advantage to compete for the strategic highland. Huawei adheres to the principle of pressure, that is, on the key factors of success and selected strategic points, it allocates resources with the strength of surpassing its main competitors, and if Huawei wants to do it, it will greatly concentrate its human, material and financial resources to achieve key breakthroughs. However, the strategy is not unchangeable. A set of strategic rectification and management mechanisms need to be established for the opportunity and for the actions according to the ability of the enterprise for gradual development. At the same time, the organization must be full of vitality, and realize the closed-loop management of strategy by examining the strategic foothold. Assessment is not for accurate orientation, but for customer value and strategic orientation.

7.3 Conclusion

In the 17 years of working in Huawei, the author experienced three critical moments of Huawei's "emergence into a butterfly" though he has not seen Huawei's entrepreneurial period "from 0 to 1". From the obstructer of the first change, to the conformer of the second, and then the promoter of the third, the author has experienced unforgettable happiness and depression, and also gained the most valuable experience and knowledge in his life.

The core of Huawei's first product R&D reform is to take the customer as the center, open up the market, R&D, delivery and other links, and form an integrated product development IPD mode. At that time, the author was the general manager of pre-research technology and deputy director of R&D general office. Before the reform, pre-research department and general office were the key executive departments of technology and product project approval review and decision-making. One of the consequences of IPD reform is to abolish the general office which is not in the new process. Therefore, the author was confused, doubtful and resistant to the change at that time. He often refused to accept the interview with IBM consultants under the excuse of being busy. Even if he accepted the interview, he also dealt with it passively. "Huawei's 100% growth rate showcases that we have unique advantages different from IBM." "IBM doesn't understand the communication industry, so why should it teach Huawei how to do it?" Similar words are often heard after the author is engaged in consulting work. In a sense, change is the redistribution of interests. Huawei has a complete set of the change management system and methods, but when the change touches the managers' own "cake", how would you face it? To embrace or to stop it?

Huawei's second revolution is about going from home to abroad. In 2001, Huawei encountered a major crisis, which is even more serious than the fourth critical moment Huawei had faced before, at this moment, the main problem is the external environment, but at that time, it was "internal and external difficulties", and even the helmsman himself was temporarily lost. The enterprise saw negative growth in its performance, and the salaries for 320 core managers were collectively reduced. As one of those who experience the pay cut, the author can take this experience lightheartedly now, but it presented as a test of human nature at that time. Huawei realized the importance of strategy and established a strategy and marketing system. Fortunately, the author served as the first head of Strategy Department of Huawei, and began to explore and systematically learn the methods for the formulation and management of the strategy. After completing the enterprise level "80X" strategic planning, in order to comply with the requirements of the enterprise's globalization reform—"those who have not been to the front line or overseas cannot be promoted", the author went overseas in early 2005. As the director of regional strategy and marketing department, I deeply experienced and understood the "iron triangle" operation mode of the front line, the front and back cooperation mechanism, the cooperation mechanism between the front line and the backline, the key account strategy and solution marketing. During this period, the author led the whole process to complete the decoding of the enterprise's strategy to the front-line region, realized the coordination and benign game between "strategy" and "campaign", and got a deeper understanding of the formulation and decoding of the strategy. But at that time, although Huawei's marketing team has been running for many years, its core responsibilities and assessment methods, as a "world problem", have been facing many challenges.

The third change of Huawei is the change of business model. When facing a small number of large commercial users in the operator market, the role of marketing is often questioned. In the face of a large number of large, medium and small business users, and even general customers, what is the role of marketing? In order to solve the "world problem" in my heart, in the third reform, I took the initiative to apply to join BG, Huawei's newly established enterprise network in 2011, and served as the project leader of MTL (Marketing To Leads). This reform has changed Huawei's history of no marketing process, and realized the closed-loop management from marketing to sales and then to cash flow through the docking of MTL and LTC. The unique value, core operation points and assessment methods of marketing are clearly presented. Through the pilot, after optimizing and solidifying the process, Huawei has made a qualitative leap in its marketing ability.

The fourth critical moment Huawei is facing marks another stage that concerns the life or death of Huawei. Under the leadership of President Ren, I believe Huawei can find a way to deal with it. Although the author has left Huawei, he still cares about Huawei and hopes that the enterprise will once again play as a phoenix survive gracefully from the difficulties, and share more experience with Chinese enterprises on the day of its victory.

After leaving Huawei, the author has been engaged in enterprise management training and consulting. After serving dozens of enterprises, he got a deeper understanding of many management methods and tools of Huawei. Against the common problems of Chinese enterprises, such as imperfect organizational system and lack of management data, on the basis of Huawei's experience and a large number of cases of other enterprises, the author developed adaptive relevant processes, methods and tools, which are expected to be more in line with the needs of Chinese enterprises that will no longer copy foreign "advanced" tools and methods. At the same time, it is hoped that the domestic counterparts will learn from each other and improve together.

Many books about Huawei can be found on the market, most of which are to explain the factors for the success of Huawei and its system for the management of the development from the perspective of analysis of Ren Zhengfei's management philosophy. This book summarizes the connotation of Huawei's three key moments from the perspective of a middle-level manager, reflecting the key issues in Huawei's development process, and extracting important management tools and methods which can be of a general reference to Chinese enterprises. Moreover, the ups and downs the author has experienced in the changes also show the importance of the reforms of the management change, and the significance of the roles of managers themselves in the changes. It is expected that this book can give readers a new feeling and understanding.

Finally, I would like to express my gratitude to my family for their silent dedication to my work and this book. I also want to thank my friends Daihui and Fan Houhua for their help in this book, as well as Jia Fuxin, general manager of Puhua Enterprise of Posts and Telecom Press, and Wang Feilong, editor-in-charge for their great support and assistance.

Bibliography

1. Moore, Geoffrey A. 2007. *Dealing with darwin: How great companies innovate at every phase of their evolution [M]*. Beijing: China Machine Press.
2. Thiel, Peter. 2015. *Zero to one: Notes on startups, or how to build the future [M]*. Beijing: CITIC Press Group.
3. Kotler, Philip. 2012. *Marketing 3.0:From products to customers to the human spirits [M]*. Beijing: China Machine Press.
4. Drucker, Peter. 2005. *The effective executive [M]*. Beijing: China Machine Press.
5. Kim, W. Chan, and Renee Mauborgne. 2005. *Blue ocean strategy: How to create uncontested market space and make the competition irrelevant [M]*. Beijing: The Commercial Press.
6. Jingsong, Liu, and Hu. Bigang. 2015. *You can if Huawei can—Product development reconfiguration upon IPD [M]*. Beijing: Peking University Press.
7. Osterwalder, Alexander, and Yves Pigneur. 2010. *Business Model Generation [M]*. New York: Wiley.
8. Qi, Qin. 2005. *Financial management for non-financial managers [M]*. Beijing: Enterprise Management Publishing House.
9. Kuichi, Matsuda. 2013. *Strategy diagram [M]*. CIT'E Publishing Ltd.—Business Weekly.
10. Lowe, Janet. 2001. *Value investing [M]*. Beijing: Huaxia Publishing House.
11. Charan, Ram, Stephen Drotter, and James Noel. 2002. *The leadership principle [M]*. Shanghai: Shanghai Jiaotong University Press.
12. Bossidy, Larry, and Ram Charan. 2004. *Execution: The discipline of getting things done [M]*. Beijing: China Machine Press.
13. Levitt, Theodore. 2008. *The marketing imagination [M]*. Beijing: China Machine Press.
14. McKinsey & Company. 2019. *McKinsey China organization management business white paper. Organizational breakthrough [M]*. Shanghai: McKinsey (China) Consulting Co., Ltd.
15. IBM Global Enterprise Consulting Service Department. 2008. *The way to revive China's manufacturing industry [M]*. Beijing: Oriental Publishing House.
16. IBM Institute for Business Value. 2007. *IBM China business value report: Strategy and management [M]*. Beijing: Oriental Publishing House.
17. Reeves, Martin, Knut Haanaes, and Jamejaya Sinha. 2016. *Your strategy needs a strategy: How to choose and execute the right approach [M]*. Beijing: CITIC Press Group.
18. Dun, Nakata. 2018. *Change: The digital transformation of digital giant GE [M]*. Beijing: China Machine Press.

L. Tao, *Huawei Wisdom*,
https://doi.org/10.1007/978-981-19-1169-9